THE WILL TO SURVIVE

By Bobby Smith
With Linda Sivertsen

VOC Publishing
Springfield, MO
www.VisionsofCourage.com
2005

Second Edition
2007

The Will To Survive

VOC Publishing
Springfield, MO
www.VisionsofCourage.com
2005

Printed in the United States of America
By: Litho Printers & Bindery
Cassville, Missouri 65625

Table of Contents:

Prologue

I wrote this book for you.

Through eleven years of being a cop and experiencing or witnessing nearly every painful thing an officer can go through in this career (and in life), through fifteen years of being a speaker for hundreds of thousands of cops throughout the world, and through becoming a "head doctor" for cops, this is the best of what I've got, both in stories and information.

People say cops don't read. Hogwash. I don't believe that for a second. What is true, however, is that cops won't take the time to read anything that's boring! What I'm about to tell you will be more than worth your valuable time, and could save your life as well! So, sit your butt down and keep reading!

As you read the chapters, I think you'll see yourself reflected back through every page.

I promise you that this book will hold your attention—even when we're talking about subjects you normally avoid, especially the pesky emotional stuff. I can make you another promise as well. If you'll read each chapter in its entirety, you're going to feel a lot better. You're going to come away from this more excited about your job, with renewed optimism and more understanding about why things affect you the way they do, and how to fortify yourself. You'll find yourself more naturally fulfilled with your family, and them more *appreciative* of you. You'll look to the future with less trepidation and more certainty because you'll know that you're handling the details, rather than sticking your head in the sand. In short, you'll be healthier and happier with yourself—as in sitting comfortably in your own skin, with more peace of mind than you can possibly imagine at this moment. I'm sure of it.

Being a cop was all I ever wanted to do. When I was shot and totally blinded by a wanna-be cop killer in 1986 and was forced to retire, I thought I'd never be able to enjoy life again. My dreams had been taken from me forever. I had no idea how wrong I was; how rich, satisfying, and bright my future would prove to be.

Along this journey, you're going to become familiar with my best friend, Jackie Coleman—talk about loyalty! When I went to Jackie and asked for his permission to write about sensitive details of our friendship for this book, he said, "Write whatever you want to cuz I'm not gonna read it anyway." As my ex partner, he refuses to accept that I lost my sight and career. Jackie knows me better than anyone, but somehow still thinks I can do no wrong. I think *he's* the one who is blind—to my faults, that is. I would hope that every officer could have a chance to have this kind of connection on the job. It makes it all so much more fun!

I can't think of a harder or more challenging road to choose than the life of a police officer. There are a million and one reasons to get stressed out in this job. I've been thinking a lot about what a life of a committed law-enforcement officer entails, from its inception at the academy to retirement and beyond (because you're never not a cop, even once you retire). We'll talk about it all—specifically how our choices affect our families, our communities, and our health—both emotional and physical. Fortunately for you, through my experience, training, and a host of brilliant mentors and friends along the way (some of whom you'll meet ahead), I believe we have invaluable information for navigating the hazards of being a cop in ways that will really serve you. We're taught at the academy, for instance, how to shoot and write accident reports, but no one really teaches us how to deal with the aftermath of tragic events—our own or those that involve the people we serve each day.

In closing, it's not easy for a blind man to write a book, so I hope this work inspires you to be your best. A whole lot of thinking and research and figuring and inter-viewing and typing and late night proofing and laughing and crying and flailing down memory lane went into this thing you've got in your hands. I hope and pray that you are better and more fulfilled because of it. Your health and safety are my greatest vision!

Dr. Bobby Smith *(formerly, Trooper Bobby Smith)*

Prior to being introduced to Bobby Smith and travel-ing to hear him talk to a room full of 150 cops, nearly three years ago, I never could have known that this would be the most meaningful working relationship of my life to date. For the hundreds of thousands—possibly millions—of cops out there who have heard Bobby speak, you know what I'm talking about. I call him the "Forrest Gump of Cops." Not because he's simple minded (or loves chocolate or shrimp, which he does), but because of his uncomplicated way of telling the truth, and his absolute and total loving affect on anyone within a two mile radius. I've never seen a person not moved by the presence of this man entering a room—gushing as if he's the most famous rock star or movie star. I am captivated every time I see him bring an entire hall full of tough-as-nails cops to their knees, laughing and weeping with equal vigor. Bobby's angelic energy and hilarious wit results in immediate relief to cops, as he talks wisely and intimately about what so few outside of law enforcement understand—the bizarre, complicated, tragic, and heroic life of a police officer.

We have written this book for you—cops—but also for the people who love you... wives, husbands, children, parents, friends, neighbors, and anyone who desires to better understand the inner workings of those on the front lines of every street in America. (To Bobby's police fans around the world, this goes for you as well.) What a lovable and fun group of men and women you are! I am both humbled and staggered by what I've learned. I will never know the kind of courage any of you have, as I'm not a cop or married to one, but how grateful I am to have played a part in bringing this message to you. May it help you to continue to bless the rest of us through your increased health, happiness, and longevity.

Throughout my career as an author and magazine editor, I've had the good fortune to interview and work with many celebrities, politicians, religious and spiritual figures, and best-selling authors. I can say without a doubt that I've never met anyone on par with Dr. Bobby Smith. I'm quite certain that God gave him a little extra of all the good stuff when He took away his eyesight. I'm not a fan of hero worship for any man, and Bobby is the first person to tell you of his faults, but believe me, you won't hear better advice from anyone. Not ever.

I hope you enjoy what we've come up with, Bobby and I. A life of selfless service (Bobby's), a lot of love, and possibly even (dare I say it?) divine intervention, is behind every word.

Linda Sivertsen

Acknowledgments:

To my wife, Janie, and our son, Brad, for the countless hours they've spent apart from me while I was writing this book. Sincere thanks go to Linda Sivertsen: an incredible writer, who over the last two and a half years has become not only my writing partner, but also a friend. Thanks to Nicole Hoppel whose editing polished this manuscript to completion. To Jackie Coleman, Mike Epps, Aubrey Futrell, and Bobby Mann four of my best friends. What can I say except thank you? I give endless thanks to God for transforming the tragedy of my blindness into a world of greater vision. Without His guiding hand, I would never be where I'm at today. This book was greatly enhanced by the input from: Special Agents Tom Golden and Dennis Lyndsey with DEA; Lt. Bill Healey of the Ohio State Highway Patrol and to Bob Douglas of the National Police Suicide Foundation. To the literally thousands of cops across this country who have been there to support me through every step of my adult life; I owe it all to you

Bobby Smith

This book is through, and I'm still pinching myself that Bobby (and this project) chose me! Wow. How did I get so fortunate? Eternal thanks to my late father, Alfred E. Tisch, for his immediate enthusiasm for and understanding of this sacred project, and for Dad's gifted help, both with the proposal, overall subject matter, and in giving the book its title. My husband, Mark Sivertsen; our son, Tosh; my sister, Carol Allen; and my dear friend Amelia Kinkade have been invaluable with their thoughtful insights, editorial suggestions, and cheerleading! Our lawyer, Tony Blain, for handling the details. My wise council—my rock in the world of publishing and business: Leeza Gibbons, Arielle Ford, Elisabeth Rapoport, Linda Northrup, & Rhonda Britten, thank you for your love, loyalty, and for holding the vision for this book from the start. My deepest gratitude goes out to all of the cops in this world who lay their lives on the line every day so that the rest of us may live with a greater sense of peace and safety. May God eternally bless you for your nearly unbelievable dedication and service to humanity!

Linda Sivertsen

CHAPTER I
The Slippery Slope: Ethics vs. Corruption

I was raised to be a man of character. My dad told me that a man's handshake or his word was a contract, and he taught me never to break those contracts. In my family, right was right and wrong was wrong. Rules were rules and not to be broken. When I took the oath to become an officer, I vowed internally and externally to uphold the law, no matter what. There were so many times—as there are for each of us—when it would have been easy to break the rules and personally benefit, but I took great pride in the fact that I was leading by a good example. For years, I resisted bribes, freebies, and even stacks of un-manned cash, all without flinching. It was easy for me to choose to tow the line because I wanted to. Even if no one knew about how "good" I was, I knew it. I could look into the mirror each night and feel pride in my actions and in myself.

All of that would change in the summer of 1976, in Monroe, Louisiana, 100 miles from my hometown of Alexandria.

I'm about to share a story with you that I've never told anyone before today, not even my twin sister or my wife. Some of you will be shocked. Many of you will think it's no big deal at all, but I'll tell you, this one incident has haunted me for over twenty-eight years.

One night while working the night shift, my partner and I received a call to check out a burglar alarm at a local drug store. That happens from time to time for reasons as simple as a change in the weather or a power surge. After securing the building, I noticed my partner standing in front of a display of sunglasses. He picked up several, trying them on and replacing them back on the rack.

"Hey man, you need a new a pair of sun shades?" he yelled over to me.

I remember walking over to him thinking, *Is he just looking at them or is he going to take a pair*? I approached the rack and began trying on the different styles with him, saying over in my mind, *what am I going to do*? My partner looked at me.

"Those look good," he said. "How do they fit?"

"They fit great," I answered, "These are some nice glasses." He took them off his face and stuck a pair in his shirt pocket.

"Those do look good," he said. "Bobby, just put them in your pocket. If the owners were here, they'd give them to you as a thank you anyway."

That was an excuse and I knew it, but it was an easy justification. If the owners were here and saw us admiring their glasses, they probably would have offered them to us. Everyone knows we're underpaid for the work we do; everyone knows we deal with death, danger, and destruction every day and could use a break. It makes sense that they'd be grateful and offer us a token of their gratitude. But they weren't here and they didn't offer. I took them off my face and put them in my shirt pocket before leaving the store, making the choice to follow my partner's lead. He was a veteran cop, eight years my senior. He was my friend. We worked together and socialized together. We lifted weights, hunted, and did everything as a team. He was a good man, an excellent cop and a very close friend. Even so, I immediately knew I had done wrong. This act was against everything that I was taught as a child and later as a cop. He didn't force me. The choice was mine and I made the wrong one.

The Will to Survive

I got in my car and we went 10-8 (back in service). For several hours, all I could think about was what I had done. For a $10 pair of sunshades, I had compromised my integrity and jeopardized my career. As soon as I could, I drove by a dumpster and threw them in. Not only did I feel guilty for stealing them, but also they had now gone to waste and the theft was for naught.

For twenty-eight years, this incident has continued to haunt me. I cannot tell you the number of times I have thought about this, questioned this, worried about this, felt ashamed of this, and regretted this selfish act. In fact, every time I'd hear someone say the word sunglasses or even see someone wearing sunglasses, I thought about what I had done. The guilt was always there, and as a result, I never wore sunshades on duty again, no matter how scorching the weather. Cops would say to me, "Bobby, it's so bright out here, why don't you get a pair of sunglasses?" and my response was, "Because they give me a headache." I couldn't have known for sure because I never tried, but I was sure at the very least they'd give me an emotional headache.

As you know from reading the introduction or the back cover of this book (or, if you have already skipped forward to the gory details in chapter three), I was shot in the face and blinded in both eyes by a man who ran through a highway checkpoint. Very soon after being shot, I had no choice but to wear shades again; large, ugly, dark ones... sun glasses to the extreme. It was not something I wanted to do by any stretch of the imagination, but it was less painful to me than forcing my buddies to see my wounds. But even today, when most blind people wear totally dark glasses to cover their eyes, I don't. By the grace of God, my scars are no longer visible, so I prefer to wear glasses that are only lightly tinted. I don't want to appear to be hiding behind anything.

Exactly ten years after I stole a $10 pair of sunglasses, I couldn't go a day without them. I guess you could say that I had one year of good vision for every dollar worth of merchandise I stole.

Isn't it ironic that the only item I ever took as a policeman would be the one I'd so desperately need just after being shot? How I wish they'd stayed in the dumpster!

Isn't it ironic that the only thing I ever took as a policeman is totally useless to me today?

For eleven years I was a "good" cop. Does this one incident make me a "bad" one? I've come to believe that it didn't, but my guilt and shame about that event made me think on some level that I was. In fact, after my writing partner, Linda, coaxed this story out of me and typed the words for all of you to read, I called my twin sister Betty to share the facts with her. After so many years of bottling this up inside, the one person I needed to confide in more than anyone else was my twin. The bonds of a twin cannot be understood fully by anyone who doesn't have one, but suffice it to say that it's like talking to the deepest part of yourself. I was nervous about what she'd think, and for good reason.

I picked up the phone, dialed tentatively, and heard the familiar crackling line as Betty said hello. I could tell she was on the handheld in the kitchen back home in Alexandria.

I gave her the news as she listened quietly...

"Bobby!" she exclaimed, "How could you? I can't believe you did that!"

Drat! I was afraid this was going to happen.

"Why'd you do that, Bobby? You've got to be joking!" She paused a moment, waiting for me to tell her it was all a farce, but I was silent. I could hear the devastation in her voice and I thought my sister was going to cry.

"I don't know, Betty," is all I could say. "I was stupid."

"But what were you thinking, Bobby?"

"I wasn't thinking, Betty," I mumbled. It's true. I wasn't.

There was nothing left to say.

I hung up the phone and realized that this one defining moment in my career colored everything else that had followed. Then I realized something else:

After twenty-eight years, it just might be time to forgive myself.

The Slippery Slope

We hear a lot about the "Slippery Slope" in the academy. If you haven't been to the academy yet, or if you're reading this to try to better understand a cop in your life, let me acquaint you with the notion of a slippery slope. Imagine a long slide with flowing water running down from the top. Think *Slip & Slide*—the yellow water slide many of us played on as kids. It's slippery and once you're on, you don't get off until you hit the bottom. In other words, the slide refers to the potential for unethical actions that start small and escalate rapidly downward. Lapses in judgment and bad choices lead to an eventual bottom, which, believe me, hurts. There are, however, some of you out there reading this who are strong-willed enough that you can get off that slide right here and now.

Our teachers do well by ingraining in us the fear that once we cross the line and get on the slide of unethical actions, there's nowhere to go but down. While this holds true in most cases, some of which I'm about to outline below, my experience has also given me a broader range of vision—of hope. I have come to find that where white meets black is gray, and our lives as cops are complicated, to say the least!

What does this all mean for you? For starters, recognize that the issue of ethics in our business is a worry in your life. Since you're reading a mental and emotional guide here, my job is to make you aware of what's bothering you even if you think it's not an issue. We'll get into denial and depression and related problems in other chapters, but the first step in making sure that you take care of yourself in this highly stressful job (and make sure that you are healthier, happier and don't burn out), is to know what you're dealing with. If you can't see the pitfalls before you, you sure as heck can't protect yourself. Delving into ethical issues may seem to add stress to your life right now, but I promise you that in the long run, you will be better off for time well spent, and your overall stresses will be eased.

If you have already slid partially down the slide already, chances are you've been beating yourself up about it and the guilt and shame you're feeling is stressing you out big time. I know; I've been there. You will need some encouragement to get off before hitting bottom, and the following examples may give you the kick-in-the-pants incentive you need. If, on the other hand, you are always on the right side of the law, you have an entirely different set of stressors to deal with. The fact that some of your comrades are tarnishing the badge and putting you and your buddies in harm's way is undoubtedly a source of tension for you.

Just in case you don't believe me, let me ask you a few questions:

*How do you feel when you hear that as a result of an undercover operation, 44 police, sheriff's department, and corrections officers from 5 law enforcement agencies were charged in January of 1998 with taking money to protect cocaine trafficking operations in Cleveland and northern Ohio?

*Do you worry about the public's perception of cops when you hear that 27 sheriff's deputies and 1 police officer were convicted in 1994 for skimming millions of dollars of drug money while they were members of an elite Los Angeles narcotics unit?

*Does it make you angry when you hear that 17 Detroit officers were indicted in June 2003 for stealing drugs, firearms and money from suspected drug dealers, and then planted evidence and falsified police reports on people, some of whom were later charged and convicted?

*How do you feel when you hear about an NYPD officer who is shot and killed by his partner so that he can't testify against him for extortion?

*What about the fact that a high percentage of officers who commit crimes and are caught, end up killing themselves because of the shame. Does that scare you?

What about those who are innocent, but caught in a web of lies around them?

You know the stats. From Los Angeles and Chicago to Cleveland, Miami, and New York, the headlines have given you the startling news of what some cops are capable of. Don't tell me this doesn't bother you. And, if it doesn't, that's a worry in itself. It should bother you, to the point that you decide today where you stand and what your limits are. While George Washington may have been accurate when he said, "*Few men have virtue to withstand the highest bidder*," I'd like to think that as police officers, we are part of that few.

The Will to Survive

Passing or Flunking the "Free" Money Test

The following true story will happen to nearly every officer in some form or another. Ask yourself what you would have done in my position…

One night I got a call to check out a local finance company in an upscale business section of town. I knew it well; it was owned by a nice gentleman who was one of those citizens who believed that we cops put our lives on the line every day for "peanuts," and he wanted to see that we were safe and taken care of during the nightshift. In the back of his finance company, a very small room with a sink and a toilet served as a back entrance to the main building, opening to the parking lot. This guy told all of us cops that if we ever needed to use the bathroom, his door was always open for us. He also added a full coffee pot to the mix every night, and consequently, cops were in and out of his place all night. This guy was smart because he was ensuring that a fairly constant stream of law-enforcement professionals regularly visited his property, and he knew that while we were there, we'd obviously check on things as well.

I was just shaking doors one night (checking buildings) because that's what you do during the nightshift when most everyone else is asleep. It was rare that I would find an unlocked door, but we always knew in the back of our minds that if we did, there might be a burglary in progress. One especially dark, cold, winter night, after getting my coffee, I was on my way out the back door and thought, "I might as well check this door while I'm here." Totally expecting the door to be locked, I damn near had a heart attack when I turned the handle and that sucker came flying open! Knowing that burglars go where the money's at, I was nervous. This *was* where the money was at, literally. Civilians ask me all the time, "Where do the burglars like to go?" and I

The Will to Survive

always say, "They don't rob the ghetto. If they need to steal something to buy crack, they go to the side of town where people have things to steal... *things they can sell for cash*." But going directly to the cash is even faster!

I had my Maglite flashlight in my left hand and my revolver in my right as I eased the door open. After taking a cursory look around the room to view the desk, phones and computers, I shoved my flashlight down the front of my pants and reached for my walkie-talkie, calling headquarters to report an open door and request back up. My partner Jim Roberts (who's now Chief of Police in Shreveport, Louisiana) and I began searching the building, trying to stay quiet in case "they" were still there. As we got about halfway through the main warehouse-style room, we looked through an entranceway to one of the cubicles and saw an open safe, with stacks of cash in plain view. We stopped and looked at each other as if to say, "Oh my God," because not only was there a fortune in bills staring at us from the safe, but a couple of stacks were lying on the floor in front of the safe. Naturally, we assumed that we had interrupted a burglary in progress. We also assumed that we might be sitting ducks; the only way the perpetrators could get out was through the unlocked back door we had just entered.

We opened the closet doors and checked around, careful not to touch anything because of the fingerprints. After a thorough search, we determined that no one was there. Displayed on one of the doors was a large sticker, stating who to call in an emergency. We called the number, and it happened to ring to the owner's home. His wife answered and she told us that her husband had been racing to the airport late that night and had realized he had forgotten cash for his trip. Since he was running late, he decided to run by the office and grab cash there. She figured that in his stress, he had hurriedly slammed shut the heavy safe door and had failed to notice when it bounced open, spilling some of its contents, which it did every once in a while. The following morning they called and confirmed that sure enough, all of the money was accounted for. We all breathed easy. No harm done.

Can you imagine what would have happened if my partner and I had been tempted to take a stack or two of the bills? I shudder to think about how easily we would have been caught, or at the very least, how fishy the situation would have looked to everyone. You never know what can happen in these situations; what seemed like an obvious foiled burglary was just a simple honest mistake. Had our actions been based on what looked like reality versus what actually had taken place, we could have been in big trouble by taking cash and blaming it on a fake "burglar." I can't imagine that the payoff of that type of phony robbery or any other fake event would ever be worth the resulting emotional guilt and turmoil and possible legal consequences.

After locking the building and getting in our unit, Jim and I wondered aloud how many cops in this country would have walked away without taking any money. We hoped that no cop would ever make a dishonest choice in that situation, but we knew better: Somewhere on that night, some cop on some beat in some small town or big city was making a very different choice—sliding further down the slide. On the plus side, cops are tempted all the time and most resist the temptation. What matters most to me now is what you do. There are plenty of people out there breaking the rules. The system will work a lot better if you are not one of them.

While I learned an invaluable lesson from stealing those glasses and would NEVER, under any circumstances do it again, some instances, I believe, are better left determined on a case-by-case basis. For example...

The Free Cup of Coffee
We've all been warned about taking the free cup of coffee or the free meal at the local restaurant. We've been warned time and again that this simple act could have a payback—that people expect us to "take care" of them when they "take care" of us. It's a constant dilemma because of the goodness behind so many of the offers, and because of the potential negative implications of some. We all have our own ways of dealing with ethical issues, and I'm hoping that some of what I've learned, both as a cop and as a therapist, will make this issue easier for you.

In the academy, we frequently had the recurring discussion of: *What's wrong with a free cup of coffee*? The argument is, of course, that once you take a freebie, you have stepped onto the slippery slide. A beginning step usually seems insignificant, which is why it's so easy to descend downward. A cup of coffee or a free meal is pretty small stuff, but your instructors know that by taking them, you have a two-fold problem on your hands. Not only is it against the rules (and rules are set up for a reason—to protect us), but it also leads to emotional and psychological stress. Perhaps you will feel guilty on some level for setting a bad example for other cops because you know that with repetition, practices like these become accepted, thereby weakening the system. After all, how can you expect your peers to stay within the guidelines of what is "right" if you are making up your own rules in front of them?

A simple act of taking a free cup of coffee can have ripple effects. For example, those who agree with your choice to accept the free coffee will feel better about following your lead in the future, saying, "Well if it's okay for him, it's okay for me." We all know that that kind of mentality can easily lead to full meals and then some. There will be cops who won't trust you if you *don't* take the free coffee or meal because they will worry that you'll rat on them when the tables are turned; you just made them look bad by paying full price. You may ask yourself, "What's wrong with doing it if it means my peers will accept me as a good cop?" This is where you have to use your head and take each incident individually. Those who disagree with your choice to take the coffee may look at you with less respect, thinking less of you for going against protocol. Is it worth it? Know who you're with and who's offering. Certainly, it can seem easier to do what your buddies are doing than to stand out and risk getting a reputation as a goody-goody, but I ask you to remember who will be staring back at you in the mirror at day's end. Sometimes a small infraction like taking a pair of glasses can wreak havoc on your life, even if you're not caught. Take it from me, and ask yourself, "Is this worth the price?" Make sure the person you are answering to is yourself.

Peer Pressure & Intimidation

> *"Values are primarily caught, not taught."*
> **Blanchard and Peale**
> *The Power of Management*, 1988

Sometimes the difference between right and wrong is a bit blurred, although according to the SOP (*Standard Operating Procedure*), there is a definite right or wrong for every situation. Trouble is rules and regulations don't account for the peer pressure we experience—a reality exacerbated by the kinds of intense bonds we face. As police officers, we are a family; many of us spend more time together than we do with our real families! If any of you think these are easy issues, you're kidding yourself. People don't know peer pressure until they've experienced it on this level because we're not just talking about school playground games and intimidations. We're talking about the bonds of men and women who lay their lives on the line every day and night for each other, and who depend on one another for mental, emotional, and physical survival.

In some respects, you're damned if you do and damned if you don't, and the area you work in adds its own negatives or positives. We didn't have a lot to worry about within our ranks in Louisiana. We didn't "play," so to speak, and had a fairly clean system. Regardless, most cops choose to act like the cops they're with. Some days we follow every rule to the letter of the law, and other days we bend the rules a tad, sometimes more. One thing you can count on, however, is that the price **you pay for the freebies you accept might not be worth it.**

The "But Look at What I've Done for You" Mentality

For me, it was always easier to say no to intimidation from outside the law-enforcement community than inside. For some reason I was totally tripped up by my partner's suggestion to help myself to those sunglasses, but I've never been tempted by bribes from the general population. That doesn't mean I don't know how insidious freebie situations can get, but I've never had trouble saying no to the bribes of someone who had previously given me a free meal. One example that comes to mind started with a local restaurant in Monroe, Louisiana, that frequently gave us police half-priced meals. We liked the food and appreciated the financial break. I was working the night shift one night and dispatch called and said, "Bobby, call this number; the guy says it's urgent." I called and the manager of the restaurant picked up and identified himself. He was frantic because he had just been stopped for speeding. See where we're going with this?

"Bobby, thank God it's you. I need a favor. One of your buddies has me pulled over; could you talk to him and help me out?" he asked.

"What did the trooper stop you for?" I said.

"I was speeding," he said.

"What do you want me to do about it?" I asked. I knew what he wanted, but I wanted him to say it out loud.

"Bobby," he continued, "Come on… How many half-priced meals have you guys been given at my restaurant?"

"I have no control over that," I said. "The trooper is just doing his job."

The man became irate. "I'll remember that the next time one of you come through my restaurant," he yelled.

What a jerk. But there are plenty of people like that out there. It's no different than the guy you pull over who says, "But I'm a mechanic and I just fixed a cop's car to-day, and all I charged him for were the parts." What are you supposed to do with that information? Sometimes they tell you this so that you'll know they are one of the good guys. Sometimes it's that simple. Sometimes not. If not, what are you going to do then? He's probably a nice guy, but does one hand really benefit from washing the other? What about when you go to buy a new car from this guy and he cuts you a great deal? What happens when one of his friends or family members gets into trouble and you're expected to pay back the favor? Can you stay true to your values then, or will his smooth talking, guilt-ridden words make you cave? The average person doesn't have this dilemma. Free meals or big discounts on cars are unheard of. When these things are offered, you've got to be smart and know your limits.

The lesson I've learned from these instances is that you've got to know whom you're dealing with. Certainly, there are people out there who appreciate the police for the job we do, and giving us a break is their way of saying thank you, but others have ulterior motives and expectations. After watching this for many years, my belief is that most businesses that offer discounts or freebies for cops do so because it's a way for them to give back. They are expressing gratitude for our role in protecting the community. But the ones who take advantage of it are the ones who plan to use it to their advantage. Ironically, it's usually not the restaurant owners who do this, but someone in the personnel, often a manager. As the academy teaches us, if you avoid this altogether by paying full price, you will avoid getting yourself into these potential conflicts, ensuring that you are at least one-step further from stepping on the slide.

I cannot tell you what to do, but I can say that these are decisions you must make early on in your career. If you don't decide ahead of time where you stand; if you stay on the fence or fool yourself into believing that these issues are no big deal, I guarantee that at some point in your career you will suffer.

Everyone Has a Price, but You Can't Afford Mine!

It was my policy as a police officer to always offer the full payment for goods and services. If someone insisted on giving me a discount, saying that they appreciated what I was doing and that it made them feel good to help out America's finest, I usually found it easier to keep from creating a scene and accept the favor. But I'd feel it out first. If the offer felt slimy in any way, I paid in full. If the offer came from a kind soul whom I trusted, I would consider the coffee or half-priced meal. If it was an entire free meal and the cashier would not take my money, I'd leave the entire cash amount on the table. Before you think that I'm so self-righteous, trust me, I have received more than my fair share of food and drink. But I accepted them knowing my limits. I knew full well that if I were asked to repay the favor at a later date, I wouldn't, no matter how tempting.

You have to be honest with yourself about your weaknesses. If you cannot stay true to your values and commitments in the face of temptation or intimidation, you cannot afford to accept favors. Point blank. Everyone has a price; however, you can't afford mine. That much I now know. I think that's true for the majority of cops in this country.

The Rich and Powerful Get Off Easy

Here's where the line, again, can get even more problematic. What do you do when the people you're trying to protect and serve believe they are above the law? This can be an enormous challenge, and disheartening for the majority of us who believe in the importance of a fair and just system. It's amazing to me how the privileged few in our society often expect something in return for a favor they've thrown your way, or even more common, strictly because of their position in the community. They think they have a free pass, based on who they are and what they do. We're talking about the influential members of a community whose families could have literally built the city hall, the hospitals, and recreation centers, and whose college libraries are named after their granddaddies. How do you tell someone with that kind of stature that they have to go to jail? How do you arrest a guy who's on the front page of the paper in

The Will to Survive

a ribbon cutting ceremony in an Armani suit and make him spend the night next to a crack addict? This city councilman, elected official, or average person of prominence might just be the creep who recently donated $1 million to build your new emergency crisis unit. People get so surprised by this phenomenon, but think about it: Doesn't it make sense that the guy who wants to get away with everything from traffic tickets to murder, selflessly "invests" in the very system he's going to need favors from? I hope it goes without saying that most wealthy benefactors are upstanding members of society. The good far outnumbers the bad, but it's important to keep your head out of the sand.

Ain't Nobody's Business If I Do

I once pulled over a fancy, uptown realtor—a man who was considered a big fish in our little pond of Monroe—who had run through a red light in front of me at a major four-lane intersection. It could have been a disaster, as drivers had to slam on their breaks to keep from hitting him in the side. He got out of his car with a big smile on his face and shook my hand enthusiastically. He tried to hand me his driver's license, and I noticed right away that it had $100 bill wrapped up around it. I put my hand down and said, "You've obviously inadvertently made a mistake in handing me your license. I don't need your money; I just need your license." It was pretty obvious by my body language that I was onto what he was doing and was giving him the opportunity to make it right. Bribing a police officer is a federal offense. The smile left his face and I said, "Now, would you like to start over?" He pulled the money away, stuck it back in his pocket, and then handed me his license. I proceeded to write him a ticket for running a red light, and when I tore the ticket out of the book and handed it to him, I said, "You can take that $100 bill you tried to hand me earlier, and let it go toward this traffic ticket. You have a nice day." When I checked later, sure enough, this guy had paid his ticket in a hurry.

Luckily, that instance turned out to be fairly benign, but the next one wasn't. One evening I got a call in reference to four teenagers in a white Buick Regal who had run a sweet old man off the highway. According to the eighty-year-old man, the boys had bumped his car with their car at a high speed on the highway and nearly scared him to death. After missing a large ditch and managing to park safely on the side of the highway, the old man watched as four boys exited their vehicle with bats in their hands and began to smash in all of his windows and doors. Fortunately, he was unharmed physically and called the police.

By the time I caught up to them and stopped their car several hours later, it was easy to see both by their demeanor and by their names that they were spoiled little rich kids. Several bats were lying on the back floorboard, in plain view. I questioned them and of course, they all denied it. I called for back up and we took them down to the station. The elderly gentleman came down and identified the boys sitting in a room. Unlike a TV show with the familiar suspense and technical mumbo jumbo, he merely pointed to the four and said, "That's the boys right there," while they sat laughing and joking around.

I immediately recognized them as the sons of four big fish citizens from the north side of town. (For those of you who grew up in newer developed areas, during the time of the railroads, railways were typically built going from east to west, as were the cities. The "south side of the tracks" was considered less desirable, and thus, influential and wealthy people moved away from the noisy tracks to the north side of town.) All four of their fathers were VERY influential. Two were sons of well-known physicians in our area. The other two kids' fathers each owned large car dealerships. I knew one of the fathers pretty well and had bought a couple of vehicles from him over the years. When I called and told him what his son had done, he said: "Bobby, weren't you a teenager at one time?" The boys were just out having a little fun." I explained to him that his son and his buddies could have killed the old man. The father started laughing, with no regard for the truth of what had happened.

The boys, who had all been drinking, were placed under arrest. After searching the car, we found stolen merchandise in the trunk as well, which started a secondary investigation. Turns out that these four boys had been burglarizing businesses throughout the city. But wait, it gets better. The sentence they received for multiple burglaries, *from a judge who was in the same social clubs as their fathers*? Public service on the order of weekends only for four consecutive weeks! Their sole sentence for nearly killing an old man, destroying his car, and robbing businesses was to clean up around city hall, which was clean to begin with! I was furious because I'd drive through the area and these boys would be out there joking around and throwing a Frisbee. All they had to do was show up. And, since they were all juveniles, it didn't even register on their records!

The "Don't You Know Who I Am?" Mentality

Some civic leaders and successful businessmen expect favors from the criminal justice system, and usually get them. Had these four kids been from the wrong side of the tracks, with daddies who were blue-collar workers, their sentence would have been much tougher, obviously. But if they had been straight up poor kids (white or black), they would have been sent right to juvenile prison.

One night I stopped a former governor's adult son, and hauled him off to jail for driving while intoxicated (DWI). This guy was weaving all over the road, and had been arrested twice before for the same offense and had never been prosecuted. He was extremely intoxicated—a danger to himself and others. After failing the field sobriety tests, I placed him under arrest for DWI. When I walked him to my unit, he looked at me and said:

"You obviously don't know who I am."

"I know exactly who you are," I told him, "but you're still under arrest."

"I'll have your job in my hand by tomorrow," he said.

"If you can get my job, you go for it," I answered.

I knew he couldn't do a thing to hurt me. I knew the law-enforcement community in Louisiana wouldn't play that game. We had a reputation for being tough, which we had earned and wanted to keep. In a strong and ethical administration, you are backed up for doing your job.

If I had cut this guy some slack and taken him home to Daddy, it would have been easier, at least in the short run; but what about the oath I took to protect and serve the people? This guy was clearly a danger, and I only had one real option.

Sometimes the line between white and black, however, truly is gray, as in the following instance…

I stopped a sheriff one night who was drunk, and what a dilemma I had on my hands with this guy! It wasn't fair of him to put me in that situation, but that didn't change the fact that I had to make an immediate decision about what to do with him. Here's the gray part: I took him home. It wasn't the "right" thing to do, but I knew I'd have to go to work with this guy every day. Sometimes we cops have to make incredibly tough decisions. If I had arrested *the* most powerful law-enforcement official in the county, how difficult would he have made my job from then on? What kind of backlash from the other officers would I have had to deal with? I don't know. All I do know is that I had a few moments on the side of a busy and dangerous highway to decide between two evils. Had I arrested him and *had* he been indicted, he would have been thrown off the force. He would have lost his livelihood and his reputation, and maybe even tried to commit suicide (losing one's reputation is the number one reason cops kill themselves). Maybe he and everyone else would have been better for it? There was no way to know if booking him would have resulted in a string of healings or a total nightmare. Did I make the right decision?

What would you have done?

People are out there thinking that we're the good guys putting the bad guys in jail. Sometimes we're the good guys wrestling with whether or not to put the other good guys in jail. Which brings us to...

Corruption: It Starts at the Top

In lecturing across the country, I've found that it's mostly the same wherever you go; every agency deals with similar ethical issues. There are, however, some departments that are "known" to be corrupt. Of course that doesn't mean that each person within those departments is careening down the slide, but it does mean that a higher proportion than normal are making negative choices. It's no surprise to find that it usually starts from the top down. This is why you can hear of a wildly corrupt precinct that gets a new commander with a high level of integrity and suddenly most of the force is transformed into doing everything by the book. **My guess is that most cops are good, even if they are making unethical choices. When someone names the problem and vows to stop the corruption, he or she will happily shape up.** No matter how clean a commander, he or she will probably never totally clean up the department, but the differences will be immediately obvious. Change can happen rapidly in these instances and it's a pleasure to witness, both for the community at large and for the cops who are trying to abide by the rules in an unruly atmosphere.

"If you want the best from people, expect it of them."

Coach Bear Bryant

The media, unfortunately, loves a sensational story, and what could be more sensational than a cop gone bad? When a department gets a reputation for widespread corruption, the media pounces on the story like lions on raw flesh, with blaring headlines that often poisons public perception. Once the level of trust from citizens is diminished, the entire police force has to work that much harder to regain the trust.

"That's what makes it hard for them, because the majority of police officers are good," says federal monitor, Sheryl Robinson—who was appointed to monitor Detroit's police department just before seventeen officers were indicted on allegations of looting money from alleged drug dealers during illegal raids and arrests in June of 2003. (*Detroit Free Press.*) She's right. Most cops *are* good. So, why does the media celebrate when cops are caught doing wrong?

Obviously, corruption sells newspapers and TV news shows. Any time you can prove a "truth" wrong, you have a headline. Think how many myth-breaking headlines you've read. "Milk Actually Causes Osteoporosis." "A High Fat Diet Will Make You Thin!" "Get Rich in Real Estate for No Money Down!" "Taxes are Unconstitutional." These headlines attract attention because they are taking a known "truth" and turning it on its ear. Milk is supposed to build strong bones. Fat *makes* you fat. Getting into real estate is only something for people with upfront money, and if you don't pay your taxes, the government will hunt you down because it's against the law. A "bad" priest or a "bad" cop goes against everything we've been taught to believe about our country, about the way things "are." Because people are not "supposed" to get ripped off by the police in the world's greatest democracy, when it does happen, the public and the media can't resist the sensational details. Everyone knows what protecting and serving means, and setting someone up or planting evidence or beating someone up in order to intimidate or steal from them does not constitute protecting and serving. But, it's a "hot" story when we do, and each headline plays on the public's fears while satisfying peoples' insatiable desire for drama.

We live in a time of great hypocrisy. Regardless of your political affiliation, it's a well-known fact that our leaders (and those around the world) frequently make up their own rules. President Richard Nixon had his Watergate. President Ronald Regan had the Iran Contra scandal. President Clinton had his Monica Lewinsky. You may not think this is such a big deal, except that these men each had the title of "Commander in Chief" when they told their lies to the public. That's no menial position! We're talking about THE commander of everything... *the* boss of every armed force in America, including the police. I'm not bashing any of them, but what I am saying is that police forces around

The Will to Survive

the world have a huge challenge to remain ethical when even those at the top have their very public criminal moments. A rookie police officer who gives a sworn statement under oath and is found to be lying (without even due process of law), will be terminated from his or her position as an officer and never allowed to be a cop again in this country. At the very least, he or she will serve a minimum sentence in a county correctional facility. Why does one man go relatively unpunished while the other loses his entire career and is branded for life? Again, powerful people often get away with breaking the law and there is little accountability with the public: that's the way it is.

Just knowing and accepting the rules of the system can make your life much easier.

A good friend of mine named Bill Healy, a retired lieutenant with the Ohio State Highway Patrol, is now one of the top experts in the world in the field of ethics and law enforcement. I don't even pretend to know all he knows about how to change the system, but he's taught me a thing or two about dealing with corruption, which I'll share with you. According to Bill, there are two key elements that make up police corruption:

1. The misuse of an officer's professional role, through "authority" or "official position."
2. The receipt or expected receipt of material rewards or personal gain.

In detecting and preventing corruption, there has to be a commitment to integrity from the top to the bottom of the department. This cannot be an abstract value statement, but rather must be reflected in the actions of the police and top commanders and field supervisors. **Loyalty has to be to**

integrity, not to colleagues, who are fallible. And, pride in the organization leads to positive peer pressure. By using better candidate screening techniques, raising educational standards and age minimums of recruits, as well as incorporating integrity training into the academy, things are getting better. Great changes have come about in policing in the past thirty years, and despite the headlines, it's getting better for all of us. By demanding an increase in command accountability, and a strong commitment to corruption control, especially by field commanders, several corrupt departments have turned around significantly.

Bill, who we lovingly call Ricochet Rabbit (because he's thin and hyper, and extremely brilliant and talks real fast), has a question he tells cops to ask themselves when tempted. It's simple. All you have to do is ask yourself:

Is what I'm about to do legal?

Some of the Good News

1. The intellectual caliber of the police has risen dramatically. American police today at all ranks are smarter, better informed, and more sophisticated than the police in the 1960s.

2. Senior police managers are more ambitious than they used to be. Chiefs and their deputies are no longer content to tend someone else's store; they want to leave their own distinctive "stamp" on their organizations. To do this, they now recognize that management is an important specialized skill that must be developed.

3. During the last thirty years, an explicit scientific mindset has taken hold in American policing that involves an appreciation of the importance of evaluation and the timely availability of information.

4. The standards of police conduct have risen. De-

spite recent, well- publicized incidents of brutality and corruption, the American police today treat the public more fairly, more equitably, and less venally than police did thirty years ago.

5. Police are remarkably more diverse in terms of race and gender than a generation ago. This amounts to a revolution in American policing, changing both its appearance and, more slowly, its behavior.

6. The work of the police has become intellectually more demanding, requiring an array of new specialized knowledge about technology, forensic analysis, and crime. This has had profound effects on recruitment, notably civilianization, organizational structure, career patterns, and operational coordination.

7. Civilian review of police discipline, once considered anathema, has gradually become accepted by police. Although the struggle is not over yet, expansion is inevitable as more and more senior police executives see that civilian review reassures the public and validates their own favorable opinion of the overall quality of police performance. This revolution has already taken place in Australia, Britain, and Canada.

Source – The Narc Officer, Dean David H. Bayley, School of Criminal Justice, State University of New York, March 1998.

The Double Standard

Despite the positive changes just discussed, the fact is that you will make mistakes. I'm the first person to say that you're only human, so you aren't going to get any flack from me. The truth of the matter is that mostly we cops get tripped up where everyone else gets tripped up by the small stuff. The minor mistakes.

While there are good cops and bad cops, just as there are good priests and bad priests, or good lawyers and bad ones, what makes a bad cop so unacceptable is his or her position of power within the community and within their own department. We're given the best weapons, the best technology, and the seal of approval from the highest levels of government. After taking a sacred oath to uphold the law, nothing less than that seems acceptable. While some cops do horrible, intentional acts to hurt people and serve their own needs, to my knowledge, it's a very small percentage. The biggest trouble for most of us in our day-to-day lives is that everyone seems to notice when we're not absolutely *perfect*, which can be totally infuriating! Let me give you several examples...

1. You're eating lunch at your favorite spot and a man walks up to you and says: "Didn't you guys just get a pay raise? What are you doing sitting in here for an hour-and-half when we only pay you for an hour?"

2. The local elementary school has a spring recital at 10:00 A.M. At 9:30, two hundred civilians leave their jobs for two hours to catch the recital, some being paid by the government. When a police officer does the same thing, people whisper about taxpayer's funds going to pay for his or her extended lunch break.

3. A person takes a stapler home from a corporation they work for, hoping to catch up on some personal mailings after arriving home from a long day. He or she is "caught," but no one cares. A police officer is caught for the same offense and is suspended from the force.

4. A surgeon working the nightshift in the ER is found asleep in the broom closet. He has slept an hour over

his break, but his actions are seen as potentially lifesaving for others. A cop working the nightshift falls asleep in his or her car, also an hour after break time, and is accused of stealing from the government.

Why the Double Standard?

I always say that being a cop is like being famous: We can't go anywhere without being stared at and talked to. Forget about a quiet meal; it just doesn't happen. But another similarity we share has to do with a double standard. How many times have you heard a celebrity complain that he or she has no privacy? They all wrestle with this problem. And the answer from the public is usually the same: "If you wanted privacy, you shouldn't have become famous." You knew what you were signing up for!" I don't think it's fair that famous people are stalked by paparazzi and it's all within the law, as if they have no feelings or personal lives. And, I don't think it's fair that cops have to be "perfect" in the eyes of the public either. I don't, however, believe that either reality is going to change any time soon.

Famous people live in a fishbowl because they WANT to be watched (either on stage, on TV, or on the big screen. We are cops because we WANT to uphold the law (or at least we should), therefore, we must uphold it more than other people do. Is that fair? No. But that's the way it is. I believe that having to walk that thin, thin line when we see people around us breaking "harmless" rules all the time adds tremendous mental and emotional pressure on us. The fact is that the public has higher expectations for us than they have for themselves. What is acceptable in the corporate or civilian world is not acceptable for cops. The sooner this sinks in for us and the sooner we come to peace with the fact that we live under a microscope, the sooner we can stop our internal tug of war and rebellion (our love/hate for our job) and the easier our job becomes because we're no longer fighting the system, even if only emotionally.

Why We Do It

It's always helpful to keep your eye on the big picture. Why did you become a cop in the first place? For me it was simple: Ever since I had to pick a career, it's all I ever wanted to do. As a kid, I played cops and robbers from sun up to sun down, and as an adult I carried that gratitude and enthusiasm with me on every shift. The joy could be found in the simplest acts that continued to happen, like this one:

Once I was driving downtown in my unit in the wee hours of the morning before daylight and a man who looked like a bum and walked with a limp was waving me down on the sidewalk. I pulled over and he walked up and showed me his VA card and said:

"I'm a WWII veteran and I hate to ask you this, officer, but I have to catch a bus to go to the hospital for tests a few hours from here and I haven't had anything to eat in a day. Can you spare a couple of dollars for a meal?"

"Sure," I said. I had been driving all night and was aching to eat breakfast myself, but I didn't get off until 6:00 A.M., and all I had was a couple of bucks in my pocket. A few doors down from us was the Pitt Grill, a greasy spoon. The hash browns were so greasy that you could squeeze the grease right out of them. I drove him there and asked him what he wanted. He ordered two eggs, ham, hash browns, and toast, with a cup of coffee. I remember thinking, "Oh well, I ain't gonna starve to death." I was able to afford a few pieces of toast and a cup of coffee for myself, while this guy had a big breakfast.

The Will to Survive

When I took my oath to be a police officer, I swore to protect and serve the public. Most cops never have a problem protecting. Protection means excitement: kickin' in doors, taking bad guys to jail, and being tough. We love that stuff. Let's just admit it right here. It's fun. Why do we take the risks we do? Because it's fun as hell! Running across a parking lot with guns drawn is exciting, adrenaline-pumping stuff. Period. I guess it all goes back to playing cops and robbers as kids. But sometimes in all the excitement, we forget about the rest of our motto: to SERVE the public. Sitting in that diner, eating my dry toast with this guy felt better than almost anything I could imagine. I felt so much pride sitting next to him. He stunk. He was diabetic and he had an old jacket on, with a foul, foul odor, but as I sat on the stool next to him, I felt so grateful to be of service. He was so appreciative, taking his time eating. Here's this old man who served our country who didn't have a nickel to his name. I'm tearing up just remembering it. That's what it's all about.

You don't see that in the headlines. Who would tune in to watch a breaking news story about a cop taking an old man out for eggs and toast? It's far more sensational to read about a cop accidentally killing a guy by mistaking his cigarette lighter for a gun. It's not like cops want anyone to know about their good deeds, either; we don't want people to think we have a soft side, even though we do. Have you ever seen a cop walk up to a cashier and declare aloud: "Hey! Breakfast for the old man—on me!" It's not going to happen. We don't do it for the pat on the back. We do it because we're supposed to take care of one another. Anytime you ask a cop on the street that's walked the beat, they've all bought an old man breakfast at one time.

You know, there are nearly 900,000 cops in this coun-

The Will to Survive

try and we're talking about maybe sixty high-profile bad cops you'll read about—a small statistic. Trouble is, people want their money's worth. Ever go to the grocery store for straw-berries? How do you feel when you find a beautiful basket of strawberries, but there's one big moldy one in the middle? The other thirty berries are great, but did you focus on the one bad one? Some do, some don't. Some people throw the whole basket in the trashcan because one berry is rotten. People like that make me angry; it's so wasteful! Why don't you just throw the one bad one away because the rest of them are good? It's just a mindset. I wish people wouldn't throw us all in the emotional trashcan when one of us is found to have gone bad, or to have made rotten choices.

While we're finishing up the subject of ethics here, I'm going to close with a very different restaurant example. This will tie in the free-meal dilemma as well, in case you're still left wondering what the heck to do about that one.

Pretend Your Mama is Watching

It's the middle of the night and you're eating dinner with your partner at the local burger joint. The place is rela-tively hopping for this time of night; it's a weekend and peo-ple have been out partying. A known dope dealer—a punk who runs prostitutes and thinks of himself as a big fish—walks in and wants everyone to think he's friendly with the police. He walks up to your table, takes your ticket and says, "I'll take care of this, you guys are doing a good job," and heads toward the counter. Suddenly you're in a quagmire because everyone's watching you—watching and judging. If he did that for the manager of ABC Furniture Company, no one would notice, but you're in a uniform and everyone is waiting to see what you'll do. What choice will you make?

You're resentful you've got to make this choice.

31

The Will to Survive

What a drag. At dinner you don't want to have to think. You don't even want to hear the specials. Just give me a burger, fries, and a Coke. Now you've got a situation on your hands. You can make a scene and say no thank you, but the guy's got your ticket and he's paying the cashier. Unlike a cop who buys a veteran a quiet breakfast and slips a five across the table, these guys want everybody to know that they've just aligned with you. Funny, this thug is out at night just like you are, but for totally different reasons. Do you allow him to buy you dinner and say, "Thank you very much, but that wasn't necessary," or do you reach in your pocket and pull out your five-dollar bill and lay it down on the table anyway? It's your choice.

Obviously you know which one I recommend.

Even if this guy has already paid my bill and left, I leave the money on the counter. The waitress just got a big tip and the public got an invaluable lesson. It all comes down to common sense. Taking coffee or a meal, in my opinion, is not wrong. I don't believe it necessarily means that you're stepping on the slippery slope. People want to help cops with no strings attached. Again, it depends on who is offering. In the Midwest, for example, with their down-home cooking and family-oriented restaurants, with fried chicken on Sunday after church, you're probably just fine accepting a free meal. If you'd do it if your mama were standing there watching, you're most likely okay.

Never Steal a Man's Blessing From Him

I've had the pastor of the church pay my ticket before. He did so quietly, with humility. People who are servants to others will do this for each other. I've had people whisper to me:

The Will to Survive

"You don't know me and I don't know you, I just know you're a cop, and one of your guys took my daughter home when she had too much to drink one night and I really appreciate it. I'd like to do this for you."

I always thank them and say, "That's not necessary," but if they insist, I take it on a case-by-case basis. I follow my gut. What's the difference between the different scenarios? The first guy is basically saying, "Look what I've done; look at me!" The second is doing it for a blessing.

I truly believe I have been so blessed in my life even with all of the trauma. It makes me feel good to help others, and I don't want anyone stealing my blessing. People often see cops and think, "I may not have much money, but I'm blessed; let me bless you in return."

It all boils down to experience, maturity, and common sense. When you're learning how to ride a bike, you won't know how to negotiate a slippery curve and will hurt yourself. It's the same thing with being an officer. You learn as you go, carefully and slowly. **With time, arrogance turns to wisdom.** The best advice I can offer you is to follow what you learn at the academy in the beginning. They do a fine job of teaching you the rules, and then it's your job to go out in the field and figure out how to apply it all. It's kind of like being a professional athlete who is extremely talented and has been taught the proper skills, but doesn't usually become exceptional in his or her position until putting three or four years in with the team. The fine-tuning is in the experience. Learn how to listen to your gut, and most of all, be the best cop you can, for yourself, above all else.

Unfortunately for me, it took losing my eyesight to gain deeper vision. If you could only see what I see, you'd know that strong, ethical behavior is the only way to make it happily through this job. We have enough to worry about with the bad guys; don't add to your pressure by having to cover up and forever look over your shoulder around the good guys!

Okay, that's enough preaching for one chapter, but let me leave you with one last thought. The next time you're wondering if this crazy job is worth the stress, remind yourself: It's about sitting on a bar stool with an old man, buying him what may be his only meal of the day.

CHAPTER II
Academy Life

Eye of the Tiger

I'll never forget my first day at the Louisiana State Police Training Academy in Baton Rouge, Louisiana. It was a bright Sunday morning, 0800 hours. There were fifty-five of us new cadets milling around and sizing each other up while waiting for our training to finally begin. In our prime and ready to take on the world, the fact that we were also naïve didn't matter much to us. What we lacked in wisdom could be overcome through sheer excitement. You could cut the anticipation with a knife because it had not been an easy road for any of us to get to this point. We had waited a long time, some of us a year, others eighteen months, and every conceivable test had been given to us in order to weed out the potential "problem children."

During that testing phase, all of us had passed rigorous oral, written, physical fitness and medical exams. Every nook and cranny of our lives had passed thorough background investigations, including the polygraph. Man, they asked us everything, including, "Have you ever stolen?" and "Have you ever used drugs?" I was amazed that they could find this many of us who made it past those two questions! Even though I was never a drug user, I understood that they allowed a candidate who had tried marijuana, for example, but I also liked the fact that they didn't allow its use within a three-year period to joining up. I didn't want no pothead having my life in his hands out in the field! You know what I mean? "Hey, sorry, dude. I didn't mean to slam your fingers in the door. I guess I wasn't paying attention!" No sir!

The Will to Survive

I also appreciated that anyone who had done hard drugs was out. I just knew there were going to be too many temptations out in the field to deal with someone with a bad habit. Basically, the attitude was, "If you've ever used LSD, cocaine or any other hard drug, you need not apply." I thought that was a good policy. So, I had made it thus far. Phew.

Because this wasn't no department store, fill out an application and you're gonna get hired organization, we knew that some of us had gotten fortunate so far but wouldn't make it all the way. I remember talking with Jackie Coleman (who later became my partner) and looking at the fifty-three others standing around us saying, "That one won't make it, that one won't make it, and that one *definitely* won't make it." By graduation day sixteen weeks later, two of the three we had chosen were gone, while five in total were sent packing. We had been wrong about one of the women. We thought she'd be gone by the end because, frankly, she was short, overweight and was just as nice as could be. She didn't seem the type. We all came to like her very much and helped her tremendously to make it through, but I didn't think she had the eye of the tiger. My feeling was that if you weren't in the best of shape, or were on the verge of not making it, you had better have the *eye of the tiger.*

Remember that linebacker-focused stare from the movie *Rocky*? You could see in Sylvester Stallone's eyes that he had it. That morning in Baton Rouge, it was fairly easy to see who had the committed type of, "I will conquer no matter what" look in their eyes. Those who didn't make it to graduation just didn't have it. They were more on the shy side, introverted, with less confidence in their stature. Since going to the academy is essentially like going to marine boot camp (our commander was a retired lieutenant colonel in the Marine Corps, and he was a bit confused because he thought he was still there), if we weren't prepared mentally and physical right from the start, we were goners.

How Did I Get Here?

Even though I loved playing cops and robbers as a kid, I never thought about actually becoming a cop until I got out of high school. My wife was a nurse and I went to school to be a juvenile probation officer. In my studies, I'd see cops around and say to myself, "Wow, I bet those guys have a lot of fun." After a while, a few of the officers said to me, "Man, that ain't gonna be fun dealing with all those troubled kids. Come be with us, kickin' in doors, and chasin' the bad guys. That's where the fun is!" The police department had a ride-along program for anyone interested who was already studying criminal justice, so I decided to check it out. Immediately upon riding with these guys, I felt like an addict. Oh, my God, it was so much fun! I couldn't wait until the next day to go have fun with these guys again.

Being from the country, I was a young, sheltered country boy. I had heard stories about murders, drug deals, and prostitution, and here it was, all in front of me. I had no idea that this stuff really went on! It was like being in New York City, or at least that's what I imagined. Every day was a brand new adventure.

Fall Out, Face North

At exactly the stroke of the hour on that first day, as we stood on the grinder (the area where we did our inspections, between the living quarters, the gym and the administration building) with our luggage at our feet, we observed five Louisiana state police troopers flying across the front parking lot racing toward us in their white Chevrolet Impala state police vehicles. It was an intimidating sight, as they appeared to be driving at mach speed! They were flying; trust me. All of our 110 eyes were focused on the cars racing right at us. The troopers bailed out of their cars with those campaign hats screwed down on their heads, running for us in full uniform screaming like a bunch of banshees.

Fall out, face north! Face north!

It was ugly. We were in shock. Every last one of us. But they had our attention, screaming at the top of their lungs. The fecal matter was about to hit the fan. For one million dollars at that moment, I could not have told you in what direction I was standing. As you can imagine, I, along with everyone else, was stressed out to the max.

They Were Evaluating Every One of Us

I came to learn that from the first moment they laid eyes upon us, these guys were watching our every move. I would also learn several weeks later when I was chosen the president of my class, and the only one who was allowed to talk to the staff, that they were looking at our reactions and responses from the get-go, and seeing how we handled stress. Everything they did was calculated to elicit a certain response from us, and our reactions were of the utmost importance! During those first two weeks, there was no play. Knowing that a certain percentage wouldn't make it, our instructors were intent on flushing out the weak right off the bat. After that point, the intensity shifted a bit. "Okay, now we've got our team. We don't have to waste any more time with those guys. Now let's go to work."

Time for a Little Philosophy Lesson

Why do you think we were told to, "Face north," and not "Face east," or "Face west?" I have never heard anyone talk about this, but I had my theories. I knew that sailors in the Navy are taught to follow the North Star if they get into trouble, and I thought there was something deep and anti-quated going on. Even if it is unconscious, we all know on some level that north is the true path. It's how, historically, we knew where we were. Our life might depend on it.

In police work, everything we do is calculated from the north. No one ever says, "turn left at 19th St. and right on Frontage Road." Instead, they say, "turn east on 19th and south on Frontage." Even in our reports, we draw a circle in the top right corner of our diagram with an arrow, facing north, as a point of reference. To me, as those officers were screaming at me to "Face north," I felt that what they were really telling me was that I needed to stay true at all times, and head in the right direction. I thought of all the times I had heard references of a deal "heading south," and knew what that meant. I was not going to be seen facing the wrong way, literally or figuratively! Now, where the heck was north?

Sir, Yes Sir!

As those five crazed troopers got to us, we scrambled to fall into formation, attempting to line up in perfect lines. This was our first experience of many of being nose-to-nose with our drill instructors, and there wasn't anything subtle about their approach as they squared up to us at 90 degrees. Clearly, it was all about intimidation and showing us who was in charge. As I stood there shaking on the inside with a steel exterior, the brim of my instructor's hat was right above my eyes. Remember that? You had better not smile, look left or right, or even blink. You had better act like these guys don't even exist and look right through them. I knew that if I looked any one of them in the eye, I'd hear, "Don't look at me boy." If nothing in my life until then had truly taught me how to focus, this would do the trick.

One winter night a sergeant woke us up at 2:00 A.M. He took us to the grinder in our boxers/briefs and bare feet and ordered us to stand at attention for one hour outside in the freezing cold, shivering and covered in goose bumps while he stood in a doorway with his arms crossed, laughing. We hated his guts. I still don't like him. But you know what? In standing there saying to myself, "You bastard; you can't break me," I got stronger. By George, I learned that I could handle whatever came my way. It may have made me a bit too proud, but to this day, I am grateful for the inner strength I gained from that experience.

This Ain't No Place for Spoiled Little Mama's Boys & Girls

Not everyone can handle being yelled at and told what to do. You can tell the type of person who's going to have trouble with this authority-driven set-up. They're the ones who never did chores at home, who cried and whined through their homework, and who basically got whatever they wanted. We called these guys "Girly Men," and we knew better NOT to call their female counterparts anything! (We had to be so cautious with the ladies. It was pretty much understood that we were to leave the girls alone. One showed up at the academy with ribbons in her hair and cute little dangly earrings, and boy, did we want to give her a hard time, but we knew better. That didn't stop me from saying, "Give me strength" under my breath.)

My experience at the academy meant more to me than I can ever put into words. I loved every minute of it, and I think that holds true for most of us. Now that my class is getting older, there probably aren't many of us who would want to repeat it now, but I'll tell you, if someone had told me at the end of those sixteen weeks that I had to turn around and do it again, I would have jumped at the chance. Nowadays it takes longer to get to graduation, about twenty-four weeks, and that would have suited me just fine. The mere fact that they chose me was overwhelming. Wow. They chose me to be a state trooper! I just didn't think life could get much better.

This Badge is Gold

On the first or second day of class, us cadets were standing in alphabetical order behind our desks at parade rest (a casual "at attention," for you non-cops) in a theater-style classroom. The door in the front of the classroom opened up, and Sgt. Vic Summers walked in and said, "Have a seat." He reached into his back pocket and pulled out his state police identification. He opened it up and held it out in front of us, displaying his gold state trooper badge.

"As you can see," he said, "this badge is gold. G-O-L-D. Every other badge in the state of Louisiana is silver."

He folded it back up and put in back in his pocket. That was all he said about that, but the message was loud and clear. *You are the Louisiana State Police and you are the very best.*

I don't know about you, but personally, I'd rather have a pound of gold than a pound of silver any day. It was pretty much known that when people saw our gold badge, they assumed we were the best. In certain instances, this bothered me because I'd arrive on the scene of an accident and the people involved would often cease talking with the police officer they had been dealing with, and run over to me. I felt bad for that officer, who was often even more qualified to do his job than I was. I didn't like the fact that in some of the public's minds, there was a pecking order and state troopers were often at the top. No wonder some cops think troopers are overconfident, but it's not always our fault.

Now, let me say this; it doesn't concern me what agency you're with, but you must have pride in your department, no matter what color your badge is. If you don't believe this from your heart, you might want to consider turning it in.

I think that a good cop is similar to a guard dog. Think about a guard dog. We've all seen some of these poor pups guarding the worst places; old grimy parking lots and junkyards. Even though they'd probably choose nicer digs if they could, they protect their spot like it's a palace. That's the way cops should be. All departments have their problems, for sure, but *you gotta dance with who brung ya.* Just as I don't want to hear that the quarterback of the Bears would rather play for Denver, a cop needs to think that his 'team' is the best there is, and work to help make it the best. This is the mindset the academy drills home.

Our badge really was gold, and boy was it pretty, but they are all beautiful. And they are all something to be proud of!

The Double-Edged Sword

From the minute we arrive at the academy, the plan is simple. They need to break us down in order to build us back up so that we can go out and take care of business. Oh, and one other detail I left out. Just before we graduate, they start knocking us back down a few notches so that we're not too overconfident or full of ourselves to get ourselves hurt. It's all necessary, but can be crazy making if you try and figure it all out while you're going through it.

When you were a kid, do you remember taking clay out of a box? Remember how it came out like a big blob? If you were like me, you'd throw it on the floor and stomp on it before picking it up and molding something cool out of it with your hands. Same idea. Young cadets are the blob. Once molded, however, we're a lean, mean, fighting machine.

To refresh your memory, the order of stages goes something like this:

1. We show up as new cadets and they let us know that we're definitely not boss. That's what all that macho screaming is about.

2. After the first six to eight weeks, they start lightening up a bit because they know that those of us who are still around are probably going to make it. (We're not officers yet, but in the back of their minds, they know they're going to be in training classes with us for the next twenty years.)

3. About a month before graduation, friends and family are invited for the "Let me explain what we've done with this person you used to know" talk. This is where they reveal why we've been acting a little weird during our nightly or weekend visits home (depending on what type of academy you're in).

4. They build us into cocky, macho invincible Supermen and women.

5. They shorten our pedestal before sending us out on our own.

Drop Down and Give Me 25

In the academy or any other quasi-military training, the purpose of the staff is to make sure that all new recruits grow into one unit. Our class of fifty-five was no different than any other; we had our screw ups. Doesn't every class have their screw ups? Those are the ones that you notice from the start and wonder if they really belong there. It was like when we were kids and had to pick our little brother for a team or game. Have you ever asked your mama:

"But why does he have to be my brother? Why can't I have so-and-so as a brother?"

"Well, that's just the way it is," she would say.

You didn't have a choice in the matter, so you learned you were going to have to find a way to like it. That's what we did at the academy. On occasion, which was usually every day, these screw ups would fulfill their ultimate purpose in life and screw up big time. One of the instructors would holler, "Drop down and give me 25."

Now, I'll be honest with you. I'm not crazy about doing punishment for some screw up, but we were a team and acted like one. So, like a bunch of fools, the rest of us fifty-four cadets would fall in the lean and rest position and do our twenty-five along with whatever notorious problem child was acting up for the moment. Why did we do this? Because it was all about…

All for One and One for All

The sergeant didn't command us *all* to drop, and would have never told us to. This was our choice as part of a team. And you can bet that later that night, a few of us cadets would go to said "screw ups" room and say, "You jerk, you screw up one more time, and …."

Our instructors were looking for the weak, trying to figure out who would remain on the team. Everything we did was wrong, even if it was right. After completing the push-ups, we jumped back to our feet and stood at attention. Outwardly, the instructor would never smile after such an act, but deep inside, he had to fight to keep a smile from his face. He knew the goal had been accomplished.

The Will to Survive

Another job of the instructor was to make us feel invincible. Remember the song, *Through the Hill*? I could sing it in my sleep: "Over the hill, around the hill. Hell no; through the hill!" The message was clear: We were studs to the max and didn't act like normal people. We were superheroes, able to handle any obstacle. Again, it's part of thinking like a team. In the military, if the drill sergeant says, "Take the hill," you aren't thinking about the bullets, you're just thinking about one thing: following orders. This mentality serves us well in times of chaos. But it can be hard on the individual.

We became a strong unit and embodied the "All for one and one for all" slogan. An example of that was demonstrated when we were on the three- or five-mile hikes (which, were no Sunday strolls). Most of us were really physically fit, but we had those few who struggled. There were always one or two who couldn't make it all the way, at least not by themselves. If they fell out of the run, this was not an individual failure, but a squadron failure. Two of us would fall back, one on each side of whomever was slowing down or dropping out, and each one would grab an arm, encouraging the cadet to keep going as we carried their load. This created a love/hate relationship because obviously, if they weren't there, life would be easier. But we knew that this was about US and not about ME.

It was the same for academics. There were some who were smarter or better test takers than others. We studied hours every night and it was tough. The ones who understood a certain topic, whether it was the revised statutes, search and seizure, or the Intoxilizer, would help the ones who were falling behind. There was always someone, no matter what subject, who excelled and readily understood the material, which made it better for everyone.

The Will to Survive

You Gotta Have the Red T-Shirt

One morning, Sgt. Futrell walked in with a load of red t-shirts and handed them out. When I say the word red, I'm sure your subconscious mind is already bringing up inferences to the color: power, danger, blood, hookers (oops, I didn't mean to say that one), or fire, to name a few. On the front of this shirt was a picture of a bulldog. There again, what images come to mind when you see the word bulldog? Maybe power, loyalty, perseverance, tenacity (the will to fight to the death). And, did I say ugly? That reminds me of Sgt. Aubrey Futrell!

Sgt. Futrell played football at Louisiana Tech University, where his teammate was Terry Bradshaw, so maybe because their mascot was the Bulldogs he got an idea or two. I was proud to put on that shirt. Encircling the logo of the bulldog on the front of the t-shirt were four words:

State Police Ride Alone

Everything the state police academy staff said or did had a purpose. There was nothing implied or assumed. The red shirt, the bulldog, the slogan; the message was obvious: *you* are the very best. You are the most prepared and equipped officers to handle danger. You have the tenacity of a bulldog and you don't want, nor do you need, back up.

Forget the irony that dogs are extremely social beings, pack animals, to be exact, and, given the chance, almost always choose *not* to be alone. But, there was something even more conflicted about the message of the shirt, which became clear to me upon leaving the academy. We had just been taught how to act like a team, no matter what. All for one and one for all. But after graduation, they'd be sending us out on our own. Alone.

All alone.

And, in going out in our new car (a chariot to us),

with our shiny badge that made us feel so proud and strong and invincible, we'd be hit with another realization. Not everyone is going to like us as much as we like ourselves. Some people will wish us dead.

More on that in a minute.

Graduation

The week of graduation was as exciting as anything that's ever happened to me. From getting my uniform and weapon, taking final exams and pictures, this was even better than high school graduation. This was the day I had envisioned for years, and each day at the academy was one more exciting day closer toward my goal of graduating. I put on my uniform and stood in front of the mirror and couldn't get that smile off my face. Behind that smile, I was so proud that I wanted to cry.

As president of my class, I had some part in the ceremony as well. Standing in the line to get my diploma, I had such anticipation. We had walked into the academy as mostly strangers, but we were walking out a family. Some of my closest friends, some of the people who would stand by me through the roughest points of my life, were friendships forged here. My heart was pounding so hard as I walked up the steps to the stage. Ohmygod, ohmygod. I was in total disbelief, as if I was living a dream. We were all speechless.

Sgt. Vic Summers pinned the badge on my chest and I was no longer "Cadet Smith." Now I was one of them. "Congratulations, Bobby," he said. I wanted to pinch myself. The only other moments that held this much importance to me were the births of my children. There is so much anticipation that builds up during a pregnancy, and for me, graduating had that same type of joy attached to it. If you ask most officers, what do you think are the two most important areas of their life? Family and Career? You bet! I was on my way.

State Police Really Do Ride Alone

As a state trooper, I found out that my closest back up was thirty minutes away. I call Jackie my partner, but the truth of it was, we worked the same county but not at the same time. When he was on, I was off. When he was off, I was on. We were taught to work as a team, but they put us out there all alone. Sometimes I wished that we had worked in a larger agency so that we could have had a two-person unit. It puts a lot of stress on officers knowing that help is a long way off if you need it. We all knew that most cops killed in the line of duty were by themselves. But that is a byproduct of budgets cuts and a lack of money. Every state is in a money crunch, which can lead to more frustration on the part of the officer—the first line of defense in times of trouble.

The Disillusioned Knight in Shining Armor

"F18, go by Miss Robert's house at 625 N. 21st St. She just called in and stated that she's pulling a homemade apple pie out of the oven and has put on a fresh pot of coffee. Go by and see her. She'll be waiting for you on the front porch. F18, enjoy yourself."

Yeah, right. You've got to be kidding! We never had such a call. Not ever. Isn't it more like this?:

"F18, see Miss Roberts in reference to a domestic complaint. Her neighbor called and said that Miss Roberts' irate drunken husband has just beaten her to a bloody pulp. He's in the back bedroom threatening to kill her. Be careful."

The Will to Survive

Think about it. When people call the police, they don't do it because they're in a great mood and just want to chat and share their baked goods. They call us when they're in trouble. They call us when they're scared. They call us when someone has overdosed or has been raped. Not when they're taking a pie out of the oven—unless they've caught the house on fire, but then they're calling our brothers and sisters with the big red trucks instead.

In the academy, life is all about dignity and honor and pride. We dream about our shiny new car, our shinier badge, and about that crisp, clean intimidating uniform. The real world, however, doesn't always mirror that vision. We're not always prepared when somebody spits in our face, calls us an f-ing pig, or gets blood on our freshly pressed shirt. What happened to the spit-shined and polished world of yes sirs and snap to's?...

Right about now, disillusionment can set in.

Oh, you mean it's not going to be fun all of the time?

Aren't they supposed to love us?

I'm putting my life on the line, aren't they supposed to at least like me?

Don't they realize I swore to protect and serve *them*?

This is when most rookie cops start to question themselves, maybe even wonder if they've made a mistake. The "I'm the man" mentality takes on a little insecurity. Some of us counter that with a few more heaping spoonfuls of arrogance. It's only natural.

The Will to Survive

There's a Thin Line Between Being Cocky and Confident

All too often, cops lean too heavily toward the cocky side. But, before you non-police personnel start chucking stones, you had better give this some thought. When you call for help, do you want the cop who steps out of his or her car to be extremely confident in their abilities, or more on the shy and uncertain side? Do you want them to protect you with a little bit of arrogance (complete with the eye of the tiger), or do you want someone to step out with body language that says, "I'm not really sure what to do here." Unfortunately, for us who wear the badge, we're expected to have the former mentality, not the latter. Do you see the dilemma placed on us? Deep down, we are compassionate. We do care. And, we have feelings, but if we show them, we could be criticized for being weak. It's so complicated! Sometimes we're damned if we do, damned if we don't!

This reminds me of a poem I've always loved.

"The Creation of Peace Officers"

When the Lord was creating peace officers, he was into his sixth day of overtime when an angel appeared and said, "You're doing a lot of fiddling around on this one."

And the Lord said, "Have you read the specs on this order? A peace officer has to be able to run five miles through alleys in the dark, scale walls, enter homes the health inspector wouldn't touch, and not wrinkle his uniform.

"He has to be able to sit in an undercover car all day on a stakeout, cover a homicide scene that night, canvass the neighborhood for witnesses, and testify in court the next day.

"He has to be in top physical condition at all times, running on black coffee and half-eaten meals. And he has to have six pairs of hands."

The Will to Survive

The angel shook her head slowly and said, "Six pairs of hands... no way."

"It's not the hands that are causing me problems," said the Lord, "it's the three pairs of eyes an officer has to have."

"That's on the standard model?" asked the angel.

The Lord nodded. One pair that sees through a bulge in a pocket before he asks, 'May I see what's in there, sir?' (When he already knows and wishes he'd taken that accounting job.) Another pair here in the side of his head for his partners' safety. And another pair of eyes here in front that can look reassuringly at a bleeding victim and say, 'You'll be all right ma'am, when he knows it isn't so."

"Lord," said the angel, touching his sleeve, "rest and work on this tomorrow."

"I can't," said the Lord, "I already have a model that can talk a 250 pound drunk into a patrol car without incident and feed a family of five on a civil service paycheck."

The angel circled the model of the peace officer very slowly, "Can it think?" she asked.

"You bet," said the Lord. "It can tell you the elements of a hundred crimes; recite Miranda warnings in its sleep; detain, investigate, search, and arrest a gang member on the street in less time than it takes five learned judges to debate the legality of the stop... and still it keeps its sense of humor.

This officer also has phenomenal personal control. He can deal with crime scenes painted in hell, coax a confession from a child abuser, comfort a murder victim's family, and then read in the daily paper how law enforcement isn't sensitive to the rights of criminal suspects."

Finally, the angel bent over and ran her finger across the cheek of the peace officer. "There's a leak," she pro-

nounced. "I told you that you were trying to put too much into this model."

> *"That's not a leak," said the lord, "it's a tear."*
>
> *"What's the tear for?" asked the angel.*
>
> *"It's for bottled-up emotions, for fallen comrades, for commitment to that funny piece of cloth called the American flag, for justice."*
>
> *"You're a genius," said the angel.*
>
> *The Lord looked somber. "I didn't put it there," he said.*

Anonymous

Rookie Cadet: This Guy's Got to Be Joking!

I'm going to tell you one of my favorite memories, and you decide if you'd rather have this wimp answer your call for help, or a more confident cop like me.

One night I went to the station to pick up a new cadet. As we were driving through town, he says:

"Where are we working tonight?"

"Booker T," I answered. This was slang, obviously, referring to the famous slave who became a hero to blacks in the 1800s.

"Isn't that a black district? You know, those people really scare me."

I looked at him and smiled, thinking, "This guy is going to be a fun partner; what a great sense of humor!" Before we even got to the district, we got a call about a fight in the area. A black officer was fighting off four blacks. I couldn't wait to get there and help my buddy. We pulled up and I raced out of the car and started *snatchin' and grabbin'* these guys off the officer. Now, we're in a battle royal, with blood everywhere. I was scared to death, but in a good way. I could taste the fear in my mouth, but had the best feeling in the world cuz we were winning and getting them all arrested.

I look up, with blood running down my chin from a busted lip, thinking, "Where is this rookie cop?" I see him sitting in the same place I left him: in the passenger seat of my unit. He's sitting like a tin soldier looking straight ahead. Like a mannequin! I walked back to the car and said,

"What the hell are you doing?" He rolled down the window, sitting with the microphone in his hand and said,

"I was manning the radio, in case they called for us."

I couldn't get this guy back to the police station fast enough. I dropped him off at the department and said, "Get Out." It was bad enough having to take care of myself alone out there much less having to baby-sit a guy who didn't have a clue. I now see that he was disillusioned, thinking it was all going to be about driving around in his shiny car, going to lunch with everybody staring at him like he was a celebrity or something. He must have been so disappointed when he saw the other side.

I was blessed to love it, gore, and all. Sure, I started off wide-eyed and as innocent, excited, and clueless as the next guy. But, when a guy would yell, "Nobody wants you here, Pig. Get off my property," that only made me want to jump in faster. I could see the reality that I was now in a love/hate job because the public either loves you or hates you, with no in-between. I had thick skin.

It Was Worth Every Drop of Sweat

The academy prepared me well. When we graduated, we really did feel like we had gone through the hill during those weeks. I could look in the mirror and know that I didn't sidestep anything. Never took the easy road. I noticed several ways to take shortcuts, but when they pinned that badge on my chest, I was glad I hadn't taken any of them. Isn't it funny how the things we accomplish in life that are the most difficult, end up being the things we're the most proud of?

I remember one rainy day, our instructor had us run fifty laps around the gym rather than risk getting us struck by lightning. There were guys who would cut across the gym when the officer left the building, or suddenly have three more laps on their tally, but not me. I was determined to earn every aspect of getting my badge. If I lost count at lap 12 or 13, I'd say that I was on lap 12. I'd rather redo a lap than miss one. One guy was a college athlete, but a slacker and would do things like pad his count. Guess what? He lasted one day on the job because he was fired for being lazy and egotistical! It was important to me to know that I deserved this position; that nobody gave it to me. I had earned it.

That's probably why it was so devastating to me when I lost my career. I was taught that I was the very best and didn't have to back down from anything.

You know, until I stole those damn glasses eleven years into it, I had full confidence in my abilities and my self worth.

I was soon to learn about a whole other reality, however. About what to do when you're no longer Superman and don't even have the courage to start going toward the hill, much less through it...

CHAPTER III
Big Boys Don't Cry & Other Myths

I was thirty-three years old when I was finally caught, and I was scared to death. I never thought I'd have to deal with being "found out." I thought I'd always get away with it—with no concept that I wouldn't be able to keep the charade going. My whole life was designed not to have to deal with this.

What was I trying so desperately to avoid?

My feelings.

My mama died on my tenth birthday. It was December 12, 1962, and she was thirty-six years old. What are the odds? There are 365 days in a year, and my beloved mama had to die on my special day! Actually, her death had double the impact: It was my twin sister Betty's birthday as well.

We knew mama was sick. In fact, we had never known her not to be sick. By a cruel twist of fate, our birth coincided with our mother having a life-threatening skin disease that was exacerbated by a previous diabetic condition. Every day of our lives mama was in constant, excruciating pain caused by huge lesions on the inside and open ones on the outside of her body. I'm not even going to try to explain the guilt that instilled in my sister and me, but you can imagine that I grew up fast, trying to be strong and capable and always upbeat for my mother. Because she was often bed ridden, I did my best never to be a burden to her, and to be the very best little boy I could possibly be.

I learned early on never to let anyone see me cry.

Heroes Aren't Supposed to Cry

"It was touching to see everyone pay their respects. I was bawling."

Detective Bobby Bell, talking in an AP report about how police officers, firefighters, sanitation workers and volunteers saluted to two police officer's bodies that were pulled out of the wreckage at the World Trade Center rubble following September 11th.

When we were kids, Superman showed us that heroes don't cry. So did John Wayne. Think about it, did you ever see any of your childhood cowboy or superhero idols break down in a tearful scene? It just didn't happen. And, chances are, the closest thing you ever knew to a superhero was a cop, and I bet he or she didn't cry either. At least not in front of you or an audience. That doesn't mean, however, that cops shouldn't cry. Some of us were told, either through our training or from other cops (often veteran officers), that crying is for "sissies," for "little girls." Even if those words were unspoken, they were understood.

Now, while it's true that there's a time and a place for everything (and we'll talk about the necessity of having a certain mentality to be a good cop in a later chapter), when we step back and look at where these "unwritten" rules come from, we see that the myths and stereotypes—usually generated by the media and from other cops—stem from fear. Fear of appearing weak. Fear of losing control. Fear of failing. In the 1940s, 50s and 60s, the movie studio heads believed that if John Wayne cried over his coffee in front of the campfire, the Indians and rogue outlaws would have the upper hand. More importantly, the generation of young male fans of the day—who were all taught to keep their upper lips stiff in post WWII America—might stop paying to see their hunky idols kick the bad guys' butts. The 1970s catapulted that mindset to a new high when the ultimate cop role model came onto the scene. Life as we knew it would never be the same...

Dirty Harry Comes to Town

You talk about the ultimate role model for cops in the twentieth century; the number one law-enforcement "ideal" ever, and you've got Clint Eastwood as "Dirty Harry" Callahan. This sucker was tough to the core. The leanest, meanest cop to ever walk the streets, and never you mind that those streets were from a Hollywood movie set. Cops didn't care that he wasn't real; it's like we were all under some mass hypnosis spell, wanting to be just like the ultra cool, rogue San Francisco cop who broke all the rules and shot first, asking questions later. I'm telling you, I loved my partners, but I would have LOVED to have had *Dirty Harry* as a partner! Me and Clint, kicking in doors. I can just see us getting our butts chewed out by the police commissioner and getting outside his office door, looking at each other and bursting out in laughter. "Hey, now let's go get somebody else..." What a policeman's dream!

Clint, as Harry, was cold, calculating, and indifferent. He didn't smile, and boy could he enforce the law! The women swooned, seeing those steely blue eyes and his perfectly chiseled face, strengthening the belief that the good guys were supposed to be even more intimidating than the bad guys.

When I was on the force, all cops could quote his signature lines, and did we ever! Starting off with the original

The Will to Survive

Dirty Harry movie, we were hooked. Who didn't love the scene at the end of the movie where Clint is standing on the dock with the villain? After firing rounds at each other, the villain finds himself at the end of the dock with two choices: jump in the water or try to get past Harry. Glaring at the villain with his gun drawn, Harry says:

"I know what you're thinking, punk. You're thinking, 'Did he fire six shots or only five?' Well, to tell you the truth, I forgot myself in all this excitement. Being that this is a .44 Magnum, the most powerful handgun in the world that'll blow your head clean off, you gotta ask yourself a question: 'Do I feel lucky?' Well, do ya, punk?"

You could hear a pin drop in the theaters during the standoff. There sure aren't any tears welling up in Harry's eyes, or any remorse registering on his face when he fires the sixth round from his .44 Magnum revolver. As the projectile strikes the villain in the chest, knocking him into the water, the crowd cheers for their new hero. I think we cops cheered the loudest. I know I fantasized about being that tough!

How about the lines: "Go ahead, punk, make my day!," or "Opinions are like assholes, everybody has one." Do you think those sayings encouraged those of us who really worked the streets to feel our pain, or care deeply about the pain of others? Many of us became men under the shadow of that role model—a cop who encouraged felons to commit crimes so that he'd have all the excuses he needed for blowing them away. For thirty years we watched Clint on the screen as detective Callahan in five different movies, and in later roles with similar characters. Each time we viewed this icon, the message was the same: Big boys *never* cry. Just listen to the way the first movie opens, and see if you think

The Will to Survive

this guy ever let his guard down:

"This is a movie about a couple of killers: Harry Callahan and a homicidal maniac. The one with the badge is Harry. There are a lot of reasons they called him Dirty, and he kept inventing new ones."

While the voiceover plays, we see Harry on the screen, shooting a driver in his car as it speeds through a busy city street.

So, you can see why we have had trouble with this pesky little issue of feeling our feelings! (And, this might have a thing or two to do with why some of us have taken shortcuts; avoided rules and regulations, even stepped on the unethical slippery slope.) As young boys, we revered the benevolent hero Superman; as teens, we dreamed of riding on the range with Mr. Stud Himself, John Wayne, but we all quickly graduated into adulthood with cold-as-ice Clint. Obviously, these were the days before Oprah, before talk shows and pop psychology jargon hit the mainstream. Guys like me didn't know we even had an inner child much less that it needed hugging or healing.

Sometimes I was as dumb as a post, and as full of myself as could be. I was a competitive power lifter and could be as macho as the next guy. I was married with a daughter, was popular on the force, and was strong and healthy and good-looking (did I mention *how* good looking?). I had everything a guy could want. Still, I had plenty to cry about, if I had taken the time to check in with myself. Instead, I preferred lifting heavy barbells in my Superman T-shirt or drinking a few too many with the boys after our shift. There was way too much pain in my past to risk seeing the demons that were locked away in that closet. It was far easier to shoot the breeze with my buddies after a long day than to go home and face my troubled marriage or my haunting childhood memories. I had made sure that those issues were locked away in the closet, so to speak, one in which I had purposely swallowed the key. Trouble was, as you may be finding in your own life, that dang closet door has a way of creeping open at the most inopportune moments, seemingly without warning. That's when everything feels like it's spiraling out of your control and there doesn't seem to be a darn thing you can do about it.

God obviously had different plans for my life than to continue on indefinitely as Mr. Macho Man. After eleven years on the force, I was about to get royally slammed out of my superhero, western, shoot 'em-up, gun slinging, cops and robbers, bigger-than-life movie icon fantasy. I was about to get a full-fledged education in crying, weeping, and sobbing.

Mr. Smith; Mr. Tough as Nails Louisiana State Trooper, was about to become an emotional cripple...

From Invincible to Helpless

One fateful moment on a lonely country highway in the dark of night, I stopped the wrong man. Actually, I stopped the right man in the wrong way, with no idea that he had a car full of weapons for the sole purpose of killing a cop like me that night. I couldn't have known that this former LSD user had fried his brain; I was high myself that night; high on the ego rush of chaining the beast, of being the hero, of taking the law into my own hands. Dirty Harry would have been proud. I knew the "shoulds" and precautions for stopping a speeding car that raced through a highway checkpoint. I knew the "safe" way to take down an idiot like this; in fact, I had successfully done that very thing only days earlier in a nearby cotton field. But I was in a hurry and following protocol would only take extra time. Besides, time had proven that I was indeed invincible. Why should this night be any different?

I used to love these driver's license checkpoint exercises. "Just doin' a little public relations," we'd say, making sure the folks all had their up-to-date licenses, registration and insurance. After eating out with a few of the guys, we got in our units and headed south on LA 15, about five miles south of Winnsboro, Louisiana.

Everything about that night was normal and easy, until a small red car heading north on LA 15 ran through our checkpoint. Although the car slowed down a bit on approach, at the last minute the driver sped up and nearly hit us. We were fit to be tied, and I immediately jumped in my unit and took off, gaining on him at about 85 mph. Suddenly the driver slammed on his breaks and I had to swerve to miss crashing into his behind. As his car pulled over to the side of the highway, I didn't want to take the time to turn my car around in a position of advantage. Instead, I hurriedly pulled up in front of him and jumped out of my vehicle.

That's when I immediately knew I was in trouble. I was a sitting duck in his blinding headlights. I couldn't see the perp, but he had full view of me. As I struggled to make out my surroundings in the severe light of his high beams in contrast to the blackness surrounding the highway, I heard the shots that would hit me square in the head. I fired back in the direction of the oncoming bullets, and the next thing I knew, I was lying face down on the center lane of the highway. I could feel blood running down my face, taking my life force with it. Unbelievably, I felt no pain. Was it my day to die? I heard a ruckus of panic around me—vehicle doors slamming, six additional shots fired, and the fearful voices of my buddies coming to my rescue.

The Will to Survive

Complete and Total Darkness

For the weeks I lived in the hospital following my shooting, I was never alone. My family and friends rallied in a way that was not to be believed. While their companionship was priceless, it didn't change the fact that I felt more alone than at any time in my life. I was glad to hear that I had shot the perpetrator and that he had died on the way to the hospital, but this victory was without celebration, as my eyesight was gone and in many ways I felt dead myself. Everyone had told me how lucky I was to have survived without brain damage. I had been such a horrible sight that night on the highway, with a face full of blood and holes where the pellets had entered my left eye and forehead. One of my buddies, who had come to my aid, ran away from me screaming after turning me over. My left eyeball had been shot from its socket and was partially lying on my cheek. The top of my scalp had been ripped off, and my hands were a bloody mess. Let's just say that I looked grotesque and it was miraculous that I had survived. It wasn't long, however, before my appearance was decent enough behind those big dark ugly glasses, and those who cared about me were both relieved and grateful.

I, on the other hand, was drowning in sorrow.

Imagine losing your beloved vocation and your eyesight in one fell swoop. All I had ever wanted to do was be a police officer, but I knew I'd never be able to drive a squad car or take down a bad guy in total darkness. Then it got worse. As I will explain in the next chapter, my wife left me six months later. Needless to say, I felt like I had just lost everything that was near and dear to me. Yes, I had experienced struggles before, but this was bigger than I could handle. My life had become a living hell.

The Will to Survive

Rivers of Tears

It took a huge knock on the head, literally, for me to get the message about the importance of feeling my feelings. Boy, did I have plenty of time to feel my feelings after that! For many months after my shooting, there didn't seem to be time for anything else *but* grieving. After losing my sight, my job, and soon thereafter my marriage, I had plenty to cry about, all day and all night. The nightmares were unbearable. Night after night I would relive my shooting in my dreams. Everything I had come to believe about myself was challenged, and everything I knew to be true about being a cop was up for grabs. Suddenly we weren't invincible. The badge didn't give total protection. And, cops *really* do cry! I wasn't the only one bawling like a baby, either. I may not have seen their tears, but plenty of my fellow officers had to leave my hospital room because they were weeping. My eyesight may have been taken, but I could still hear their sobs.

The tough guy who rarely grieved (that would be me) suddenly became the guy who could do little else (that would be me all the time). Every time someone would leave and I'd be left alone in my house, I'd go straight to my room and curl up in the corner and have an anxiety attack, weeping for hours at a time. This was not the me that I knew. This was crazy! I didn't know how to stop the downturn and was beginning to think of committing suicide. My doctor recommended that I go to see a psychiatrist because my panic attacks and the uncontrollable bouts of crying were paralyzing. I had no interest whatsoever in seeing a shrink. Cops don't like shrinks. People ask me why cops don't like head doctors and I say, "Because they're all nuts!" At least I thought they were. Sure enough, on my first visit to the doctor it took me about ten minutes to realize that this guy was nuts. Whacked out. Crazier than a run-over dog.

I left and found another doctor. I kept going until I found one who I could trust and respect. Just in case you're tempted to think, "Forget it, I'm not going to work that hard. I won't be able to find a good one," I ask you:

Are there bad teachers?

Bad doctors?

Bad cops?

Of course there are! Do you pull your kid out of school forever if you don't like his teacher? No! You transfer him into another class or find him a different school, but you don't give up on your son. I'm asking you not to give up on yourself either if you think you might need help. As we age, we all have to become our own parents at some point; I just had to do that a lot sooner than most. Thankfully, I didn't let a few bad experiences stop me from getting extra help. And it was worth every minute of searching through a slew of bad "head doctors" to find the right one. Therapy not only helped me to begin to have fun again, but it probably saved my life.

Closed Emotional Doors

Dr. Bryant—my kind-hearted and brilliant therapist was someone I could finally trust. That much I knew. Maybe that's why his efforts were starting to sink in and seep through my emotional armor. This still wasn't my idea of having a good time, but I was starting to feel safe with this man; things were starting to shift. Ever since going blind, I had been hanging on by a thread, waiting for someone to cheer me out of my misery or put me out of it.

"Bobby," he said one afternoon. "What I'd like to do today, with your permission, is to have you answer a very important question for me... *Who* is Bobby Smith?" At the time, I didn't immediately know what he was asking, but now that I'm a therapist, I understand the importance of gathering as many pieces of the puzzle as possible from a client, in order to see the complete picture.

"I grew up on a small farm," I answered slowly. "We were very poor. Although my dad was an extremely hard worker and I never recall him missing a day's work, my mother's illness caused a serious financial burden on our family. We were monetarily poor, but were extremely wealthy in our love for one another." I began to share details about my dad, my two older brothers (who were incredible athletes, as well as my mentors), and my twin sister, who was and still is one of my best friends.

As I began to talk about my mama, however, my whole demeanor changed. My facial expressions, my body language, and my voice inflections all shifted. For a man trained in reading body language, it was obvious to him that I had locked away a lot of pain around the topic of my mama.

This was Dr. Bryant's lucky day. This is why any good therapist does what he or she does: for the breakthroughs. Dr. Bryant knew that he had just found an emotional closet, filled with grief and loss. Being totally blind, I am not distracted by things around me and as I began talking about my mama, it was as if I had drifted away all alone, blowing wide open for the first time the doors of grief and loss in my subconscious. There was no doubt in my mind at that particular moment that Dr. Bryant placed his tablet of paper and pen in his lap, picked up his cup of coffee from the table in front of him, and leaned back with a smile because he realized that he had just found what he was looking for. The closet door had eased open.

The Will to Survive

In a nutshell, here is what I shared with him...

I told him about my childhood, sitting in the middle of mama's bed at night while she told my two older brothers and Betty and me stories. My mother loved to tell stories (guess where I got that trait from?), and she loved to hear us kids sing to her when we visited her at the hospital. We would stand around her bed and sing at our very best. We weren't the Osmond's, but I'm sure it was beautiful to her. Mama would always cry when the four of us sang.

"Dad, maybe we shouldn't sing to mama anymore," I said on the way home from the hospital one evening. "Every time we do, she cries. I don't like to see mama cry." Dad replied, "Son, you just keep on singing." He knew something we children hadn't thought of: Our mama treasured each time she heard us sing because she knew at all times that it could be her last.

I then told Dr. Bryant about our tenth birthday, so many years ago, yet still so fresh in my mind. I explained how Betty and I could barely contain our excitement at school that day, racing toward the bus at the last bell. During the 8-mile drive home we chatted excitedly about what kind of dinner awaited us and what presents we might hope to open. We jumped off the bus at our stop, noticing that the driveway was full of cars. That didn't seem too unusual, however, because this was a very special day. We raced each other to the front door; I got there first. People were everywhere, but they should have been, it was obviously a party for us! But almost immediately, I could tell that something was wrong. Everyone appeared to be sad. Most were crying.

Our aunt Irma walked over to us with tears streaming down her face. She knelt down in front of us, reached out and hugged Betty and then me before saying,

"I'm so sorry children, but your mother is dead."

The Will to Survive

When I tell people this story, they are often surprised by my aunt's blunt speech. "Couldn't she have found a more gentle way to tell you two?" they ask. No. Not where I come from. This was the country, and life was hard. Being tough was just a reality of life. People talked in facts, no matter how harsh those facts were.

Sitting in Dr. Bryant's office at the age of thirty-three, I began to cry. Only several months ago, my shooting had brought forth a geyser of hidden pain from my past. As I began to sob, it hit me that this was the first time I had truly grieved the death of my mama. It was horrible. I was hysterical, with my face in my hands, blubbering on and on. Cops feel so much shame when they break down like this. I tried to cover the shame on my face with my hands, as if I could mask my embarrassment by hiding my face from view.

Why? Because…

Big Boys Don't Cry

After what seemed like a very long time, I began to gain my emotional composure. Dr. Bryant took a deep breath and said, "Bobby, why has it taken you twenty-three years to grieve the loss of your mother?" I had a pretty good idea why. "The same afternoon that my mama died," I explained, "one of my uncles walked over to me, put his arms around me, and said, 'Son, I know this is a difficult time for you, but you're going to have to be strong for your sister. *Remember now, big boys don't cry.'*"

I recall sitting on the front pew of the church at the funeral, looking at my mom lying there in the casket. Betty was sitting next to me; I was holding her hand and she was sobbing. But not me. Big boys don't cry. I wanted to yell out in church. I wanted to scream: *"How could a loving God take our mama on our birthday? Couldn't you have waited*

The Will to Survive

a week?" As my mind raced, I knew I had just lost three things: my beloved mama, my faith in God, and the ability to ever again celebrate on what was supposed to be my special day. It was clear to me on that day that God was punishing me and that life wasn't fair, which would prove to be true many times in the future. But another thing was also true: I was now a big boy and I had a job to do—to stay strong for my family. Sometimes that didn't work too well.

During the following two years, I failed so many classes that I was forced to repeat the sixth grade. I realized many years later that my sixth-grade teacher, Miss Maxine Deville, had become my surrogate mom. I loved her and I didn't want to leave her class.

Like it was yesterday, I remember sitting at my desk one morning as the principal's voice blared out over the intercom: "Miss Deville, bring Bobby to my office." A Rhodes scholar I was not, but I was a good kid. I never got into trouble. All the eyes of the children were fixed on me. Everyone knew what was about to take place.

Miss Deville walked over to my desk extending her hand and said, "Come on, Bobby, I'll go with you." Hand in hand, we walked down the hallway. No words were spoken as we entered the administrative offices leading into the principal's room. The principal looked up from his desk and advised me to have a seat, telling Miss Deville to return to her class. I sat in the chair in front of his desk with my head down, shaking. I knew what was coming. This was 1963 in Louisiana. If you did something wrong, you didn't get a letter sent home to your mama and daddy; you got your butt tore up and then got sent back to class. Things were different then. Adults had all the power.

The principal stood up from behind his desk with a three-foot long wooden paddle with holes drilled in the end

The Will to Survive

(for added pain), and walked toward me yelling:

"Boy, what's wrong with you? There's no sense in you failing the same grade two years in a row! I'm about to adjust your attitude."

His rhetorical questions continued and once again he yelled, "Boy, what's wrong with you?"

I remember sitting in fear thinking, "If you *really* want to know, I'll tell you what's wrong with me: I want my mama. I want her to come home. I don't want my mama to be dead anymore. I just want her to come home and tell me that everything's going to be all right."

Did I ever grieve for my mama? Not as a child. I was the family mascot—busy being the extroverted, fun-loving kid around the house. My dad was an introvert; a soft-spoken and hard-working man. I needed to balance him and keep up the fun my mother always seemed to be able to bring, in spite of her pain. That was my job. I felt that if I broke down and lost it, my family would fall apart. I placed the loss of my mama in the closet and boarded it up with big nails. There was so much loss, primarily of expectation. There would be no mama to watch me ever again on the football field. No mama would ever get to meet my girlfriends or watch me walking down the aisle. That was too much to face at such a young age.

Don't worry, I'm not going to ask you to all stand up, do a group hug, and sing *Kumbayah*. I'm not going to ask you to sit down and cry about your childhood or write in a journal about all the horrors you've seen. You don't have to sign up for therapy or learn to meditate and come to earth-shattering understandings about yourself. All I am asking you to do right now is to begin to be aware of what you feel, when you feel it. Pay attention to what is going on with you. Slow down and watch yourself. Are you reaching for a beer when you really need to talk to someone? Are you short with your wife or children simply because you're reacting to your day? Are you choosing to avoid something because it doesn't feel good? Just begin by noticing the details. This is a process and you don't have to master it by tomorrow. Take one step at a time, one day at a time. The more you read in the chapters ahead and sit with the ideas I'm outlining, the more natural the process will become.

Tears Can Actually Help Those You Serve

What I came to find is that tears help relieve pain, and not just our own. It is so ironic that the people we serve in the course of a day—many of whom have been victimized and are in trauma—actually appreciate seeing genuine emotion from us. In times of chaos or tragedy, superficial beliefs and behaviors often make way for deeper truth and emotions to surface. The very soul of a person is often front-and-center in traumatic situations. I have found that if you try to hide your feelings and act like a Clint Eastwood character (giving people a false front when it would be more appropriate to be vulnerable), they'll smell it a mile away. If they can't immediately tell that you're covering, they will know that something isn't quite right. They may not be conscious of why they don't trust you, but your emotional distance and in-authenticity will leave a bad taste in their mouth.

So, contrary to stereotypes, don't be afraid to show your humanity. The people we serve need to see us exhibit real emotions, and I'm talking about the gamut, from sadness to joy and everything in-between. Sometimes the only thing to do is cry. I'll never forget the night I got a call about a traffic accident on our local highway. When I arrived, it was immediately clear what had happened: two cars had collided in a head-on crash and a nine-year-old girl was thrown from

The Will to Survive

the car and was killed. Her mother, who was hysterical, spotted me driving up to the scene and began running toward me screaming, "Officer, please save my little girl," as she pointed to the lifeless body laying in a ditch. She repeated herself over and over until she was standing before me. There were plenty of paramedics on the scene—the guys and gals who knew better than I how to handle the situation—but she was focused only on me. Something about the motto, "To Protect and Serve" sticks in people's minds and they don't identify with other branches of emergency responders the way they do with us.

When the mother reached me, she was still screaming, begging me to save her daughter. There was nothing I could offer her but to open my arms. She flung herself into them, continuing her plea, even while knowing that nothing could breathe life into her child's lifeless form. What she really wanted from me was emotional support. She wanted to be hugged and to be understood. She wanted me to grieve *with* her. As my eyes filled with tears, I almost turned away. I could barely keep it together. I was speechless. All I could think about was *my* little girl at home—about the same age— and how this could be her little figure lying there in the dirt. I couldn't imagine what it must feel like to lose your child. I wanted to run, to be anywhere but on that road. Give me a good old drug bust or bank robbery anytime; just don't make me witness the death of a child. *Anything but the death of a child.* Without a word, I hugged her, and as my own tears gently flowed, I stroked the back of her head as she sobbed. Our mutual tears helped soothe us both, to a degree.

Was it easy? Hell no! That was one of the toughest nights I ever faced in my eleven years as a cop, but I had no choice but to do my job that night, and frankly, neither do you. It's the game we've chosen, no matter how brutal, and the trick is to know how to play it without risking your emotional or physical health, or burning out. At the time, I was tempted to "handle" the situation by putting on my Stone Cold Austin face (or, in those days, it was Hulk Hogan) and distance myself emotionally from the scene. But what happened when I cried? I have learned that my tears probably helped make the entire episode *less* frightening. My sadness gave silent permission to the young mother before me to feel her immense despair. It gave us both the room to be human. While I don't advise going to town with your emotions and bawling like a baby in front of others—which would necessitate that the focus turn toward you—I believe that authentic tears are not only appropriate, but appreciated. And, you won't have to hammer another nail into that closet door that will only burst open later and mess up your life.

When thinking about the far end of this spectrum, the funeral scenes on television following the police and fireman deaths at the World Trade Center come to mind. Clearly, the public needed to witness uniformed heroes crying along with them. If we hadn't cried, we would have seemed cold-hearted. It was our individual and collective tears that helped to heal not only us, but also the nation. Our vulnerability and sorrow gave permission for others to feel their pain. Through our common anguish, we gained strength together, a little at a time. The healing process had begun.

I'm not saying that it's easy to be on duty and feel your feelings at the same time. After all, you're paid to do a job—to protect and to serve—and that's not easily done if you're sad or grieving. There are so many unique stresses we face as cops, and you obviously have to be on top of your game. But, you must find the balance between being real with yourself and real with those around you. If you're

The Will to Survive

trying to hold back a world of grief and pretend that you're Superman, you're only making life harder on yourself, I can promise you that.

Pay Me Now or Pay Me Later

Feelings are like taxes. You either deal with them regularly, or pay dearly down the line, with interest! I don't know how old you are, but some of you will remember an old Fram Oil filter commercial. I love this commercial because it's so true about life. A mechanic stands in front of a smoking automobile with an orange oil filter in his hands. He's trying to convince a customer to spend a little money now to put in a new oil filter, vs. spending a lot of money later with a smoking engine. He says, "You have a choice. You can pay me $2.50 now (pointing to the filter), or you can pay me $2,500 later (pointing to the burning engine)." Very effective!

I have been pleasantly surprised to learn that crying wasn't always so frowned upon throughout history. A man by the name of Tom Lutz, Ph.D.—an associate professor of English at the University of Iowa and author of a book called *Crying: The Natural and Cultural History of Tears*—writes that crying was fairly normal for men and women prior to the Industrial Revolution. And, "Heroic epics from Greek times through the Middle Ages are soggy with weeping of all sorts," Lutz says in *Crying*. When Roland, the most famous warrior of medieval France died, 20,000 knights supposedly wept so profusely they fainted and fell from their horses.

Since feeling your feelings is no longer so socially acceptable, how do you do it without going overboard or being a total downer? There are so many instances that will come up where you will feel conflicted. Do I repress my emotions or let them out? Do I shed a tear or grit my teeth? Remember that gray area we talked about? The challenge is to stay open to what each new experience brings without becoming robotic or hardened. Each of us has to face these tough issues in our own way, and the first step is to start noticing that you have feelings. (This is often even harder for female officers, who try to stay especially strong in front of their male counterparts to ease concerns about women's emotional natures.) How, for instance, do you put on your dress blues to attend the funeral of a fellow officer and not break down like a baby at the service? Is it okay to break down, and how do you express your pain and get it out without falling apart in front of everyone? (See Chapter 9 for protocol etiquette.) Most of us will go to work the next day with a heart of steel that won't break again, or so we hope.

"I'll never forget the first time I had to go to court to protect a nine-year-old boy who was being sexually molested by his uncle. He was terrified to face his relatives—who denied the charges. I told him not to worry; that I'd be his strength. He was so afraid of making eye contact with the people he loved so dearly, the very people who had allowed the abuse to continue. I told him, 'Look at me when you want to look at them. Keep your eyes on me and I will give you courage.' The trouble was, I didn't anticipate how devastatingly hard it would be to be strong for him. All I wanted to do was cry myself, but I couldn't. The enormity of the situation was almost too much to handle. There they were—the creeps who were ruining this young boy's life, and lying to get away with it. I held back my tears as well as I could, but I'll tell you, I drove home and let them flow. I yelled a bit too. I knew this would eat at me for a long time if I didn't get those emotions out."

Julie Stranahan, LAPD

The Will to Survive

Detective Stranahan loves handling sexual assault cases, especially the part where she gets to put the bad guy in jail for a "really long time." She has learned that she has an effect on these children; they send her birthday cards and Christmas presents. But Julie says that it's the smile on these kid's faces that's the biggest gift of all. She's smart. Detective Stranahan understands that after days like the one just described, if she doesn't find a way to let her anger and grief out, those repressed emotions will catch up with her later!

As a cop, there will be many different situations like these that will pull on your heartstrings and cause you deep sadness. Obviously, there are more appropriate times to cry or break down than others. In the case of giving courage to a young child in court, tears could hurt the situation, but you will have to use your judgment about what works for you and those you serve. Stifling tears now will lead to greater sadness, even despair in the future. There is no way to avoid the grieving process; it has a way of sneaking up on all of us. The longer you try and hold your feelings at bay, the more you risk having your pain come out inappropriately. You can only put so much water in a cup!

Have You Ever Yelled When You Wanted to Cry?

*"Bobby, how do I know when showing my emotions is appropriate?"

*"I'm not comfortable crying in public. How can I cry without appearing weak?"

*"Where do I start? I don't want to end up burned out or worse!"

These are the questions both male and female officers frequently ask me after my lectures. Whether they are federal agents, state police, city cops, rural cops, supervisors or narcotics officers, the questions and concerns are the same. There is a general awareness that the old stoic Dirty Harry way of doing our job is outdated, but many are still unsure of how to change what has been the status quo for so long. Fortunately, it's getting easier and easier as awareness grows. The younger officers are blessed with better training and a more conscious mentality than we had in my day. I'm happy to report that the rumor that each generation grows from the mistakes of those they follow is true. And, there is plenty of help out there within departments, but unfortunately, many cops tell me that they still feel a stigma about going for that help. Some fear that if they tell a department counselor about their problems, whom the court can then subpoena, it's too risky. Tell someone who can screw up my life? I'd rather keep it locked up inside!

Hopefully I've got your attention, and maybe, just maybe you're wondering about steps you can take to get a little more help. Keep reading! I commend you for getting this far already (who says cops don't like to read?). Chapter 5 will give you further insights as to what to do, and there is a glossary of contact names and organizations in the back of the book if you desire immediate help. In the meantime, I will continue to give suggestions in each chapter, and through my story, you will continue to learn about what to do, who you are, and why you chose this job in the first place, which leads me to...

Why the Superman Mentality?

We cops are a unique breed, with distinct predictable personality characteristics. Whenever I talk about what we have in common in front of large groups of cops, the feedback is hilarious. We laugh and laugh, and the consensus is nearly unanimous. We have a lot in common, us cops. See if you can relate to any of the "norms."

Research Tells Me That:

1. The things that make us good cops can also make us bad cops.

2. A large percentage of us were the oldest or the dominant children in our families. If this applies to you, think back to when your parents would leave you at home with your younger siblings and put you "in charge." Do you think your siblings appreciated your newfound chargeness? Probably not, but the feeling of power and responsibility suited most of us just fine.

3. We are extroverted and like things fast-paced. No driving in the right lane like grandma for us!

4. We are, as a group, average students who prefer sports to class (we are stellar athletes).

5. We are very competitive and want to win at all costs.

6. We marry our high school sweethearts, the first time.

By our very nature, therefore, we are not the type to easily emote or analyze our feelings. Our heart is not taped to our sleeve. But no one taught us that when you hold in your feelings, you become overwhelmed with what's going on in your emotional closet and have trouble living in the moment. The majority of us didn't graduate at the top of our class, but we're smart and could have used that information! It's overwhelming to see a child killed, for example, and unless you deal with the horrific things you see and hear on this job—things that most "normal" people will never encounter in their lives even once, much less many times—you will get distracted and you will start to have problems in all areas of your life. You could get lazy and shot. Your closet will be stuffed full, bulging ever more with each new trauma and tragedy.

If you keep your emotional closet doors shut because you think that only sissy-wimps ask for help, and that Superman would handle any challenge *alone*, you're tempting fate. If you believe the motto "State Police Ride Alone" you're tempting fate. In my experience, becoming a statistic starts with walking with an attitude of superiority and machismo (ladies, I'm talking to you as well). This reminds me of my favorite motto. I beg of you; please remember it…

You Cannot Heal Until You Feel

You cannot heal from the losses you experience as a cop, or from life for that matter, until you feel the pain and sadness connected to each event and grieve those losses. I'm talking about all of them: the death of your first dog, moving away from your best friend, the divorce of your parents, the death of a grandparent, all the way to what you see and experience daily on this job—the rapes, the murders, the child abuse and the fatality accidents. If you don't take the time to feel your pain, it's going to come out in detrimental ways, like inappropriate humor, excessive anger, headaches, accidents, and so on.

Before you can deal with your present, you have to deal with your past.

Those of us who are left behind when an officer is killed on the job or who have witnessed the unthinkable, must cope and continue, which is a tall order. Being both a cop and a psychologist, I guess you could say that I know the drill from both sides of the fence. I know how hard it is to deal with emotions when you're a cop, and I know how much harder it will be if you don't deal with them. I have seen the disastrous after-effects, both in my own life and in the thousands of men and women I have counseled.

Opening the closet may mean becoming angry, often with yourself and with people you love, but you will get through it in time. The anger will turn to understanding and forgiveness, but only if you face it head on. I tell my clients and fellow officers, "*The* most important thing you need to understand here is that there are no Supermen. You have to accept your losses. You don't have to like them (I will never like the fact that I'm blind), but the only way to heal is through acceptance." That's usually when they start to cry, as they realize that they've got to let go. As I mentioned in the *Prologue*, we're taught in the academy how to shoot and write accident reports, but no one can really teach us how to deal with the aftermath of tragic events. That, unfortunately, is a learned skill. I didn't know how to deal with losing my sight and my career until I was faced with those realities. Learning came through the experience of doing. I truly believe that if you begin the process of feeling now, you will have less pain to deal with in the future.

Grieving Ain't No Foot Race

Wouldn't it be great if there were a designated starting point and a clearly delineated distance to travel in order to get rid of grief? When you crossed the finish line, you'd be finished. Man, I would love that! All we'd have to do is just go the distance and it'd all be over. No more tears, no more regret, and no more blindsiding sadness.

That's just not realistic. Some things heal with time; other things will never totally go away—the emotional pain of a disability, for instance, or the death of a child. While

The Will to Survive

there is some truth to the fact that time heals all wounds, time cannot erase all of our scars.

I have learned to live with being blind, but every time I hear a bird chirping and can't determine if it's perched on a tree limb, my roof, or a power line, I am reminded of my limitations. I am always learning how to live with this pain.

I'm going to close here with a short story. As you will see, it's incredibly symbolic to what this chapter is about.

About two years ago, I was sitting in my room in an Embassy Suites Hotel, getting prepared for an 8:30 A.M. lecture. I turned on the TV to occupy my mind before going to speak and realized I had turned to a show I had seen many times prior to my shooting; a show about family, character, integrity, and the importance of loyalty. It was *Little House on the Prairie.* Most of us remember Michael Landon's character of Charles Ingalls, or "Pa," the adoring husband and father, but do you remember his sidekick, Mr. Edwards? Mr. Edwards was a rough, mountain man; loud, obnoxious, and, Charles' best friend, although totally different in personality. As I walked back and forth getting dressed, it dawned on me that I remembered this particular episode. It had been fifteen or twenty years since I had watched the show, but I could see the actors in my mind's eye. The dialogue between the two characters caught my attention and I sat down on the edge of the bed, listening intently as Laura Ingalls talked lovingly with Mr. Edwards about why he had just called off his engagement with a woman many years his junior, with whom he was very much in love. (Incidentally, she happened to be blind, as was Laura's older sister, Mary, but that wasn't the focus of this episode.)

Their conversation went something like this:

The Will to Survive

"Mr. Edwards, why have you called off your engagement when you love her so much and she is so much in love with you?" Laura asked.

"Well, I'm just an old man and it's not fair to her because she's so young and beautiful. I'll probably be dead before she even reaches the prime of her life, so it just wouldn't be fair to her," he answered.

"Mr. Edwards, are you sad?"

"Yes, I'm very sad."

"Do you want to cry?"

"No. I don't want to cry," he said, "I want to laugh. But I know before I can ever laugh again, I must first learn to cry."

I rose to my feet, pointing at the TV with my right hand, damn near spilling my coffee. "Mr. Edwards," I shouted, "that's what I've been trying to tell them for ten years! That's what I'm about to lecture on to a room full of police officers!

That's what I'm *always* trying to say!"

Somewhere on some studio lot, nearly twenty years ago, some writer knew the perfect thing for Mr. Edwards to tell Laura. It sounded to me as if he or she also knew a thing or two about dealing with loss. Maybe this writer had learned through experience that you cannot heal until you feel. Maybe he or she also understood that big boys really do cry.

The Will to Survive

CHAPTER IV
No Cops Allowed at Home:
This is Where Mama & Daddy Live

I'm sitting upstairs in my office in our new home. It's been a good day. My board of directors just left an hour ago after a successful brainstorming meeting for the **FORTE** Foundation (Foundation for Officers Recovering from Traumatic Events). It looks like we're going to be breaking ground soon on the trauma center—the first ever in the U.S. for police officers, and I'm excited that we'll finally have a place for cops to go when they're burned out and dealing with issues like Posttraumatic stress disorder. As I think of my world at this moment, I'm feeling peaceful, grateful, and relaxed about where I am in my life and about what kind of value my work is bringing to others.

The sound of voices outside takes me out of my revere. Sounds like several people are getting ready to start a game or something. "Hey! Want to join us?" I hear a man's voice yell in the distance, headed in the direction of our house. "Yeah, I'll be right there!" my son Brad yells back from the side yard. At this point I can hear balls being caught and can tell they're starting a game of pitch. The chatter becomes muffled and I can't make out many words, but I can tell that several father-and-son duos are joining up.

I hear the back door fling open and Brad's familiar steps racing through the kitchen with the usual excitement of a thirteen-year-old about to play. He runs through the house, up the stairs to his room, where I assume he's getting his glove, and then as he's rounding the stairs towards where I'm sitting he yells,

The Will to Survive

"Hey Dad! Do you want to…" He catches himself and stops running. The excitement in his gait disappears and he slowly walks toward me.

"I'm sorry Dad, I forgot. I'll get one of the other dads to play pitch with me."

The next sound I hear is of Brad going down the stairs and exiting the house. As the door shuts behind him, tears begin to roll from my eyes like rain off a gutter. Another day in the life of a blind father.

I bet you can guess what the moral of this chapter is, huh? You got that right if you thought: **Appreciate Your Family!!!Every second you get with them.**

I didn't always know how to be a good husband and father. Some things, I'm afraid, are learned the hard way.

I married my high school sweetheart. The first time, like a gagillion cops before and after me. Actually, I married my elementary school sweetheart, who I was lucky enough to be with throughout high school. I fell in love with Jackie Crooks during my second year of sixth grade. (Yeah, I married a crook. I told her that if she married me and took my name, she wouldn't have to be crook no more.)

I'll never forget the first day Jackie walked into class from being transferred. She was tall and thin, at least a foot taller than me. Everyone wanted to get to know the new girl, especially me.

It didn't take long for me to win Jackie over with my charm—really it was my Mallow Cups (like a *Reeses Peanut Butter Cup*, with marshmallow cream inside). I got my first kiss that year from Jackie while standing next to the band building after a junior high football game. She played clarinet in the band, and we were in band together until they kicked me out for not knowing which of the three keys to press to make a "C" on my baritone.

Mr. Martinez, the band director, was so mad that day at my inabilities that he took his skinny white, ivory orchestra stick and was hitting his music stand with such force that the stick shattered across the floor. With a beet red face he yelled, "Get out! You haven't learned one single thing since you've been here." It was just as well because my brother Danny had clearly explained: "There will be no toot toot players in the Smith family. We're athletes, Boy!"

She Was My Whole Life

Thankfully, the one thing I didn't have to give up was Jackie. My family loved her from sixth grade right on through high school. She was the only girlfriend I ever had, and we dated from elementary school until the day we were married the year we graduated. I knew I was marrying a nurse because that's all Jackie ever talked about. But she didn't have a clue she was marrying a cop because I had no real plans. I had always worked construction in the summertime and had thought about being an electrician, which I did before I went to college, but all she knew was that she would have a husband who worked for a living. When I told her of my goal to become an officer, it wasn't a big deal. By that time, she was used to the idea of trauma because she was a trauma nurse and saw police officers in the emergency room all the time. It is amazing how many police officers marry nurses because we're all accustomed to trauma and caretaking and protecting and serving.

Jackie and I had our problems, but we got through them and we were happy. Within about a year and a half of my being a cop, however, things shifted. Kim, our daughter, was born and I was working for the Monroe PD, and Jackie would say: "Bobby, have you noticed that you've changed?

The Will to Survive

You don't talk to me anymore. Ever since you became a cop, you're not the man I married."

Was Jackie telling the truth? You'd better believe it.

I Didn't Feel It Coming

I wasn't dealing with half of the crap that LAPD or NYPD deal with, but it's all relative. We had fewer officers on the street, and we were taking a lot of calls.

Personally, I didn't see the changes in me because it was all so subtle. I didn't realize that I had consistently been putting my job before my family, nor did I understand that I had started to disconnect from them. I knew that I was more stressed out than I used to be, but I was just trying to survive. I had been taught by my superiors not to talk about my feelings and emotions—signs of weakness—because it would only scare my family. In fact, my field-training officer had actually said to me, "Bobby, if you want to be a good cop, the job will become your wife, your God, and will fulfill everything you've ever wanted out of life." I don't know how I could possibly have believed that, but I did.

Like so many other macho types, I fell in love with a young girl, decided to save the world, and married the girl/woman who believed in me and my big plans. How was I to know my plans would change?

Kim was only two years old when Jackie announced that she was leaving me and taking our daughter with her. By the time she was headed out the door, she was through. She said that I hadn't paid attention when she pleaded with me to spend more time at home with them. As my mind raced to make sense of it all, I saw that she was right; I *had* chosen to work overtime and hang out in bars after work with my buddies and go fishing with the guys on my days off. It wasn't until that moment that I really realized that I needed to be more intimate with the females in my home. But, I just didn't have it in me to tell her so. Jackie never saw me cry or even fight to keep her despite how much I loved her.

Jackie's leaving was a tragedy really, because as she left with her broken heart and our little girl in tow, my heart was also broken. All I could do was go numb and watch them leave.

Round Two

Five years later I tried it again. My second marriage lasted a little longer, but was even less successful. At least Jackie and I are still good friends. She's happily married to a great man, and she still feels like family in some ways. We will always have the love for our daughter Kim to keep us bonded. But the second wife and I got off on the wrong foot right from the get-go. When we first got engaged, she got cold feet and returned my ring. Later, once she committed, it turned out that I didn't feel so sure. Knowing that she wasn't necessarily the love of my life couldn't have been easy on her. I wasn't exactly voted "groom of the year" on our wedding night when I told her that I might have made a mistake getting married. You could say that I was kind of a chump. I didn't mean to hurt her; I just had a bad feeling that night and couldn't *not* tell her.

We decided to try and make it work despite the dead elephant bleeding under the carpet, but I imagine that my lack of romantic loyalty made her a little less loyal after my shooting. I'm quite certain that she would have left me anyway, but taking care of my now totally dependent self was just more than she had bargained for. She dumped me like a hot potato while my blind butt could barely walk to the mailbox! I can't say that I blame her, but man, that hurt!

The Will to Survive

Why We Often Marry Our High School Sweethearts

This is just my opinion, but in thinking about this topic and talking to a lot of cops, I've determined that we are very loyal. When we meet someone special in high school, we are intensely devoted to that person, hence why we often marry them. The flip side of this coin is that we are the same guys who can be controlling in relationships because we are mission minded and task oriented—the type of personality that can sweep a woman off her feet and then tell her what kind of shoes to wear. When this personality type wants something, he puts his whole heart and soul into it—all of his efforts. But later, when this same man finds *other* things he likes (a demanding job, a group of buddies, a hobby), you can bet he'll devote himself with the same kind of energy and enthusiasm he showed when courting his wife, only now there may not be room for everything and everyone to receive his quality attention.

People ask me all of the time why the divorce rate for cops is so high. Why don't we talk to our spouses more, they ask. Why don't we open up more—let it all out? Surely the person we marry wants to hear what's bothering us; wants to share our grief so they can help relieve our stress. Hmmm.

This is what I usually say to those folks: Imagine you're a cop on your way home for dinner with your new wife. It's been a hard day, to say the least. You're exhausted and shut down. You arrested a man who killed his two-year-old son with cigarette burns and a baseball bat. You're so pissed off by the day's end that you feel like driving up to Hillcrest road and taking your car clear off the 200-foot drop. If it weren't for the fact that someone is waiting at home who loves and cares about you, you just might do it.

You walk through the door and your beautiful wife is

excited to see you. She has had a wonderful day gardening and catching up with old friends and says, "How was your day, honey?"

You have several choices. You can share the pain of what you've been experiencing, possibly ruining her good mood (not to mention her view of life in general), requiring that you relive your cruddy day when it was bad enough the first time! Or, you can talk around it, change the subject, drink or become a zombie in front of the television. People wonder why we cops don't talk to our families. We often wonder how the heck we can do that and still *have* a family?"

Men, as you know, go into their caves, just like the author John Gray talks about in his book *Men Are From Mars, Women Are From Venus*. We think we can handle it all and don't necessarily relish chatting about our stress. Women, too, are at risk of holding WAY too much in this job. Maybe because they hang out with so many of us cave dwellers!

Manic Matrimony

The young man or woman who marries the new cop is usually unprepared for the sudden changes in their spouse. The once fun-loving, jovial best friend starts to withdraw and stay out late. The spouse left at home feels lonely and often jealous of the time their partner spends at work or hanging with "the guys." Resentment builds, and once happy couples begin to grow apart unless the officer works hard to keep this from happening.

So, what are we to do? How can we appreciate our family and let them into our lives without depressing or alienating them? Ah, I wish I knew! Just kidding. I think, actually, that I've got some pretty good ideas about that—what with having gone through the gamut of miserable to happy family experiences. Before I get to too many "answers" however, let's cover one of the more amusing challenges of staying happily married as a police officer.

Women Really Do Love a Man in Uniform!

People make jokes about women loving a man in uniform, and before I became a cop, I figured that was true… sometimes. I had no idea how widespread this uniform-loving phenomenon really is. Talk about danger. For those of us who are married, this can be one of the greatest dangers we face!

One summer evening, I was working at the Monroe PD when I got a call in reference to a report. I went to the address, knocked on the apartment door and heard a woman's voice say, "Come in." I opened the door and a stunning tanned woman with long blonde hair was sitting Indian style brushing her hair on the carpet in the middle of her living room.

Did I mention that she was totally NUDE?

My first thought was, "Man, them butt heads. My buddies have set me up!" Since we were always pulling pranks on each other, my next thought was, "Them suckers are probably in the closet with a video camera, ready to record every last act we do."

"Ma'am," I said, as I stepped back from the door "you need to put a robe on before I can come into your house." After a few minutes, she came to the door dressed in a robe.

"Do you *really* need anything?" I asked.

"Nah, I saw you and wanted to meet you, so I called the department and asked if you were working," she answered. "I just wanted you to come over."

On another evening I was in my unit in a Sears parking lot, jotting a few things down into my notebook when

The Will to Survive

I heard, "Sir, can you help me out?" A gorgeous woman leaned up against my car and put her face level with my open window. As we were talking, she took her hand and reached over, laying it on the inside of my thigh.

"Baby, you can't do that," I said as I took her hand. "I appreciate the compliment, but I'll get in a lot of trouble if you keep your hand there."

"Oookaaaaaaay," she said, as she slowly withdrew her hand with a huge smile across her face.

Like rock stars, we've got our fans—police groupies. It takes a fairly strong man to walk away from such a willing playmate. Especially if his partner at home—if he's got one—is not as ready, willing, and able. Add to that the fact that the officer is working long hours often far from home, in an area where no one knows his name, and you've got a recipe for dangerous liaisons.

I've got a news flash for you: **Female Officers Cheat Too!** Often with other officers because they're the ones they spend the most time with and who understand them and share their experiences. It can get pretty crazy out there, and it's nice to be in a relationship with someone who knows what you're going through. Let's just say that both sexes love an officer in uniform!

Now, before some of you get your feelings hurt and your panties or boxers in a bunch, know that not every cop demonstrates this type of behavior. So, if the shoe don't fit, don't wear it and don't be sending me your ugly emails and letters and phone calls trying to tell me how perfect you are. I know there are quite a few of you monogamous ones out there. God love you! We need more like you!

Obviously the issue of not being faithful while we're out in the field is a big one, but our marriage woes go deeper than that. A large part of the problems we experience in our relationships stem from the stress of our jobs. It's logical: if you're coming home filled with stress, what kind of partner and parent do you think you're going to be?

On Being Combat Ready

Everyone knows that half of all marriages end in divorce in this country, but the ratio is much higher for police officers—one of the highest for an occupational group—with estimates ranging from sixty to seventy-five percent. Cops want to be a safe haven for their families, but fifty percent of us will also abuse our families in some way. To that horrifying statistic, I say, it's okay to be angry, ***it's just not okay to take it out on your spouse and kids!***

While the issue of stress will be explored more in-depth in the following chapter, I'd like to briefly cover a few things.

First, are you aware that when you prepare to start your shift as a police officer, you immediately go into a mild to moderate state of fight or flight reaction? You know the purpose of fight or flight—to prepare you for crisis, battle and danger. It's a survival technique that your average accountant, sales rep or computer programmer doesn't experience much on the job. The exact *American Heritage Dictionary* definition of fight or flight reaction is:

Fight-or-flight reaction: n. A set of physiological changes, such as increases in heart rate, arterial blood pressure, and blood glucose, initiated by the sympathetic nervous system to mobilize body systems in response to stress.

Yuck. That's what we're living with every time we put on our uniform. Now, give the above definition some thought and then answer this question:

The Will to Survive

If you're in this level of stress before you go into service in the morning, what level do you think you're going to be in at the end of a ten- or twelve-hour shift?

What distinguishes us from the average working person in America is that when we hear the words fight or flight, we think, "Yeah, so? It's not that big of a deal." In comparison, when civilians hear these words (in reference to the emotional and physical conditions we work under) they think, "Oh God, how does anyone live like that?"

Cops. We're a different breed. We're warriors, with the mentality of soldiers going into battle. We know our job is dangerous, but we like the excitement. We prefer living on the edge, not knowing what's around every corner. It helps us to feel alive. Going to an office in a business suit, sitting at a desk all day? Now that's scary! But, there can be a big difference between excitement and fun.

Venting on the Wrong Person

I want you to be straight with yourself. How many times have you made a traffic stop for someone going 45 in a 15 mph school zone and you walked up to the violator in a furious state? (The example doesn't have to be exact, but you get the idea.) The driver may have looked at you with a confused look on his or her face, wondering why you were hollering at them to give you their driver's license.

What the violator didn't realize was that three weeks prior you worked a fatality accident at this same school zone. A seven-year-old little girl was walking across the street in this "protected" area and was struck by a driver who just happened to be late for a hair tinting appointment. You had the privilege (as an officer) to go to that little girl's house and tell her mother that her daughter was dead.

The Will to Survive

Does anyone need further explanation as to why this officer is so upset? It's not about *this* particular speeding incident; it's about all the past little girls who were hurt or killed, and the unconscious nature of the way in which people live their lives! It's about feeling helpless as we realize that no matter how hard we try, no matter how good we are at our jobs, there will be an endless stream of accidents and wrongdoings that we cannot control. It's about knowing that we cannot clean up the inner cities with the budgets we're given, that we cannot stop the virus of crime and abuse running rampant in the world, and that we cannot be at all places at once. Life is, at least on the face of it, hopelessly unfair, and that's not an easy pill for any of us to swallow.

Sometimes you're going to be rude or short with people when working under this stress. You're going to write the driver a ticket, tell him or her to sign in the appropriate place, rip it out of the book and throw it into their lap. This is not proper procedure, nor the appropriate way to handle a speeder. Remember, you cannot heal until you feel, and these calls aren't going to go away. For the next ten or twelve hours (or however long your shift may be), it's going to be calls like this all day. It's going to be the domestic violence calls (where you may walk in to find a woman who is unrecognizable because she's been beaten by her drunken husband), it's going to be child abuse calls, sexual torture cases, and even murders.

I know you work these stories every day, so what's my point? My point is this:

After a day like this, think about what kind of energy you will carry into your home at the end of your shift.

Is Your Place of Dwelling a House or a Home?
What kind of a partner to your spouse or parent to

your children are you after weeks and months and even years of shifts like these? Scary thought, isn't it?

We've all been there. We're all guilty. You drive home and you're still thinking (but trying not to) of all the calls you've taken during the day—and some from days, even weeks ago. You've been told over and over not to get emotionally involved but you don't see how that's possible. Whatever happened to that cute eight-year-old boy who was thrown from his daddy's truck last week? You haven't heard since you dropped him at the emergency room. You make a mental note to check on his status tomorrow. What about the drunk, illegal immigrant who inadvertently ran a family off the road going the wrong way on the off ramp? Was he deported, and is the grandmother from the other car still on life support? Your mind drifts off to the sketch artist the captain hired to catch the serial rapist in the county, and you pray that she has enough leads to prove to be accurate enough to work the magic she has in the past. You can't wait to see that bastard put away, where he'll be on the receiving end of the fine art of being victimized. You daydream about personally strapping him into *Old Sparky* down in Angola State Prison when you pull into your driveway.

You park your car and walk toward the house in a daze. As you enter the back door, you're unaware that you're stressed to the max, still in the fight or flight "I'm ready for battle" mode. It has slipped your mind that you have a responsibility to your family, yourself, and the people you serve to keep emptying your emotional glass so that each moment, each case stands on its own, rather than building into an avalanche of stress and unexpressed anger. Right now you're beat, you have a headache, and you don't necessarily care if you bring down everyone around you.

The Will to Survive

The Cop in the House Will Destroy the Home

Again, the examples I'm about to give will not apply to all of you. There are many cops in this country who know how to handle stress. They come home as Mom or Dad and act appropriately. Some, as I'll explain, have rituals that allow them to leave their work behind before entering their home. No matter how healthy you are, however, I don't know that there's a parent alive who hasn't said or done something they regret. Even the best of parents get stressed out on occasion and act in ways in which they wouldn't otherwise.

For those of you who feel good about the way you act at home, you may want to use these stories as warnings of what *not* to do.

As you walk into your house in a fog, there isn't an ounce of energy left within you to help shake off your day. All you want is a good meal, some peace and quiet, and a mind-numbing sitcom to lull you to sleep. Your high school sweetheart—your wife of eight years—is standing in the kitchen preparing dinner. You enter the door and trip on a skateboard. The sound of your teenage son's blaring music immediately hits your frayed nerves. You throw your briefcase down on the kitchen counter, look over at the stove and glare at your wife and grumble an insincere hello. Your tone of voice and demeanor says, "I'm not real pleased right now. Is it too much to ask to have the house clean and quiet when I get home?" She turns to make eye contact with you with apprehension because she's been in this position too many times. You yell:

"Please don't tell me you've fixed another damn tuna casserole again! That's the second time this week. Do you know how to cook anything other than those damn, stinkin' casseroles?"

You both know that there's no need for her to defend

herself; no answer will be good enough. As you walk down the hallway and pass your first son's room, you glance inside. You're not necessarily checking to see how his day was, but rather you've been trained never to walk past an open door without looking in. Your son is sitting on the floor playing Nintendo and his room is a mess. You begin to vent:

> *"Clean up this crap. I work my butt off to give you the very best I can afford and you just throw it all over the floor?"*

You continue on down the hall toward the blaring music in your second son's room. You open the door and the volume shocks your senses.

> *"Turn that crud off! Haven't I told you enough? How many times do I have to tell you? Do you want to be deaf or something?"*

You walk into your bedroom, change your clothes and throw on a pair of shorts. You walk back into the den and sit down in your favorite recliner and grab the remote control to watch the evening news. When your kids come running through the den laughing and playing (they're children; they're loud), Daddy (you) is still prepared for battle. You jump to your feet and begin to yell:

> *"Boy, come here! Stand right here. Look at me when I talk to you (which really means, "Look at me while I verbally abuse you"). Stop that crying or I'll give you something to cry about."*

Sound familiar? As you stand over your son in your combat-ready stance, screaming and yelling only inches from his face, he cannot hear a thing you're saying because he's terrified. He's so scared, in fact, that he too is in a fight-or-flight mode. And, he's developed a nasty little thing called **"Audio Exclusion,"** which will keep him from being able to hear you at all.

All of your screaming and hollering from this point on is in vain—pointless. Do you have any idea that you, Mr. macho-man cop, are the one who needs to do the changing?

What is Audio Exclusion?

Have you ever noticed that when you're involved in a traumatic event, everything moves in slow motion? You experience "tunnel vision" and may not even be able to hear very loud noises nearby. Your sole focus becomes the danger at hand—usually a weapon creating the danger.

Cops interviewed after a bank robbery, for example, say that once a gun is in plain view, everything moves as if under water. Regardless of how loud the surrounding screams of warnings may be, the only thing the officer can concentrate on is the location of the gun. All else fades into the distance.

How could this be? It's a form of protection, really, as our mind and body work together to force us to focus on the most critical thing endangering our life in this moment—in this case, a hunk of metal pointed straight at our head.

Now, doesn't it make sense that if this kind of audio exclusion happens to us as grown adults, that the response in our children could be even greater? You cannot expect them to hear any of your so-called wisdom when all they see is a great volcanic rage spewing their way, looking as if it has the power to take them out. Your disfigured red face is all they can focus on when you stand over your child screaming bloody murder. They will not be able to hear a thing you say, no matter how wise and valid your information. And, the saddest part is that they may never forget that look of rage and hate in your eyes. The subconscious mind is extremely powerful and remembers absolutely everything, so these incidents may just stay with them for a lifetime, making your children wonder deep down on some level if you really do hate them after all. Can you imagine the fear and insecurity this could instill in your child—the one you're hoping will grow up to be a strong and capable adult? Is this really the legacy you want to leave?

Of course not!

Rage Poisons the Entire Family

As you scream, there's not a damn thing your kids can do about it. They are helpless because Daddy is bigger, stronger, and the head (or king) of the household. They know that Mommy must be hearing this and they fear that she is torn and afraid wherever she is in the house. How many times have they seen her cry in these instances? They know that Mommy doesn't want to go against her husband and that she wrestles with her loyalty and commitment to both parties (the man she swore to love and honor, and the flesh and blood she brought into this world). Daddy is not acting like the kind of father or king they have seen in the movies—the benevolent leader or ruler who protects those in his jurisdiction. If Mommy doesn't step in, who *will* protect them?

At this point, no one is in control. Well, maybe the Devil. As you lord over your child, dumping out your verbal vomit, every hormone in Mama's body related to protecting her offspring is on full alert! Would you expect it to be any other way? Would you expect a mama lion to allow her cubs to be left alone with an angry hyena? Get real.

This mama has heard enough.

She turns off the oven and races out of the kitchen, heading toward the den. She will do her best to stop you before your rage escalates into something even more violent. As she approaches you, standing between you and your sons, she knows she is taking a terrible risk. She knows that you could turn on her, as you've done before, and that her marriage is in jeopardy. She also knows that she is physically weaker than you are, and prays that her presence doesn't further your aggression. But your punishment went way past fitting the "crime" many minutes ago, and the panic in her children's voices is all the fuel she needs to make it worth the risk. You can't really expect her not to get in your way, can you?

"Get out of my face or you can get some of the same!" you scream.

Mama is now in fight or flight herself, with her adrenaline hitting the roof. You push her down and yell, "Get out of my face." She hits the coffee table, and down she goes. The kids are screaming and crying. Mama is crying from the emotional and physical pain. She yells, "All I have to do is make one phone call and you're through with your career," which adds fuel to your rage. (For those of you who haven't heard, there is now a federal law that states that if a police officer is involved in domestic violence that is corroborated by an investigation, the officer loses his or her career.)

Who's Protecting Your Family?

Anyone within hearing distance, be it relatives, friends or neighbors, also has to deal with their concern about what to do while hearing your verbal tirade. Neighbors may wonder if they should call the police. Relatives may stress about not wanting to get involved, but fearing they should. Everyone within ear-shot worries for the health and safety of your children. You may not care about these "side players," but put yourself in their shoes for a moment. Think about how you feel when you take a domestic abuse call and walk toward a house hearing the very thing you are now doing. It's not pretty, is it? I'm certain that your instincts are to protect the children, just as theirs are.

Do you see how selfish you have become? You have just thrown a world of crap onto your family and loved ones, all because you were too ignorant or lazy or selfish to deal with your pain and issues. The payback will be astronomical. Yes, they suffer, but I venture to say that your suffering will be even greater in the long run. This is a lose-lose situation, in which your children will learn that they cannot trust their own father, and will blame themselves for not being good enough. You, however, will learn something even worse; that you cannot trust yourself. Your feelings of moral bankruptcy will lead you into further self-sabotage, where drugs, alcohol, increased rage or some other demon will bring you to your knees. Until that moment, whenever that is, you will never know if the love and respect you receive from your family is genuine or born from fear. Deep down you will know that you could end up alone one day, and the only one to blame would be yourself. In essence, you are chipping away at everything that is precious to you, everything you have worked hard to build. And, the spiral will continue until you take responsibility for your actions and learn how to control yourself.

Does this stress you out? I feel sad for you if it doesn't. Okay, maybe you don't blow up about skateboards or loud music or tuna casseroles. You're more controlled than that. It takes something bigger, more expensive to rattle your nerves. How about this?

You come home from work and see your sixteen-year-old daughter, who just got her driver's license, back out of the driveway in your new Ford Bronco. She crashes into your large wrought iron mailbox—the one that took you an entire Saturday afternoon to put in—toppling it to the ground.

Could that send you off the deep end, screaming and swearing for everyone to hear?

"I knew better than to let you get your license. How difficult is it to back down the driveway without hitting the mailbox? Are you retarded? I've done it thousands of times. Give me your license. You're grounded."

There you are, Mr. or Mrs. Public Servant, standing in your driveway in full uniform, screaming at your daughter over a stupid mailbox. Can you imagine her humiliation as you put more importance on a meaningless object than on her feelings?

Hardly any of us hasn't gotten mad at a situation like this. And, hardly any of us hasn't hit or run over something, minor or major, while learning how to drive. But is this what Dad is really mad about? Not to this degree. Again, he's yelling at the driver who killed that little girl in the crosswalk or any one of the many injustices he deals with.

Everybody loses in a domestic abuse situation. Who would want to live in this type of disloyal, walking-on-eggshells environment? Would you want to be the kid growing up in this house? Not a chance. Yet cops in this country create these environments day after day, for two reasons:

We do not know how to deal with our feelings and emotions and we do not understand the root cause of our anger.

I don't like justifying a cop's inappropriate behavior in any way, but I surely understand it. Most of us have been in situations similar to at least one of the two I've just described. If you think for a second that any one of us truly enjoys acting out on our families, your head is full of holes! What we're really dealing with here is FEAR.

The Will to Survive

The Root Cause of Anger is Fear

When you yell at your spouse or your kids, your fear is showing. As Rhonda Britten, author of Fearless Living and the founder of the *Fearless Living* Institute teaches, "Whenever you get angry, you're basically posting a billboard of your fears for the world to see."

In your calm moments, if I asked you, "Is this rage-filled display of anger the way you want to treat your family?" you would say, "Absolutely not." If I asked you if your display of anger is something you're proud of, you would also say, "Absolutely not."

Then, why do you do it? I'll tell you why. Because you, Mr. Macho cop, are **scared to death!** And, male police officers aren't the only ones involved in this behavior. This has less to do with gender than it does a mindset. I've had female officers say to me, "Bobby, I come home and scream and yell at my husband and slap my son across the face." They tell me that they have gone to get help because they didn't like the people they were becoming. One woman told me that her husband was scared to death of her. An athlete in college, she was tough and ruled the roost—a "wom-man," the "po-lice." So, you, Miss Machoettes, this applies to you as well.

Back to the skateboard example: Cop Dad steps out of his car and sees the skateboard. Rather than choose to step over it (which he's done countless times and is tired of doing), he chooses to kick it. Does he really want to break the board or his toe or knock a gouge into the garage wall that will have to be repaired? No! He's just afraid. He loves his job, but he hates his job. He loves his family, but he hates the stress of being a family man—at least on days like today. And the worst part is that he's only two years into his career and doesn't see any kind of light at the end of the tunnel. The tunnel, leading to retirement, seems to go on forever. Thus, the stress is "never" going to end and Cop Dad is losing it.

We human animals tend to play out the things in our life that we think about. Cop Dad hadn't been thinking of kicking a skateboard today—that wasn't even a desire, but he did want to kick the punk on the street this afternoon who flicked him off and cursed him out in front of all his buddies. There wasn't a damn thing he could do but listen because it's not against the law to verbally abuse an officer. Free speech allows these guys to say whatever they want, and that's a major downside to freedom.

I hated dealing with these situations! I've been flipped off, called every vulgar name you can imagine. I remember one guy pulled down his pants in front of me, grabbed his business and shook it at me as he said, "Hey pig, you want some of this? Suck this," as he laughed like a hyena. Sure, I could have arrested the guy for indecent exposure, but in the end, is it worth the paperwork? No, and they know it.

No father really wants to break his son's $150 skateboard. But he might want to smash in his sergeant's face, who's been nothing but unreasonable lately, having forgotten where he came from. Cop Dad can't do anything about that either. Anger begins to build and build, until you're a volcano waiting to explode on your family.

Don't get me wrong, I'm not saying that kids are easy. They don't say that parenting is a thankless job for nothing! But there's another saying you might have heard as well:

The fruit don't fall far from the tree.

Our kids are a product of all that we are. Yes, I believe they come here with their own destiny and must be held responsible for their actions, but did you know that they often act out our unexpressed emotions? When a parent (or two) is repressed, depressed or angry, it's common for a child to be wild and out of control from the unexpressed anger or sadness enveloping the home. Does it make sense to punish your child for something they have little conscious control over—something you've either taught them by bad example, or instilled in them through your own emotional blocks?

I talk to a lot of officers who tell me about the repercussions of walking through their door in fight or flight mode. I've been there myself. We couldn't care less if we have to eat tuna again this week. As a matter of fact, that casserole is pretty darn good. It's just that so many feelings and emotions have built up that the officer doesn't know what to do with. Taking it out on some dead fish just seems like the thing to do, but then all hell breaks loose and children learn not to cope with their own issues, much less yours.

Cop Dad loves his wife. He would lay down his life without even considering it for his two children. The last thing in the world he wants to do is to take his anger out on these people. But it happens, and then he feels like a pile of cow dung for doing it. He is now in a cycle in which the abuser has become the victim of his own shame and guilt.

See Your Actions Through the Eyes of Your Kids

Obviously, if you're screaming uncontrollably over your child, you're not leading well by example. Your job is to protect and serve, not to terrorize your family. Kids know that. They watch everything and hear even more. You don't want them growing up thinking that Mommy or Daddy is the bad guy, but when they hear you talking on the phone about some "loser" you just put away, they might think, "But wait a minute, how are you any different than that guy?" If you could climb into the body of your child and watch your behavior from their eyes, what would you think of yourself? Would your behavior match your words and intentions?

The Will to Survive

Just the Facts Ma'am

You know, it makes sense to me why we often come home with an attitude or a chip on our shoulder. We have to be so distant and even cold when dealing with hoodlums, and thus, in order to protect ourselves, it's tempting to become harsh and business-like with most people, including loved ones. Since we're often running short on staff and on time, and because most cops are left-brain thinkers (rational, practical, filled with common sense) as opposed to right brain thinkers (who are more emotional and fanciful), we just want to hear the facts without a lot of fluff. Don't give me a bunch of reasons why you or someone else did something; just tell me what happened. Give me the facts.

Doesn't it set you off when your kid or your spouse gives you twenty-seven excuses for their negative behavior rather than simply taking responsibility?

Every story has two sides, and one of the great things about being oriented this way is that we cops often see the big picture of something right up front. We can go into a situation and see exactly what needs to be done. We have a strong sixth sense and an uncanny ability to read situations. Please excuse my French, but we have incredible bullshit detectors. Still, that doesn't give us any right to treat our family members like punks on the street.

We're taught not to waste words at work, but our families often need just the opposite—to talk and express and emote. It's true that we may be asked to prove everything we've said on a case in front of a court of law, and it's true that judges and juries and defense attorneys can't use our opinions and that we can even get in trouble for documenting our beliefs about a case, but our families are made up of emotional beings who are separate and apart from the system we work in. You may be frustrated at work because your job requires that you stick to the rules. Just the "facts," when your intuition may be telling you otherwise, so you become a machine and spit out the details of a case, often ignoring your own feelings and beliefs. But, you don't have to be like that at home! You can use that great intuition of yours and your big-picture skills to tap into the people you live with, communicating in a way that is deep and layered and more fulfilling than the limited way in which you have to deal on the street.

What's Cop Dad So Afraid Of?

Cops, like most people, are afraid of being vulnerable. To be honest, Cop Dad is probably afraid that his wife will eventually realize that he doesn't make a whole lot of money. He's afraid she will wake up one day and say, "I'm so tired of having so little; I'm so tired of the constant disruptions that come with your job," and walk out the door, never to return. He is afraid that their lack of shared experiences will pull her away from him, toward a life where her needs will be better met. He has been on many calls where a wife is packing up and leaving her husband (usually for her own safety), while that husband stands in the yard with his hands on his hips, glaring. Cops hate these calls because these are the saddest and most dangerous calls to get. First, the officer is seeing the dissolution of a family; the ending to what was once an idealistic beginning. And, this is where, statistically, most police shootings take place. We all know that when a wife calls the cops on her husband and the cop handcuffs the man for beating his wife, he had better watch his back because she might just hit the officer on the back of his head with a frying pan.

We may look macho and powerful, but these situations make us highly insecure. It's not uncommon to be scared to death out there, and our self-esteem gets battered and bruised. When we come home to see a messy room that looks like chaos, with blaring music that sounds like chaos, it reminds us of all of the chaos we've just witnessed and couldn't do a damn thing to stop.

No matter who says otherwise, we're not a bunch of *dad-gum* monsters just because we wear a badge, but unless we keep our emotional glasses emptied, these stress-filled family scenes are all too common.

There's hope, even though this may sound hopeless. As you start to recognize your patterns and get more comfortable feeling your feelings and taking responsibility for your actions, these negative behaviors will disappear naturally. You won't have to use great will power; you won't even have to sit on your hands or bite your tongue to avoid being a jerk with your family. You will naturally begin to slow down and make smarter, healthier choices. You'll find yourself making time for your spouse in ways you haven't done since you were dating—like going on dates without the kids, to dinner, to movies, and even dancing. Your emotional exhaustion will ease, and you will find yourself less stoic and distant. Becoming more communicative and expressive with your family—two of the great keys, I believe, toward creating a happy marriage and home life—will be the fulfilling end result. It will take time and you may sometimes feel that you're taking two steps forward and three steps back, but you will become the man or woman you are meant to be—the companion your spouse deserves to have. I've seen it many times. There is great hope.

Third Time's the Charm

Sometimes it still boggles my mind that my beautiful wife married a blind guy who had never even made eye

The Will to Survive

contact with her and had two failed marriages already! What was she thinking? Thankfully, Janie was totally centered in her heart when she met me, most likely the result of having lived through an abusive marriage and having nearly given up on men entirely.

Janie and I were introduced by my cousin at the hospital, where I was visiting a friend who had just had back surgery and Janie was working as a dietician. We immediately felt a spark between us and had loads to talk about, but she was a little put off by my weight at the time, my thick beard, and a bad bulging fake eye that no one had bothered to tell me about. I had no idea that I was a walking Frankenstein, scaring little kids and young women in my path! Still, we hit it off and she told me later that she heard a loud voice in her head tell her upon meeting me that I was "the one." Janie had been praying to God to bring her the "right man," and she trusted that despite not being her "type," God knew what He was doing.

Janie and I got along so well that I decided to make it a little easier on her by losing the weight, shaving the beard and fixing the eye (the least I could do). At any rate, we were married three months after we met, and we've been going strong for nearly sixteen years now.

People ask me if I ever feel rage toward my family. Well, duh! Despite being very happily married, Janie, was a complete slob! I say that with love now because she's stopped tripping me by leaving the dishwasher door open or the laundry basket in the middle of the living room or her high heels in front of the bed. I can tell you that I've never laid a hand on a woman, but I was tempted to take her out after getting a few bloody shins and kneecaps.

Compared to getting smacked in the head with an open cabinet door, however, having a teenage boy in the

The Will to Survive

house can be even more painful! Kids can break your heart with their attitude, and even though Brad is a loyal and loving kid and easy most of the time, he's still a teenager and has the ability to totally disrupt our family. We can be ready to go out on the town after looking forward to eating out all day long and it takes him about five minutes to completely destroy all I've been waiting for with his sarcastic mouth or attitude. I will feel like just slapping him across the face, which of course I've never done.

Kids have this "it's all about me" mentality that's so frustrating, especially when you're trying to give your kids the world. Trust me, being blind does not help! It really affects my patience because I can't just go take care of business like I used to. I don't have "the look" that can instill fear. I have to depend on my son to be more responsible than other kids, and I need him to pick up the slack and do things I can't do. Even though I can take out the trash and mow the lawn or sweep the carport, these things are stressful when you can't see, and I often prefer Brad to do those chores. Even folding clothes becomes confusing, but I'll often do it just because I ache to be normal and productive. Brad and Janie are the same size, and I will sometimes put Brad's things in her stack or vice versa. Brad will occasionally come in and say, "Dad. You put the blue socks with the black ones again. I wish you wouldn't even mess with that stuff." Crap. I'm doing the best I can with this little disability here and I can't see all that well. I just want to be normal. If only kids knew how hurtful their sarcastic remarks are.

People say that the 60's were rebellious, but I don't think they were anything compared to today. Teens are watching these horrible shows and cartoons, where kids are telling their parents that they're stupid and worthless, basically ridiculing all authority figures (if I remember correctly,

The Will to Survive

in the late 60's every kid was watching "Gilligan's Island" and "The Brady Bunch"). Today's programming is filled with totally disrespectful stuff; rebellious to the max. When you're an officer, you're dealing with punks all day long on the street who don't seem to have an ounce of respect for authority. Even when I worked twenty years ago, these twelve-to fourteen-year-old kids would say, "What are you going to do about it, Pig? I'm only a juvy (juvenile) and there's nothing you can do to stop me." They were right. And like the old Ma Belle commercials, I wanted to reach out and touch someone (and I don't mean over the phone)!

So, as cops, we're walking through our own house, minding our business and we walk into our kid's room just because. Our teenager looks at us with a glare that says, "What are you doing in my room?" and we snap. I may not be able to do anything about the punk on the street, but I can reach out and touch someone in my own house!

I have found through my experiences with my son Brad, that he has a tendency to act out through sarcasm or disrespect when he is angry or has had his feelings hurt. Children are just like Mom and Dad and they display their true feelings and emotions at home more often than they do in the outside world. That is, as long as the home is a safe environment in which to display their disappointments. Kids have to know that they can safely vent at home without being squashed, otherwise they will take their disrespect and anger to school for their teachers and playmates to experience. I have seen enough school bullies over the years to know that you can go right back to the home and see that that child is either expressing what's going on inside the home, or expressing what he or she is not allowed to display there. It's so important that children can grow emotionally in a safe environment. Instead of hollering and screaming at them, sit

The Will to Survive

down and say, "What's going on? What are you so angry about?" Show them that they can freely tell you their situation without being yelled at or lectured to.

What Happens When You Are No Longer Their Hero?

I am not a child psychologist and there are excellent experts in the subject of childrearing out there, but I do know that research shows that cop children often act up even more than normal brats, I mean, kids. In reality, children are hard on any marriage. I once heard a statistic that most divorces happen within the first year of having a child, and I believe that's probably true because everyone I've ever known who's had a kid has told me how much harder it is than they expected. In countless ways, kids add pressure to a normal life, much less someone with a cop's responsibilities and schedule (and dreaded shift changes). When you figure the added expenses involved, the extra work around the house required, and the stress of worrying about them and taking care of their on-going daily needs, we're talking about a major commitment to have children. Combine that with our already enormous obligations, and it's not uncommon for cop's children to feel the pressure and become very difficult in conscious and unconscious ways. At first I didn't understand why, but it didn't take much research to see the phenomenon more clearly.

There is so much pressure on cop's kids to be little grown ups, to perform better than other children. Just as higher expectations are placed on preacher's kids, cop's kids are expected to be perfect as well. Their mamas and daddies take an oath to protect and serve and enforce the laws of the land and that's just about as high and mighty as it gets.

But kids are kids. With the added pressure NOT to make mistakes, when they do make them, it's bad. The ridicule from other parents, as well as their own goes something like this… "Well, you of all kids should have known better! You know good and well not to do such and such." These kids run the risk of getting squashed emotionally, and when that happens, they rebel, just as any good little teenager would. Their attitude may be, "I'm sick and tired of the pressure. I'm not the one who chose to be a police officer's kid. I didn't choose to be the enforcer of the law. Why are you making me act like you?" Society watches these kids like hawks because their parents are the po-lice. And, the higher the rank, the higher the expectations placed on that child by parents and society. If your daddy is the Chief of Police, heaven help you!

Step into your kid's shoes and imagine for a moment being the child of a police officer. You'd get so bottled up. All the other kids make mistakes, yet you're the only one who gets crucified for yours. Cut these kids some slack because if you don't, I can almost guarantee that they're going to lash out something fierce eventually, even if you're not being disrespectful to them but especially so if you are!

The Off Duty Cop Mom or Dad

The fact that your work is so demanding makes it even more important that you're present with your family when you're off the clock. But that gets complicated, doesn't it? Everywhere you go, people expect you to be on duty, even when you're not. You can make this challenge harder than it needs to be, however, and hopefully this section will give you better tools about how to say no to certain societal demands.

Do you know, for instance, that it's okay for you to be a normal bystander? How many of us have been off duty, gone to a baseball game, seen a fight break out and think we have to handle it because we're an authority figure and our authority counts? It's so easy to mix the line between being on duty and off duty, but that's where some of our overwhelming stress comes from because we never feel like we catch a break—another example where white fades into gray.

Also, we have to guard against using these situations as an excuse to exert our authority when we should be spending time as a "Mom" or "Dad" for a day at the park.

Who do you think would take care of the disturbance if you weren't there? I'm quite certain that someone would call the police and a marked unit would show up to handle the situation because that's the job of whomever is on duty, right? Does this make you feel like jumping out of your skin? I know, me too. But, these are the things you've got to take into account if you want to start taking better care of yourself and your family. You don't have to do it all. Heck, you CAN'T do it all! Besides, no one said that you had to be the authority figure at all times in every situation.

It's So Tempting to Work Long Hours!

We're scared to death to be left out. Some of us are adrenaline junkies and can't stand to miss out on the action. We adore our families and would die any day to protect them, but man, there's stuff going on down the street and we've got to be there. You're home on a Sunday, but you jump up and run when you hear the scanner in the garage. "They're going to need some help, I'd better go." No, they didn't ask for your help. Relax and get your butt back into the family room.

In my case, while I really did love hanging out with my buddies and staying on the case after hours even when the department didn't have the extra funds to pay me for those hours, I was also trying to avoid something at home. My words said, "My family is everything to me," but my actions proved otherwise. The reality was that I needed help emotionally and I didn't know how to be available (i.e. intimate) for my family. It was easier to work.

When Duty Calls

There are going to be times when you just can't go home, no matter what is planned. You're on your way to your daughter's fifth birthday party, but you get a call that there's a body waiting at the morgue and you're the only one to handle it. You've just called home and said, "Hey baby, Daddy's en route," and I'll be damn, just as you say that they announce your name on the intercom. I can't tell you how many times that happened to me. Here I was, about ready to switch into husband and father mode and a shooting, a robbery, or a murder pulled me away. These are things we can't help because we're the officer or the agent on call.

But some things we can help.

Here are a few things to do, and they're quite easy.

1. **When you're off**, really BE off, and spend time with your wife or husband and your kids *before* you spend time with your friends! Your buddies may not like it, but they should understand. If you lose them, they probably weren't the best of friends anyway. Many cops I talk with are very happily married and tell me that their spouses actually help a great deal in lessening their stress. If this is the case for you, keep up the good work and continue to nurture your relationship each and every day.

2. **Social companionship** and spending time with people you love in fun and recreational activities is a great

stress reliever. Instead of going fishing with the guys, how about taking a camping trip with two families, or going hiking or exploring with the neighbors or your son's best friends' family? That way your spouse and children are included in the fun, and you're still able to get away.

3. **Be expressive and talk** to your spouse, often! Talk, talk, talk (don't forget to listen!). By the way, before you can sit down and talk with someone for hours, you have to develop a relationship. I wonder how many of you know as much about your spouse as you do about your job? I hear you guys, especially, at these conferences I go to, and you spend hours and hours telling war stories to each other, laughing and cutting up and bonding over your job. That's okay to do once in a while, but if all that yapping makes you go home at the end of the day and give your family the silent treatment because you've already had your fill of communication, you might want to rethink that.

4. **For God's sake, please take your pagers off** at the movies and at your children's piano recitals! The world will continue to revolve in your absence!

5. **When you go out with your wife or family**, resist the temptation to clip your badge onto the front of your belt. I know you love your identity and get a lot of your sense of self from being an officer, but it's also important to identify with being a husband and father.

6. **When you get home after a long day** and your kid says, "Dad, can you come here for a minute?" think twice before you say, "Son, I'm really tired. I'll help you out later." What if you got a call at work about a child who needed help. Would you say, "Not now. I'm too tired?" Of course not. I'm just talking about a change of mindset. There's no reason we can't be as loyal and committed to our family as we are to the people we serve. "Sure, son." Take that call.

The Will to Survive

7. If you find that you and your spouse can't seem to get it together, don't be afraid to get your butts in a therapist's office! You know how much I used to hate therapy, but I've got to tell ya, it works wonders for helping couples learn how to communicate. A man and a wife with healthy coping skills will be able to weather whatever stressors this job brings. That's great news, don't you think? Isn't your family worth it?

Do You Really Need That Extra Money?

A big trap a lot of us cops fall into is over-spending. We are a proud and we like to have the nice things—big houses, good schools, hot cars. The drag is that these things are expensive and we're not rich.

"Dad, I thought you were off on the weekends?"
"Baby, I am usually, but this is an extra detail."
"But dad, you don't *have* to work. Just tell them no."

Your child knows you are rationalizing when you say, "You know, honey, we bought this new house last year and we're trying to give you the extras." That may be the case, but you have to ask yourself, what are you really saying? Are you telling your kid that you'd rather put them up in a façade (the nice cars, the beautiful house), to keep up with the Jones's? Because, if you make acquiring a lot of stuff all-important, Mommy or Daddy (or both) is going to have to work a lot more, which is extremely challenging because more than anything kids need their parent's time and attention. They don't want us in bits and pieces. I remember seeing a sign on the front lawn of a church once that I've never forgotten. It said:

The Will to Survive

"Kids don't care how much you know until they know how much you care."

There is nothing wrong with wanting nice things for your children, but what motives are behind your desires? Couldn't you be just as successful living and working on the other side of town? It's something to think about.

Too Late for Quality Time

Even though I wasn't allowed to continue working with the state police, I was starting to see a future for myself in the speaking world. Sgt. Aubrey Futrell and I were being asked to travel to local departments and talk to other officers about my incident. *The Bobby Smith Story* was a good warning of what not to do, and I was told I was a good storyteller as well. The bookings continued to increase, eventually around the country, all without any effort. It was quite amazing. Officers laughed and cried at my tales. Over and over, people told me that my shooting had not been in vain, that perhaps it had been "destined," "meant to be," so that I could help others. I was starting to feel of value, and letters began pouring into my office about how sharing my experiences were saving people's marriages, lives and sanity.

I decided that if I was going to be in the business of helping people, I'd better go back to school and get me a little bit of that education. It was time to become a head doctor myself. I signed up for college against the warnings of the administrators, who felt that the curriculum would be too difficult for a blind man, but their concerns fell on deaf ears. I believed that I was destined to be in the mental-health field because whenever there were traumatic events while I was on duty, I was usually the one called to go talk to the people involved. I knew I could do it. (Besides, one of the

The Will to Survive

upsides of going to hell and back is that not a lot scares you after that.) I learned to take notes by tape recorder, memorizing each lecture, and somehow graduated in 1991 at the top of my class with a 3.9 grade point average. The highlight of that day was when Kim, then a junior in high school, proudly escorted her daddy on stage while an audience of 10,000 cheered us on. Kim leaned into me and said, "Daddy, they're giving you a standing ovation." As I walked to the podium to receive my diploma, it was all I could do not to bawl like a little baby in front of the crowd.

Nine years later, I received my doctorate in counseling psychology.

I, *Mr. Big Shot Doctor Man*, was soon to need those psychological skills I learned in school (and had been preaching to others) when I got a call one night in September of 1997 from my first wife.

"Bobby!" she screamed, "It's Kim! She's been in a terrible car accident and the doctors don't think she's going to make it."

I'm going to spare you the play-by-play that followed, because I didn't write this book to depress you. Lord knows you've got enough of your own pain to deal with. But, I will tell you that Kim didn't make it. That single event—the death of my daughter—was harder on me emotionally than my own shooting. I've said it before and I'll say it until the day I die, there is nothing as painful as the death of your own child! Nothing.

Let me tell you what I hear all the time:

"Bobby, you don't understand. I don't have time to spend with my kids."

"Oh, really?" I tell them, "but isn't it amazing that you can go out to the gym each day and get in your two-hour workout?"

The Will to Survive

We take our kids for granted. We think that they'll always be here tomorrow to play ball with, to read to.

I used to think that way too, but guess what? *The only quality time I get to spend now with my daughter Kim is in a graveyard.* When I use that in my speeches I hear parents in the audience begin to cry. Man, that line gets their attention. It's so true. If I would have known then what I know now I would have at the very least eaten regular meals with my family. If I was working the night shift, I would have eaten a hearty breakfast with Kim and Jackie in the morning when I got off, and then I would have taken Kim to school, no matter how tired I was. It wouldn't have killed me to get one less hour of sleep several days a week. If I were working the day shift, I would have been there for dinner every dang night! Okay, maybe I wouldn't have been able to be a competitive power lifter who benched 450 pounds, but does that really matter? Come on.

A cop called me one day and said:

"Bobby, I heard you speak two weeks ago. Yesterday I was sitting at home reading my paper and my son came up and said, 'Hey Dad, do you want to go throw the football?' 'Yes son, maybe later,' I answered. I had just gotten the word 'later' out of my mouth when I heard you in my mind saying, 'but later may never come.' I threw the newspaper down on the floor and said, 'Wait, I'd love to pass the football with you.' I was really tired, Bobby. I had had a rough day, but I don't ever want to push my children away again."

Doing It Right

Most of us have enough physical strength that we could throw someone through a brick wall if we wanted, but we don't. Most of us choose compassion and wisdom when arrogance would come easier. Most of us walk into a violent

The Will to Survive

or emotional situation and use soothing words to settle domestic disputes when banging someone's head in would be a lot more fun (and even deserving when dealing with some folks!). Many of us use our brains over our brawn every day and take care of business coming home to be loving to our families.

These are the sides people don't see. They watch Rodney King getting his butt kicked repeatedly on television and think we're all out of control monsters to be feared and loathed. For every Rodney King incident in this country, how many acts of compassion and caring do you think we perform daily? Millions.

I encourage you to take stock of where you are now and where you want to see yourself in five years. What kind of a husband or wife do you want to be? What kind of a father or mother? It sounds corny, but it might help to imagine your own funeral and see not only what you imagine other people would say about you right NOW, but what you would LIKE them to say in the future—then figure out what you have to do to get from here to there. Dare to dream on this one. Choose the BEST of what you could hear. The best of what you *want* to hear, the best of who you truly are. The legacy you leave your family in deed and in reputation is up to you.

While you imagine your best self, aspire to be that person. I'm not talking about being a saint. I'm talking about being a real and honest and true-blue officer and human being who does his or her emotional work and treats people cleanly, fairly. I'm talking about trusting that there's enough for everyone, trusting that your needs will be met, trusting that making the right choices will lead you to fulfillment. I'm talking about being or becoming someone you and your family are proud of, now and always. You know you have it in you. You've had strains of that person within you all along no matter how distant, most likely starting at the academy—heck, starting back in childhood!

Dare to dream big here because *only you determine the outcome of your humanity.*

I'd like to ask you to raise your right hand right now and commit to being your best self from this day forward. Do it now. If not, you're under arrest. Repeat after me…

"I, Officer _____, commit today to be the best person I can be, to myself, my family and the people I protect and serve and work with. I commit to getting and staying healthy, both emotionally and physically. I commit to release my emotions in a positive way, through healthy outlets, and to get help somehow, some way when I need it. I understand that I can't do it alone, and that I need to reach out to the people I love and who love me every day."

Today is a new day. Start by being the parent who takes off early to go to your kid's soccer game. Turn in your slips for *K-time* (comp off-time) to attend your daughter's dance recital. Be the cop who has enough sense to keep the cop outside of the house, allowing only Daddy or Mommy to enter your home, your haven. Be the officer who walks in the door and gives his casserole-cooking wife the appreciative hug and the kiss she deserves. "How was your day, honey? Man, it's great to be home!" Gratitude will expand your riches beyond belief. Try it, I dare you!

If Only You Could See Her!

On several occasions Brad has sat down with his mom and cried, asking why he doesn't have a "normal" dad. My being blind is hard on both Brad and Janie much of the time, for obvious reasons (like having to take care of me and drive my blind self around) and for some not quite so obvi-

The Will to Survive

ous...

We live in a large gated community in Springfield, Missouri, and our neighbors are very social. I've encouraged Janie to belong to groups and spend a lot of time with her friends because I'm on the road about half of every week and I don't want her getting lonely. Recently she went to one of our neighborhood parties while I stayed home with Brad doing homework. It was just before 10:00 P.M. and I got a phone call from one of the women who had been at the function.

"Bobby," she said, "it's me, Lisa. Janie is on her way home, but I wanted to talk with you before she gets there. Bobby, if you could only have seen your wife tonight! She was absolutely gorgeous. She was glowing—*the* most beautiful woman at the party! I just wish you could see her. I wish you could see how beautiful she is!"

Wow. I didn't quite know what to say. This was no small compliment from our friend. Janie and I live in an upscale area filled with women who take great care of themselves and show pride in their appearance. They work out, wear beautiful clothes and have big diamonds on their fingers. I always compliment Janie because I know she's beautiful, and because I know women love being appreciated for their looks and being noticed by their husbands. "Here, do you want to feel my outfit?" she'll say. "I've got a shirt and a sweater on and my hair...feel my hair; I just got highlights." "Oh yes, baby, you're gorgeous," I say, and we laugh. I feel badly that I can't see and appreciate my wife visually.

To think that my wife is a vision of beauty that everyone gets to enjoy but me is a real drag. I would love to see what they see. You know, I married this woman who thought her husband was probably going to get his sight back one day. That obviously hasn't happened. Janie's got a great attitude and we have a beautiful life, but I know it isn't always easy on her. My loved ones have also paid dearly for my winning-at-all-costs attitude.

I've Been Married to Him for Ten Years!

I was recently at a police conference that was open to spouses and kids. After one of my talks, a lady walked up to me and said:

"Mr. Smith, my husband has been a cop for twenty plus years, and I'm glad to hear you talk about the good ones who come home and love their families. I had been married to him for ten years when I noticed one day that he was standing at the garage entrance. I usually heard him drive up, but I had never paid attention until he was well into the house. On that day, I noticed that as he walked up to a bush in the yard that he kind of bunched up in front of it. I thought, 'What in the world is he doing?' He was acting as if he was taking off his jacket, but it was summertime and he didn't have one on. My husband laid that imaginary jacket across the bush and turned around. I could hear him talking, but I didn't have a clue what he was saying. He walked back toward the house in a nonchalant way, and then caught a glimpse of me starring at him with a look of total confusion on my face. He had a huge smile on his. I said, 'What are you doing honey?'

'Oh,' he answered, 'I was taking off my uniform and leaving it outside,' explaining that he did this every day. I couldn't believe that he had been performing this ritual for ten years, yet I had never seen it before. My husband and I have had our fair share of disagreements over the years, but you know, that ritual must work because he has never once brought the cop inside our home."

I wonder if this officer had some wise mentor out

there somewhere who taught him early on how to do that, or if he came up with that idea on his own? Either way, when I think of this family, I imagine this warrior husband arriving home after a long day of battle. I see him lay down his sword and reach out to hold the hands of the people he loves, bowing his head to say grace, and give thanks that his wife and children don't have to live in the environment in which he works every day.

Life is so precious. I hope that the next time you're tempted to cut corners or act like a superhero, you'll stop and think twice and remember the rules (and call for back up when needed). And, I pray that the next time your son or daughter wants you to play with them, be it a game of pitch or hide-and-go-seek (I'm really good at that one), you'll take the time to stop what you're doing and give it your all even if you're still in uniform. There's nothing more touching than seeing an officer in uniform playing catch or a game with his or her children in the yard before dinner. I'm certain that you'll enjoy being with your family as much as they enjoy being with you.

As a reminder, you might want to post a little visible sign somewhere in your house that says:

Why don't cops belong in the house?"
"Because Mama and Daddy live here!"

Amen to that!

The Will to Survive

CHAPTER V
Stress: When Thy Cup Runneth Over

"Cops are like landfills. We collect trash every day, and we store it until it overflows."

Reverend Robert Douglas, police chaplain and the executive director of the National Police Suicide Foundation

Allow me to get into your head for a minute and read your mind—uncover a deep, dark secret you've been hiding. Ready? Here goes: How long has it been since you've had *the dream*? You know, *THE* dream! I bet you haven't discussed this nightmare with your buddies. I bet you don't even know that they have the same dream you do, maybe worse than yours. You're not alone; most cops are unaware that the officers standing near them at roll call are also awakened in the middle of the night by similar frightening visions.

You cops have something else in common. When asked, everyone agrees that they don't know how to stop the dream. No one seems to understand the secret to keeping it at bay. It's just a byproduct of being a cop and everyone silently tries to accept it.

What is this nightmare? Imagine that…

you're face-to-face with a cold-blooded killer. He draws his gun and points it at your heart. You are certain that gunfight is inevitable. You pull out your gun just in time, but as you attempt to fire, the unthinkable happens… Your bullets are stuck—lodged inside the barrel. The bad guy now has the upper hand, and as you fumble to recover from your shock, you pray that some miracle happens and he doesn't

The Will to Survive

have time to kill you…

Sometimes your bullets do come out in the dream, but they're made of water and cascade to the ground. Other times hard steel bullets blast forth, only to drop with a thud or float through the air with the ease and lightness of a fading balloon. Maybe you watch as the bullets fly with great speed toward the assailant, but miss him altogether or swerve around him as if playing chase with an invisible playmate.

Most everyone has this dream in some form or another within their vocations. A successful sportscaster dreams of seeing his favorite athlete—the one he's always wanted to interview—at a party and spends the entire dream trying to get up the nerve up to talk to him, unsuccessfully. Well-known actors reveal to Oprah and Jay Leno that they have repeated dreams of getting on stage and forgetting their lines. They even have a name for that—it's called "The actor's nightmare." A grandfather chess enthusiast I once knew complained of a repeated dream in which he couldn't find his chess piece and would freeze in his chair, unable to make his next move.

My training as a therapist has taught me that for people in all fields, these dreams represent a fear of lack of personal control. There isn't a person alive who doesn't fear something, and when you're in a career that involves high stakes, it's logical that your mind will deal with that stress during your sleep time, when the subconscious mind attempts to make sense of everything.

The Odds are In Your Favor

It's quite remarkable, really, and almost unbelievable to civilians when I tell them that very few of us cops (statistically speaking) will ever fire a gun at another person or be fired upon. Most of us will never be shot in this job; most of

The Will to Survive

us will live safely to retirement. But, it's the constant *possibility* of danger and violence and the repeated witnessing of violent and tragic events that keeps us on edge and stresses us out.

Before my shooting, I had never been involved in a shooting before. In fact, I had never even fired my weapon in the line of duty prior to that March night in 1986. In eleven years there were only three cases where I had to pull out my weapon, where I was fixing for a shoot out, and many other times where I pulled it out only because a situation called for me to have a weapon in my hands. But, actually firing it at someone didn't happen until the evening I shot my assailant. Because most of us never fire our weapons in our whole career, we run the risk of feeling a false sense of security when it comes to danger. Man, did that ever happen to me! It works both ways, though. The longer you go without ever having to use your weapon, the more you may assume that you're getting closer to having to use it.

For those of us who *do* get shot, there's a part of us that can't believe someone actually intended to kill us. "Are you kidding me? I stand for law and order and you dare pull a gun on me? Are you crazy? I'm a police officer!"

We've already covered many of the stressors we cops face in previous chapters, and this chapter will be devoted to filling out that picture a bit more (especially considering the newest types of challenges we're up against), and giving further hints about how to get the most out of this career—how to love your job. I sure hope this book doesn't scare any of you away from being an officer, especially if you're new to this career, as it's not my intention to *add* stress to any of you! I'm a big fan of the saying, "To be forewarned is to be forearmed," and I believe with all of my heart that knowing the potential pitfalls and being better able to negotiate them

The Will to Survive

is half of the battle toward a successful life and career.

The New Face of Police Stressors

The nasty stressors listed below were not much of a problem if at all for cops a generation ago, but have made our jobs infinitely more complicated and stressful as of late. Directly following the list, you'll find more details on each subject...

1. Terrorism: working on the front lines of global drama
2. The media & public's insatiable desire for gossip and information
3. Dealing with a massive influx of immigrants, with their many languages
4. The effect of having cameras in our cars that record our every action
5. Natural disasters: protecting the masses in an increasingly fragile environmental era

1. **We're the First Line of Defense**

The police are now on the front lines of a new kind of war, and for the first time in this country we find ourselves vulnerable on our own turf. We've seen what's happened to our brothers and sisters involved in the September 11 terrorist attacks—perhaps we knew someone who was killed or has quit as a result. We officers now have a whole new world of stressors to take into account.

Every cop knows that when he or she raises their hand to protect and serve, there is a chance they will die in upholding the honor of that oath. But at least put us in a situation where we have a fighting chance to win! We're well trained to deal with people who break the law, but this new type of terror is foreign to us—the people out there who want to take us out have no fear of dying. Most violators we've become accustomed to dealing with have an inherent drive toward self-preservation. Nine times out of ten, the person you have face down on the ground doesn't want to die. Americans, as a rule, value life, and until recently cops have had the edge over civilians because people hated the thought of their own demise. Now we've lost some degree of that edge because we're seeing extremist fundamentalists from other countries who view it as an honor—a notch on their spiritual belt—to murder you and kill themselves in the process.

I never had the time to do so, but I know many cops who also work as extra security for corporations and wealthy individuals on their off hours or upon retirement. A lot of these officers have been put in charge of guarding places like our nuclear facilities. How much stress do you think that little detail causes them in this day and age? You've got some nut who hates our government and steals an 18-wheeler filled with fuel and sends it racing towards a nuclear plant. I was talking to an officer guarding one of these places recently and he said:

"Bobby, I'm standing in front of a massive facility imagining what I'd do if I looked up and saw one of these psychos traveling 60-70 mph straight for me. I'm just standing there by my marked unit, thinking that I'm an invisible wall   that nothing can penetrate, which of course I'm not! Am I supposed to jump out with my 12-gauge shotgun and fire rounds into the front of his truck? Is that going to stop terrorism?"

What is he supposed to do when an airplane comes flying over his head twenty feet off the ground? Should he start firing rounds at the plane? Even if he gets lucky enough to actually hit the pilot, the plane is going to crash and he's probably going to die along with it. Talk about a no-win situation for that officer!

Do you think a little added stress has popped up on the streets since 9-11?

Not only do you police officers have to worry about the usual dangers, like opening a door and having some perp blow you out of your shoes, but now you've got to worry about some extremist who's traveled to our shores and wants to blow everybody up! For a guy like this the higher the body count the better because bodies earn him brownie points in his view of the afterlife. And, who's sitting at the front gate? It's you, a police officer.

As you know, cops are often in the military as well. A recent ABC News survey of America's state troopers found that in 29 states, between 5 and 10% of the troopers belong to the National Guard or Reserves. These officers could be called up at any time to serve, increasing their level of stress. A 2004 poll of more than 2,100 law enforcement agencies by the Police Executive Research Forum found that 44% of police forces have lost personnel to call ups for the war in Iraq. This not only puts undue pressure on the departments and personnel at home, but adds great stress to the family of the officer, with the added strain of separation and concern over personal safety.

2. Did All Those Media Helicopters Really Need to Follow O.J.'s Bronco?

Considering the very real danger of what we've just talked about, how do you think most cops feel about dealing with the blown-out-of-proportion scandals like we've seen in Los Angeles during the infamous car chase and murder trial of O.J. Simpson? My God. Give me strength! We've

The Will to Survive

got *The Juice* being followed for miles by a fleet of marked cars traveling down the interstate at an absolute crawl (while thousands of fans wave and hold up signs...they call this a chase?) and every time O.J. picks his nose, the cameras zoom in to see what he's going to do with the booger. All we saw on television was that dang Bronco. You can't tell me there wasn't a cop somewhere in Los Angeles County at the same time who wasn't saving someone's life. Where were the cameras for that?

You know, cities like L.A. and N.Y. have helicopters in the air at all times, with scanners monitoring every movement below, like a hawk circling from above searching the landscape for rodents. The networks bank on the fact that something *big* is going to happen at any moment, and it usually does. Every few minutes there's going to be a car chase, a bank robbery, or a killing, and they're going to get the scoop. With satellites working 24/7 and choppers in the sky (and a blood thirsty society in which violence sells), the stress on you as the officer trying to do your job in this environment is tangible, unless you can view this as just an absurd part of the game, as opposed to an insult to your intelligence and training, and an assault to your senses.

I can imagine what it was like to be one of the cops ordered to handle the Michael Jackson case. We're hired to follow some celebrity around as he travels around in a dark, tinted-windowed SUV as choppers rage overhead and we think, "I did not take this job for this kind of nonsense!" (Just because cops work in a place like Tinsel Town doesn't mean they always enjoy being part of the crazy circus out there— so don't be too hard on your brothers and sisters working out on the left coast.)

3. Being Bi- or Tri-Lingual Ain't Enough Anymore

The world, as you know, is getting smaller and it seems that everyone still wants to come to America. In the big cities it sometimes feels like everyone is already here. As a cop on the street, it's not like working in some small town, where the bad guys and good guys are clearly identifiable because you know them—you know their mamas and daddies and where they live and where they hang out. In the big cities in this country—New York, Los Angeles, Chicago, Detroit, New Orleans, Miami, Dallas, and so on, you've got to be joking. Think about being a cop in Miami. You could speak five different languages and dialects in that city and it still wouldn't be enough to effectively communicate with everyone. As a blind man, when I fly into any airport I'm totally at the mercy of the people who work there to help me find my way. It never fails that the Miami airport has been the toughest location for me to navigate. When they bring me to my gate it's usually the case that no one can speak English. If you're from Cuba or South America, you're in like flint, but try finding someone who can help a blind gringo from Louisiana.

There is great stress in trying to protect and serve (and even arrest) people of other nationalities. They start speaking and we can't understand their needs, their problems, or often even their crimes. Many cops in these areas are getting trained in learning key words so that they will know what dangers may be being communicated right in front of them, and so that they can better protect themselves and help people in need. The cops of tomorrow are going to have to be much more skilled than most of us currently are in knowing how to bridge these language barriers.

The Will to Survive

4. Big Brother is Watching Us, in Our Own Cars!

Putting cameras in our squad cars was intended to help us out, to cover our butts, and it often does. Sometimes someone we stop on the side of the road has a gun and takes us hostage and we thank our lucky stars later that it was all caught on tape. But these cameras are double-edge swords. While they can help us put more bad guys away, they also take away some of our edge.

For example, you make traffic stop and you know the camera is rolling. You walk up to the car and after interviewing your violator you realize that something's just not right. The suspect keeps diverting his eyes away from you and keeps moving his hands toward the back of his pants. You are being very cautious to be politically correct and diplomatic because you're being watched and recorded (heaven forbid we offend some punk violator). In dealing with criminals or a criminal element, you had better be able to speak their language, but because you're on tape, you instead remind the man politely for a third time to please place his hands in front of his body.

In my professional opinion, you've just lost your edge in dealing with a suspected criminal because you cannot talk with him in a way in which he understands. In nature, when a lion or even a dog wants to reprimand their young, they don't do it by being gentle. They grab their offspring by the neck and throw them to the ground. Specific words and intonations used with authority have that affect on a perpetrator as well. The odds of this guy getting the upper hand are greater when that fear factor isn't there. Maybe the violator reaching for his pants has a weapon and intends to use it. If you were to scare him with your intensity by talking to him in a threatening tone, in his language, perhaps he wouldn't dare take the chance. In a split second you have to decide

135

which is more important: going by the book and guarding against getting sued or having a complaint filed (should this guy criticize your treatment of him later), or possibly saving your own butt by stopping him before he gets started.

Remember the old show "Sanford and Son"? It was one of my favorites, and hilarious. The two main characters—Redd Fox, as Fred, and Demond Wilson, as Lamont—were each black, but were always talking very diplomatic, like they were whiter than white. My experience on the street has taught me that people usually talk in the same style of their neighborhood. Most white people in small country towns speak differently than most white people in big cities. Country talk is often more casual, less rule-oriented (in other words, the proper grammar ain't that important). I have friends who are proud of living in the "backwoods," as they call it, and are the first people to say that they have a hick way of speaking. These are our dialects, if you will.

Blacks in a white neighborhood are more likely to talk "city white" than blacks in a black neighborhood. While cameras are put in place to help preserve evidence and protect a cop from liability, they also add stress to the officer who now has to walk the fine line of not saying or doing anything inappropriate. But what do you do when you go into east L.A. and you're dealing with a street gang where the members are swearing at you, calling you a Mother-Fer? Your training has showed you that when you talk to them in their style, at their level, they will give you more respect. But not according to policy and procedure. That can be challenging!

5. Natural Disasters Hit with Greater Abundance
Protecting people and property is a tough thing to do during a natural disaster! Whether or not you believe in

The Will to Survive

global warming (my writer Linda does; I'm not so sure), we have seen a rise in natural disasters over the last decade due in part to growing populations, fire raging through dying forests, floods, hurricanes and tornadoes. (The looting experienced in Los Angeles wasn't too bad after the Northridge earthquake. It couldn't compare to the looting officers had to deal with during the riots there in 1992.)

When I was working for the swat team for the state police in Louisiana, we had a hurricane hit on an island called Grand Isle, on the Gulf of Mexico. It was a six-and-a-half-hour drive away for me, but when you're "near" one of these danger zones, you know that at any second when they say "go," you've got to be on your way. Basically, we troopers were packed and ready to go all of the time.

As I got closer to the coming hurricane zone, I thought to myself, *"Did I miss the hurricane training class at the academy? Did I miss that part of the tactical training that tells us what to do in an emergency like this? What am I supposed to do in a hurricane?"* It's not like there was some defense I could create, some barrier between the populace and the winds and water, but everyone expects us cops to be where the danger is. The media and the government help squelch people's fears by saying, "Troopers are on the scene." I suppose I can do a good job at evacuating folks and protecting some property, but it feels to me like it's the illusion of safety that we're really offering here.

People around us might feel safer, but what about our safety?

Boredom: Praying for a Violator

Then there are the stressors that have been around as long as policing has. When you hear the word stress, you probably think of danger, trauma, emotional situations and physical challenges. But sometimes stress can result from inactivity. Plain old boredom.

You have to understand that we cops are type A-personalities and we love excitement, which is one of the reasons we go into this field to begin with. Put us in an office with a pile of paperwork and we go nuts. Put us in a police car at 2 o'clock in the morning on a state highway somewhere in the middle of nowhere with one car coming by every two hours, and my brotha, you're going to experience some serious boredom! I've been in this thankless situation and you're just hoping and praying that that sucker driving toward you is speeding! Give me some probable cause to stop somebody soon because I need a break.

Not only do I need relief from this boredom, I need some contact, even if it's a speeder. I won't write 'em a ticket; just give me someone to talk to! Can you feel my pain?

Out on these lonely highways, I have gotten out of my unit and run laps around my car, done hundreds of side-straddle hops (jumping jacks) and slapped myself across my face while screaming like a banshee, just to keep from falling asleep on the job or going mad. I did once actually fall asleep in my unit, sending me clear into a ditch. The winter temperature was cold; my heater was on, and I was lulled to sleep like a baby—probably drooling. The next thing I knew, I was three feet from a state highway sign. Thank God there wasn't any traffic that night. That little incident woke me up real quick. With my adrenaline pumping, I turned my car around and headed back toward the Tensas Parish Sheriff's Office, grabbing my microphone:

"F-18 to St. Joe."

"Go ahead Bobby."

"Waldo (who was about as "country" as a pile of horse crap), my brother, you've got to put on a pot of coffee,

The Will to Survive

I can't take no more. I'm en route."

I went back to the office and sat there for an hour with this guy. Sometimes you need companionship, just to stay awake. There are two things going on here that pertain to most cops. **We *hate* extreme boredom and we love to talk to people.** Police officers may seem very self-contained, but we are social animals who thrive on human contact.

City cops don't experience the same amount of boredom rural cops do. I worked in New Orleans during Mardi Gras one year and experienced the other side of the pendulum big time. (It's often too little or too much with us.) The big-city experience can be non-stop! Once we got done with our briefing and hit the streets for our shift, we were already 35 calls down and playing catch-up all night. Which way do I prefer to work? That's easy! Give me the fast-paced, snatchin' and grabbin' anytime, where the shift goes a lot faster and excitement rules. Like any cop, I love problem-solving, interaction, and taking care of business.

One of the ways I learned to take care of myself on these busy nights was to make sure to take a breather every time I found myself getting overly stressed out. When you get that harried it's too easy to push yourself to work all night without taking a break. When necessary, we all learned not to call 10-8 when we were done with a specific call, and would instead run and grab a quick cup of coffee or juice or a snack.

There's a big difference between the slugs who don't take their calls, and the honest officer who just needs a 10-minute breather to maintain focus and productivity. I encourage you to take the extended calls that will help you avoid burnout. Be smart, though. If you're not catching your calls, someone else is catching them for you, and I don't even have to tell you how important loyalty is in this job! You never

The Will to Survive

want others to be forced to carry your load.

Cops Love a Good Jolt

When I was a competitive power lifter, my three team members and I worked out at the YMCA in a cement box-like room we called the dungeon. That's where we challenged each other to lift as much weight as possible, and where we cranked the tunes full blast to help us pound the poundage with gusto. Trust me on this; we weren't working out to Lawrence Welk music! Unfortunately for us, we listened to AC/DC and Black Sabbath. I can still hear the screeching chorus of "Highway to Hell" blaring through those speakers. Although we didn't have the choice of listening to rap back then, I suppose we might have been tempted to because we were looking for the pump and we wanted our heart rates up. Frenetic music enabled us to pump like crazy and better imagine that we were Superman.

No Rap Music for You!

Sorry to tell you this guys (I'd say gals, too, but I don't know too many of you who listen to rap), but there's no rap music allowed in your car or home stereo any longer! I'm not trying to be a drag, but if you go out into the field listening to songs that hype up your adrenaline and your bloodstream, you're tempting fate. You'll be more likely to act like I did—like some macho superjerk—and get yourself shot.

I've told you somewhere before (but I can't tell you where because I can't read) that we act the way we think. By listening to intensely negative lyrics that spill blame-filled hate into your energy field, you're bound to end up breaking the rules or doing something stupid. And, you'll be sending out a vibe to everyone you meet that you're full of yourself and a danger to deal with, making others even more defensive in your presence. Lucifer wasn't in charge of music in heaven for nothing! Why do you think that so many of the kids who commit suicide or shoot up their schools are found to have practically worn out their depressing and violent music CDs? The negative words become an anthem that gives people permission, even orders, to maim and hurt others or themselves.

Now, I know some of you cops love listening to your rap music. You're a swat team guy and living with your blood pumpin' is what makes you tick. Besides, you get tired from the long hours and this heavy-hitting stuff keeps you on your toes, helps you stay alert.

Don't even try that kind of B.S. justification with me! I know you're tired. I was too, and we'll be talking about sleep and nutrition a little later. I don't enjoy that boring, easy-listening, classical elevator music, either, and I'm not expecting you to, even though it lowers our heart rate. But, I am expecting that you take your mental health seriously and start looking for music that energizes you and stays clear of violent and angry images because anyone who is ignorant enough to think that our role models don't influence us is a total dumb ass. If rap music is what we're listening to all day, it's no wonder that our lives are all about violence and killing.

Officers on the road will say to me, "Bobby, I just listen to it occasionally." But you know what? Even when you erase a document on your computer, a ghost image of it is still available to a technician who knows how to find it. The same thing with your brain (and a trained therapist). If you're listening to a song about killing whores, raping women, and drive-by shootings (not to mention cop killings), those thoughts of trauma and rage are locked in your subconscious mind, even if the beat makes you want to dance. Give yourself a break and listen to Will Smith or some other music that makes you feel powerful without eliciting thoughts of brutality and cruelty.

I'm sure you can guess that I have similar opinions about cops viewing violent movies and playing violent video games. You may not see many male cops with their nose in a book at the library, nor do you see them taking their wives to many movies, but you do see plenty of them at shoot 'em up movies, usually with each other. We love cop movies; man, we could watch those things all day long! I watched those macho films when I was a cop, too, but I also loved the other stuff, especially the comedies. Remember, what you see becomes a reality for you, so since you're already seeing so much negativity in your work, my feeling is that your time off shouldn't be spent looking at more of the same. Use your common sense, and keep it tempered. You can see an occasional shoot-em-up movie (and I recommend playing football or basketball video games instead of the angry ones), but balance them with ones that make you laugh. And, you're not a sissy if you take your wife to a chick flick either! Hey, you never know, you might find it rewarding. And, your woman will appreciate you for your trouble and for your openness (crying during the film will score you major bonus points as well).

Speaking of comedies, one of the most important things you can do in this job is to...

Keep Your Sense of Humor

Your health and happiness goals are closer within reach than you think because your attitude is the one thing you can control. The next time you're around a bunch of off-duty cops, notice how much fun, joking, and laughing is taking place. Am I right? But as soon as these same people put on their uniforms, it all becomes about being tough. It doesn't have to be that way.

Not a day went by where I went to work with a bad attitude! Not ever. I LOVED my job and I loved the people I served. If I was stopping them for speeding, I felt honored to help them be more careful. I'd smile at them when it was time to go, telling them to have a good day. "Slow down, buddy. Take care of yourself." I loved talking to the little old ladies and the shopkeepers and the people who worked at the restaurants. There was so much more to my job than kicking in doors and taking people to jail. But that's in part because of the way in which I chose to think about my job and act while I was on duty.

I ask you: ***Do you really enjoy being a cop?*** (In my experience, most of you will say, "Yes!" and I believe you.) Then, why don't you show it? When people love something, they SHOW it. I'm sure you wear your enthusiasm and passion for some things on your sleeve, whether it's your kid, your Harley, or your favorite band. Everyone who knows you can tell us where your passion lies! Why don't you do that with regard to your job? It's okay to smile and show people that you're happy to be of service.

Police stations are predominately negative environments. You've got your investigators walking through the halls, who at any one time are working on several rapes, murders, and/or child abuse cases. They've got one thing on their minds—solving these hideous crimes. No games are played in the squad rooms; the business is just too serious. We start off our days in briefing, where we're told what to look out for and what to expect for the day. The game consists of people and their heavy, heavy problems, and we're over-serious and taking it all too personal (especially when we're wearing twenty-seven hats and working holidays).

Seek Out Healthy Fun!

I expect you to also take the job of solving these crimes seriously. And I know that when making an arrest, you're bringing in folks who don't want to be there and hate you for catching them. Your reward is a pile of paperwork that you don't want to do. (Remember how much you hated homework back in school?) Add to that that there isn't a moment of quiet time in the busy departments, and it's difficult to be laughing and joking when you've got so much crud on your plate. You might not be able to laugh much during your shift, but you sure as heck can turn off those scanners when you get home, watch a Jim Carrey movie with your family after dinner, or play a card- or board-game that brings excitement, fun, and friendly competition to the mix.

Janie and Brad and I have a blast with different games in our house—especially basketball (I'm still pretty good, believe it or not) and bike riding, where they let me steer in a wide parking lot with my wife on the handlebars, barking directions. Now that's some serious FUN, especially when she doesn't know the difference between her left and her right! You should see how wild and adrenaline inducing it is to play with a blind man! When you stop being a cop and turn on a sitcom and wrestle with your kids or play cards with the neighbors or even your parents, you have made the choice to empty your stress-filled glass for the day and decompress.

You alone are the one who chooses to be a grouch or a blessing.

Cops and coroners are the most hilarious people I've ever met. We crack each other up! What else are you going to do after seeing what we see? You either become a monster yourself or laugh about the sickest things. It's a form of release.

I caution you to be careful, however, and not take your humor out on the people you love. Being funny shouldn't include being mean. I've seen many cops cut people at the knees with their jokes and think it's okay for the sake of a laugh, but that's not fair.

You might never have thought of this, but it's possible to use your humor as a form of avoidance, just like anger or depression or alcohol or drugs. The trick for us is to be able to hold onto our very necessary sense of humor without turning spiteful and using it as a weapon against others, or even as a deterrent to intimacy, which will ultimately give you more stress to deal with.

Stress...Shmess...What is it Anyway?

The exact *American Heritage Dictionary* definition of stress is:

stress: n. A mentally or emotionally disruptive or upsetting condition occurring in response to adverse external influences and capable of affecting physical health, usually characterized by increased heart rate, a rise in blood pressure, muscular tension, irritability, and depression.

Just in case you don't like the word stress (personally, I abhor it), here are a few others with similar meanings. Take your pick.

Worry   Tension   Anxiety   Nervousness
Trauma   Pressure   Strain

The Will to Survive

Here's more of what stress looks and feels like:
Headaches - Loss of Weight - Stomach Pains - Shortness of Breath - Insomnia - Boredom - Forgetfulness - Negative Thinking - Low Productivity - Increased Mistakes - Feeling Overwhelmed - Irritability

Fear - Depression - Frustration - Loss of Joy - Increased Smoking

Increased Alcohol/Drug Use - Social Withdrawal - Emotional Outbursts - Increased Rage - More Sick Days - Problems with Co-Workers

Stress is inevitable for nearly all people. In the following pages we'll outline a few other stressors, as well as some of the inappropriate coping mechanisms people use that are especially tempting to those of us in law enforcement. See if you partake in any of these activities. And finally I'll talk about my top stress relievers—more appropriate ways to handle your tension, strain, anxiety, and so on.

Maybe I'll Just Drink it Away

Depression + Alcohol = More depression

Cops are notorious for being large alcohol consumers, and some stats say that as many as 25% to 50% of us have serious drinking problems. Holy crud. Been there myself. Where else can a person get PAID to hang out in bars? What a strange set up! Our job is to follow some low-life drug dealer around all night and watch his movements, even befriend him. He hangs out at the local tavern, and thus, so do we. Hour after hour we pretend to be one of his kind. Only problem is that we can easily slide down the slope and *become* one of his kind.

That's not our sole temptation with alcohol, either. I wish it were. The dang stuff is incredibly helpful in helping us to forget our problems. And, talk about expressing ourselves and letting go of stress; we feel so much less inhibited and more able to talk with our buddies honestly, so much more able to cry or laugh or feel our feelings when we're under the influence. It feels good. No, it feels great, and it's cheap, legal, and accepted. After working long hours in dangerous situations, it's no wonder that we often gather after work with each other and bond over those familiar war stories told over a brew that makes us warm and happy. We're too scared to turn towards the mental health system for emotional support, so instead we turn toward substances and make a u-turn at getting to the heart of our issues.

Sometimes we're not even looking to drink, but we're hoping to further bond with other officers. Maybe our goal is to be promoted and the bosses are partying down the street. If you work longer and harder, you've seen that you're rewarded, so chances are if you party longer and harder with them as well, it can't help but wear off in the popularity department, right? Maybe in the short run, but not for the long run. You can't do your career any good from rehab or an early grave.

After my shooting, when I was dealing with so much emotional pain and Debbie had just left me, I'd get one of my buddies to pick me up some Jack Daniels to numb the pain. I'd be home alone and start crying and feeling sorry for myself; I just wanted the anguish to go away. I'd fix myself a mixed drink and sometimes I'd have two or three. It would help me sleep a little bit, too, because I was having so much trouble getting rest. One evening after everybody had left and gone home, I realized that I was having a drink every night before bed. Alcohol had become my crutch.

Luckily, I remembered that I was taking medications, and my anti-depressants weren't supposed to be taken with alcohol. It dawned on me that I was making my problems worse by mixing the two, and although I looked forward to nighttime for this most inappropriate of coping mechanisms, I forced myself to stop. I figured that my problems were bad enough and that this was not helping matters.

Some of you won't be able to walk away from alcohol as easily as I did. You're only human. Take it from me, you can never get drunk enough to cover up the sadness and trauma of what you've seen, of what you're holding down deep inside. Drinking will only add a flame to your gasoline-drenched troubles.

Pushing Your Body to the Brink

Another reason we can get mixed up with drugs and alcohol is because of the emotional and energetic roller coasters we live on. We pump ourselves up to get out there for every shift, jumping right into fight-or-flight mode, as we discussed in chapter four. Then, we must keep our energy up throughout our shift, despite the fact that we may be running low on sleep and vitality, exacerbated by often poor eating habits on the road. We're hyper-vigilant for hours on end, only to have to return home at the end of our shift and try to be relaxed, loving, present, and available for our other job—that of spouse and/or parent.

As my friends Dennis Lindsey and Lt. Sean Kelly teach, the demands of our body to relax and rejuvenate are in conflict with the needs of a healthy family life. Here are some differences we experience in the on- and off-duty modes:

The Will to Survive

<u>**On Duty**</u>
Alive   **Alert**   **Energetic**   **Involved**   **Humorous**
Quick Thinking   **Over-Invested**

<u>**Off Duty**</u>
Tired Detached   **Isolated**   **Apathetic**   **Angry**
Exhaustion   **Social Isolation**   **Under-Invested**

Counting Sheep

As you can see by the above lists of words, any one of them (especially exhaustion) is influenced by not getting enough quality sleep. Twenty percent of adults experience chronic insomnia at some point, and ever since I got shot eighteen years ago, I've been right in there with them. My sleep patterns have been seriously messed up, even though I never had trouble finding sleep before the incident. My restless nights started in the hospital, and continued after I was released. Being an emotional train wreck didn't make getting rest any easier. I couldn't believe I was so emotional. If anyone had ever asked me, "Bobby, do you think anything could ever happen to make you emotionally bankrupt?" I would have said, "I don't think so. I have too much confidence in myself."

As a trooper, I was used to being involved in incidents where I had at least *some* control over the outcome (or perceived control). If you look at the psychological test they give to determine stress levels, I now had the highest ranking you could get—what with losing my wife, my job, and everything else you already know about. Only by the grace of God did I not suck on that Glock lollipop.

When you have severe trauma, post-traumatic stress disorder (which we'll talk about before this chapter ends) creates actual caverns in the brain, carving little ditches, which can cause fear, paranoia, and insomnia. Sleep disorders based on trauma are all about fear. Because of my blindness, I no longer know the difference between night and day. Because the eyes take in light and pick up Melatonin—a natural hormone that regulates the human biological clock—I no longer have that ability and therefore my brain doesn't pick up the twelve hours of light that says, "It's time for you to go to bed now." I've taken Melatonin and everything else you can buy, but nothing works other than sleeping pills, and those don't even get me REM sleep. For any of you sleep gurus out there, if you've discovered techniques other than Jack Daniels, feel free to give me a call!

I'm lucky if I get to sleep three or four hours before waking up. I say a prayer and tell myself to go back to sleep. If I can get a couple of more hours, I feel fortunate. There are days during the week where I get no sleep at all. I will go to bed at 11:00 and wake up at 12:00 and then go to my computer to write, literally staying up all night long. I'm physically and mentally drained the next day, but I've got lots of stuff to do and just keep moving. I'm almost fifty-one years old, so it must not be affecting me too badly. I'm in great shape physically, but there's no telling what more I could accomplish with eight hours of nightly rest.

A few helpful hits the sleep experts have shared with me:

1. Alcohol leads to a decrease in REM sleep, so keep your intake moderate.

2. Avoid heavy meals, spicy food, and caffeine before bed.

3. Engage in a period of relaxation (not TV related) before bed.

4. When you're able, try to get to sleep at the same time each night.

5. Use your bed for sleep and sex only.

The Will to Survive

6. Avoid heavy exercise and stimulating activities before bedtime.

7. Exercising during the day will help you sleep better at night.

8. Turn off the phone and turn on the air conditioner (white noise).

9. Get shades that block out all light (or try wearing an eye mask and even ear plugs, if necessary).

Sleep is an issue for most cops, which isn't surprising based on what we just learned about food, caffeine intake and bedtimes, especially. But aside from those issues, cops are also vulnerable to sleep disorders when they have been involved in serious life events, repeated traumas. I've had cops tell me they think they're going crazy with visions of past crashes they've worked that haunt them at night. We've all seen multiple accidents involving children, or cases of child abuse where the kid is still in the home. We worry about these kids all the time. Everyone likes to keep the family together, but if they're getting the hell beat out of them, how do you turn this off? It's normal to see their little faces when you close your eyes. You're compassionate and it breaks your heart.

An officer's lack of sleep is a serious problem on the job. We're dealing with high-stress and high-speed environments where we need to be alert and capable. People's lives are in our hands. Severe lack of sleep is tantamount to being drunk. According to the Australian Transport Safety Bureau in *Driver Fatigue: An Accident Waiting to Happen* (on www.science.org), ..."a person kept awake for 17 hours will perform at a standard comparable to that of someone with a blood alcohol concentration (BAC) of 0.05... After 24 hours without sleep, a person will have capabilities similar to someone with a BAC of 0.10 percent."

All the more reason to dump the dirty water out of your glass!

Sweet dreams.

The Us vs. Them Mentality

All of the stressors we face (including our lack of quality sleep) add to our feelings of isolation and our mistaken belief that we're alone and that it's us (and people like us—other cops) against the world.

One of our biggest challenges is the change within our own psyche. The transformation from civilian to officer goes something like this: You're a new cop with a mission: to help your corner of the world live in peace. You know it won't be easy, but you're young, energetic, physically fit and excited to serve your community and make it a safer place for your children to grow up in. You kicked butt at the academy and have an overall positive outlook about life and your abilities.

You begin driving around at night in your black and white. Your friends and family are tucked away in bed, sound asleep and relatively peaceful. You begin seeing things that you've never seen before, things you didn't realize were going on so consistently all around you. Things you don't want to share with your friends or family, for fear that they will live with constant worry. Suddenly the world starts to alter. Nothing looks the way it used to. Everyone becomes suspect.

Night after night, your trust in people wanes and you find yourself getting cynical. The world becomes a complicated place, with fewer familiar faces. You begin to withdraw and lose your optimism and enthusiasm. Life isn't as

The Will to Survive

fun as it used to be, as you second-guess even the dearest people in your life more readily. You seek things out that are easy to control, since you feel like you have so little control in the world. Winning the game, whatever game you happen to be involved with, takes precedent; even if it alienates you from the people you care the most about. You mostly befriend other cops and begin to separate from old friends and family members because they don't understand you anymore. Besides, they nag you and expect too much from you. You're tired and want to be left alone much of the time.

In your attempt to protect and serve, you quickly lose your sense of inner protection (or the opposite, feeling invisible), and run the risk of losing your desire to serve altogether (or serve recklessly, as was my case).

The Brotherhood of Silence: The Blind Leading the Blind
If the above sounds too close to home, I implore you to continue reading and know that you're going to have to open up and communicate with someone before it's too late—before you become a statistic! Don't rationalize and think that you're going to talk to your partner in the morning. Only talking to our partners is a self-fulfilling prophecy of doom. If you're both in the same boat at the same time, you'll be drowning together!

Again, in the back of this book, I've listed organizations you can contact (both on the Web and of the brick-and-mortar variety) for further information and/or help.

High Stress Calls
I once had to kick in a door on a domestic abuse call where a guy was beating his wife. Her face was all busted up and her eyes were closed and her nose was split and bleeding. This guy was using his wife as a punching bag.

The Will to Survive

He'd been drinking, but he wasn't drunk. Their kid—a little girl—was only three or four years old, and ran straight into my arms, laying her head on my shoulder while she trembled and cried.

The father looked at me through his rage and said, "If you weren't wearing that badge, I'd kick your ass, too." I wanted to pummel this guy. I took my badge off and put it in my pocket (not cool... an instance where I could have been fired). "Well, if that's what's holding you back, Bro, I've just taken care of that problem. You're in luck. For the next fifteen minutes, I'm off duty." This wasn't about me being the police anymore; this was man to man. I dropped my hands and I said, "Go ahead," as I stood two feet from his face. He said, "I'm going to take you out." "Come on, I'll give you the first lick," I said. I was screaming at him, calling him every name in the book. I threw him against the wall and screamed, "What's wrong? You only got enough guts to beat up women?" He hesitated, looking suddenly scared. I didn't really want to kill this guy, but I thought he needed to be dead in that moment. "You're breathing good air, punk." I turned him around, handcuffed him and took him to jail. (Before I read him his rights, I pinned my badge back on.)

Calls like these are highly stressful because people are injured (in this case the wife) and kids need to be protected while you spring into action. This type of call definitely adds to your stress level, but there are worse calls, as you know.

PTSD (Posttraumatic Stress Disorder)

Ah, this is the Big Daddy of disorders we all have to watch out for.

You can look up the technical terminology and characteristics of Posttraumatic Stress Disorder in the *DSM-IV*

The Will to Survive

(the *Diagnostic and Statistical Manual of Mental Disorders*) put out by the American Psychiatric Association, but for layman's purposes here, let's just say that PTSD is a nasty condition that is associated with exposure to death and violence and can shake even the strongest officer's belief systems to the core. Symptoms often appear after experiencing a critical incident or a series of stressors that add up until the camels' back, so to speak, is broken, and the officer's normal coping skills no longer give relief.

A friend of mine was a helicopter pilot in Oklahoma City after the bombing in April of 1995. He was one of the first ones on the scene, and with infrared technology, his task was to look for survivors amongst the dead bodies. After working 18-20 hours for 20+ days in a row, pulling out dead children and body parts, he went off the deep end and had to check himself into a rehab center because a person can only take so much of that junk. Just as we saw in New York following 9-11, thousands of cops and fireman joined the effort from across the country and exhausted themselves in an attempt to make a difference. No one was left emotionally unharmed and many experienced delayed onset PTSD, where you think everything's okay and then suddenly you're barraged by repeated intense memories and grief that can persist for prolonged periods—a virtual avalanche of images you didn't even know had been affecting you and can paralyze your ability to function.

Denial is to be expected because it's necessary for us to put aside our own feelings and emotions when dealing with an emergency. If we're helping a community that's just been hit by a tornado, for example, or we're pulling people out of the rubble of a bombing, we can't be expected to feel our feelings at the time. Someone's got to take charge. Someone's got to be the hero. But, when the dust settles and the funerals are over, nightmares of what we've seen may threaten to steal our sleep like a thief in the night. In the old days they called it "shell shock." The effects are the same.

If you are experiencing any of the following, you might be dealing with PTSD:

1. Becoming emotionally distant with people you love

2. Loss of sex drive

3. Becoming either clingy and dependent or cold and impatient

4. Engaging in dangerous activities, like radical driving or motorcycling

5. Reverting back to old habits, like smoking, drinking or drug use

6. Cheating on your spouse

There isn't time in a book of this size to give extensive guidance in treating conditions like PTSD, but if you think this is an issue for you or someone you care about, I seriously encourage you to seek out the help of a good therapist. The symptoms can be greatly eased or eradicated with the use of therapy and/or medication. Do something. It won't go away on its own and may get worse.

We All Express Our Denial in Different Ways

My good friend Trooper Mike Epps dealt with his pain and denial concerning my shooting in his own way. He drove three and a half hours out of his way from West Monroe to Baton Rouge to the crime lab to find my bloodstained shirt. He took my badge and all of my pins and ribbons off the shirt, and soaked them in alcohol and then cleaned them meticulously with a toothbrush. Mike then drove back to my house, opened my closet door, found a clean uniform hanging there and proceeded to put everything in order before hanging the shirt back in my closet.

I was so grateful! I'd rather see a guy deal with his symptoms this way than drowning his sorrows in a fifth of gin!

Transfers: Maybe Another Division Would Be Better

Some officers try to handle their stress load by looking for a way out through a move or transfer. It's common to be led astray by the misconception that moving to another division will be less demanding, less stressful. That's what I thought.

I always wanted to be a narcotic's agent. It seemed so intriguing. Back then, Don Johnson was the slick-haired, thousand-dollar-suit-wearing, Porsche-driving Miami vice ideal. I ask you, how many cops do you know who can afford thousand-dollar suits and drive a Porsche? But again, these TV-land creations were our training films, and they usually had just enough realism in them for us to hold onto our fantasies. Young cops would see these popular characters solve all the crimes and would say, "Wow, wouldn't it be great if my job was like that?"

I talked to my chief and said, "Get me into narcotics." These plain-clothes guys were cool, with their long hair, beards, and Cameros and Z28s. They didn't work a shift; they just worked whenever, usually taking weekends off and acting like their own bosses. Already divorced, I was determined to spend more time with Kim and this was my ticket. I'd still be a cop, with that identity, but would be more like a secret agent.

In the beginning, I had to spend many hours learning the ropes of working narcßíics. Unlike patrol, where you work a traffic accident and take reports and then turn them over to someone else, the hours required for investigation and working undercover felt endless.

Mastering the underworld takes both time and skill.

Once I was assigned to a major case, I was constantly doing surveillance work, getting informants, trying to meet the bad guys. My goal was to buy dope from them—to get them booked for distribution of illegal narcotics. But, here's one of the challenges. If you score a pound of cocaine, you want 100 pounds. If you get one ounce of crack, why not a kilo? The bigger the case, the more chance you have of getting these scumbags off the street. It's a battle we'll never win.

I was having fun, though, even though I was working mega hours. It was nothing for me to work eighty-hour weeks. I didn't have to, but I loved it. Once you get into it, you realize it's no longer about taking a report and punching out, you've got a caseload and you're the one in charge. This is no longer the squad's case. This is YOUR case and your responsibility!

I'd get calls from Jackie. "Bobby, I'm so sick of this. You're not a dad. Kim wants to see you and has been crying, asking why her daddy isn't coming to pick her up!" I may be slow, but I'm not stupid. I was so caught up in the excitement, but it only took me a year to realize that this life was not a life I could do half way. After that year, I went back to being a trooper and being grateful for my time off.

Further Recommended Stress Relievers

You already know what it takes to be healthy and happy (i.e. get more sleep, take naps, get to a therapist, allow yourself to cry by renting a tear-jerking movie if you need to—open up to the people you love, avoid self medication, treat others with respect, take your Prozac, and so on), but let me remind you of other helpful actions to take because chances are you're still stressed out, right? If you follow the ideas and suggestions explained below, I guarantee you're going to feel better and be less stressed out!

1. Engage in ritual
2. Eat for health and energy
3. Exercise at least 20 minutes a day, four days a week
4. Write it out
5. Try a little "empty chair therapy"
6. Keep the faith

1. **The Freeing Power of Rituals**

I have found that the use of rituals is powerful in dealing with the stressors of our job. We talked in chapter four about the importance of engaging in symbolic rituals, like taking your imaginary jacket off each night before entering your home. Having daily rituals in place to better connect with your family when you're working long hours—things like connecting around the same time on the phone to help with homework, even for a few minutes, or talking with your family about their day after dinner, helps create bonds in your absence.

The police family needs to work diligently at establishing rituals in order to fortify the normal ups and downs of marriage and raising kids. When I'm on the road, I'll often use a tape recorder to tape notes to myself of what I want to tell Janie and Brad so that I don't forget the moments or thoughts I want to share with them. You can write things down on your shift—stories you want to tell your family, maybe things you've forgotten in the rush of your morning.

There are other important times for us to engage in

The Will to Survive

ritual as well—more formal rituals. When you've had a relationship with someone who has died, for example, I highly recommend that you observe and engage in some kind of ritual on significant dates, like his or her birthday, an anniversary, or even on the date of their death. These exercises help to bring closure to our losses. The closer you are to someone who dies, the more difficult it is to deal with their absence and the more powerful the ritual will be.

The subconscious mind is very influential and doesn't forget a thing. It will slowly begin opening the closet doors to your memories and repressed pain as the event draws near. Have you ever noticed how a specific time of year will remind you of a past event? The sensory input from a certain fragrance in the air or the rustle of leaves blowing down a sidewalk may stir up powerful feelings and memories in the subconscious mind after a traumatic event or loss. As an example, if your father died in the fall, it's normal to start feeling melancholy and sad toward the end of summer, when the trees begin changing colors and the air turns crisp. Marking the date with a ritual will help ease your stress significantly.

I believe in celebrating the birthday of someone who has passed away, even the anniversary of their death. If you and a friend went to the local jazz concert together each spring, I advise that you continue to go to the festival despite the fact that they are no longer there. As you indulge in your wine and cheese (or soda and burgers), set up an extra glass for your loved one and say a toast to him or her. You're not focusing on death when you do this, but rather you're commemorating a loved one's life—remembering the good times.

The anniversary of my shooting will be here in a few weeks, and I prepare for this anniversary every year—not to honor the shooting, but to celebrate my survival.

The Will to Survive

Returning to the Scene of the Crime

On the first anniversary of my shooting in 1987, my buddy Sammy Rogers took me to the site of the gunfight. I was still in bad shape emotionally, but I knew that I was getting better and I wanted to face what had happened to me. Sammy took me to the precise location of the shooting, and he said that even a year later, a faint imprint of blood was still visible on the pavement. We parked fifty yards from the spot, and I got out of the car. Sammy walked me to the spot, and then I asked him to leave me alone for a few minutes.

As I stood on the shoulder of the highway trying to relive as many moments of my shooting as I could recall, I remembered jumping out of my car, being caught in the brightness of those headlights, and then laying face down in a pool of blood. I also prayed that day while I was there that God would restore my sight in the exact place in which I had lost it, but mostly I was there to attempt to connect spiritually with Trooper Bobby Smith, who I missed so dearly and still didn't quite understand. I needed to remember him and find out why he had been so careless. I think I also wanted to forgive him.

I wish I could say that I experienced a true mystical moment that day. I'm sorry to report that there were no bells or whistles; no gale-force winds with crashing thunder and crackling lightening. I wasn't taken up heavenward in a flaming chariot like Elijah. But I did realize something invaluable:

I was still alive!

I still commemorate this anniversary every year because I find it empowering to celebrate being a survivor, which is why I also have a yearly celebration for Kim's birthday. Sometimes I get a cake, sometimes only a muffin and coffee, but I always bow my head and thank God for her life, for the beauty of having Kim in my family. And, her mother and I always talk on that day and express our feelings and end up crying together.

I invite you to create rituals for whatever feels important to you. You can do it for practically anything, even a divorce. There is a time in any marriage where the two people involved were once in love. A divorce is a death of sorts—an emotional death. Performing some kind of ritual (maybe through lighting a candle, writing in a journal, saying a prayer, or taking yourself on a trip or out to a special dinner) around the marriage that once was is an opportunity to reflect upon the positives of the union, rather than any hollering and screaming (and restraining orders) that may have come later.

2. **Eat Your Vegetables!**

Cops are notoriously bad eaters. We're always on the run and even when we do sit down in a restaurant we're often interrupted. Talk about stress eating! We eat like we're in the military and hope and pray to at least get our food down our throats before our pagers go off. It's tempting to just drive by any fast-food joints and grab whatever food we can. And, while you're at it, give me some caffeine to wash this junk down with.

When you eat a diet heavy in fats, grease and fast food (in a rush, no less), you might find that antacids like Rolaids become your candy. "Cop candy." One night my buddy Ray Clary (we called him Haas) and I were driving during our night shift. I was a rookie and Ray—a cop's cop—had been on the force for years.

It was cold outside and Ray says, "Bobby, reach in my briefcase and hand me my gloves." I leaned over the seat

The Will to Survive

and found the typical police briefcase, worn black leather, with a broken handle (cops aren't going to walk around with no stream-lined, panty waist, name-brand briefcase... we're cops, not CEOs). This sucker was more like a box than a briefcase; one side was smashed in. It probably fell out of the back of his car or trunk and then got beat up as he drove over it. The latches didn't work; the only thing holding it together was a cop's *other* best friend (other than his weapon)... duck tape.

We were at S. 6th and Winnssboro Rd. and I reached back to this piece of junk, pulled loose the duck tape, and retrieved a 500-count bottle of Rolaids. Now, I hadn't eaten ten Rolaids in my entire life, so I said

"Ray, what in the world are you doing with this huge bottle of..."

"Boy, after you've been a cop for about five years, ask me that question again.

And, since you got your hands in there, go ahead and pass me a couple."

Those guys I worked with were constantly popping *Cop Candy* into their mouths.

I can't say it enough; cut yourself some slack and stop making life harder on yourself than it needs to be! Cops already have a much higher risk of cancer and heart disease than the normal population (due to our habits and levels of stress), so get creative. Bringing celery and carrots and fruit in the car won't take away the fact that you're eating a greasy burger, but they'll help make the effects less damaging. Grab the bean burrito with lettuce and tomato instead of the beef taco. Have the ice tea instead of the soda; the croissant instead of the donut (I had to include the "D" word at least once in this book or civilians wouldn't believe this was a cop book). It's not too complicated. The only thing stopping you from eating better is laziness.

3. Exercise As If Your Heart Depends on It

In doing your job, you want to make sure that you're physically fit, mentally alert and properly trained. Personally, I took that overboard by spending more time at the gym than with my family, but it's smart for your own protection and even your mental, emotional and physical health, to be in good shape.

Studies have shown that if a cop doesn't win a hand-to-hand confrontation within the first three minutes, the bad guy will win. We've all heard stories of a violator getting away because the cop was too exhausted from fighting. Sometimes they even get shot and killed with their own weapon taken during the struggle.

In these traumatic situations, especially when the cop is injured, there are two forces vying for power: the will to survive and the desire to let go. The push/pull of the two forces becomes a battle over life and death, and you're far more likely to triumph if your body (which helps fuel your will) is strong and powerful.

After my shooting, during the first meeting I had with Dr. Steven Charles, my eye surgeon, I was sitting in his exam room and he pulled his chair right up in front of me, placed his hand on my knee and said: "Bobby, I just got through reviewing your charts and I wondered, 'How the hell did this guy even make it?' After looking at you, I'm going to tell you right now, you shouldn't even be here. But it's very obvious that you work out. The only reason you made it is because you're so physically fit.'"

I know I've basically just told you not to be a work-out-aholic like I was, and now I'm telling you that it saved my life. But, there's a balance for everything. I believe that I still would have pulled through even if I hadn't been a power lifter. Exercising twenty minutes a day, four days a week is enough, I believe, to keep a body strong, and stress at bay. You'll figure out what's right for you.

4. **Write It Out**

Sometimes you're not going to want to talk with anyone. You're not going to "go" anywhere to get help. You're stubborn (I know who you are) and don't want to be told what to do. I get that. But, please, try this: get a journal or a pad of paper, and start writing your thoughts down. Jot down whatever comes to mind.

> What's bothering you?
> What's making you angry?
> Who's pissing you off at work?
> What are you thankful for?
> Who do you love?
> What do you want?

Write it all out. At first you may not be able to think of anything. Sit there anyway. If you can force yourself to sit and write five or ten minutes a day, you will be surprised at what comes forth. Don't judge it, either. It may look like gibberish. Keep it up. It's important to get it out of you and down on the page where its power to hurt you lessens dramatically. If you can't stand the thought of having a record of your thoughts, burn it. Just get it out.

5. **Tell it to an Empty Chair**

In that same line of thinking, you can express great emotion—as in get it OUT of you—by sitting and talking to whomever you need to talk to, in the safety and quiet of your car or your home. It's only you, but you are talking to whoever has hurt you; whomever has caused you pain—even God, if that's what feels right.

I learned this technique from my therapist. In a session one day, he asked me to talk to my old self—the Bobby Smith whose carelessness pulled me into a life of total darkness. At first I didn't want to do it—didn't see the point. How could talking to some invisible imaginary person do any good at all? Boy, was I wrong!

Talking to my old self in my therapist's office was one of the most cathartic things I've ever done. I yelled at him. I talked to him. I cried to him with such forcefulness that it was as if the therapist was gone and I was really speaking with Trooper Smith directly. Then I forgave him… I forgave *me*. There are no words to express how powerful this was for my psyche. Try it. Make up your own rules. You're the one in control.

6. Faith Works Miracles

I have a strong faith in God that's helped me to believe that there's a reason things happen, a reason for everything. People ask me all of the time how I deal with the loss of my sight. My first answer is this: *Because I'm not paralyzed!* Then I explain how I was lying flat on my back in the hospital looking up at the ceiling after I was shot when I realized that I was looking UP. Isn't it a shame that God will allow us to be put on our back to force us to look up?"

Personally, in case you haven't noticed by now, I'm a Christian and Janie and Brad and I find great peace and support through our religious faith. Regardless of your faith, you might find solace in going to a church or temple or to a religious/spiritual setting to reach out for help. You might find it to be a wonderful source of community as well. I rec-

The Will to Survive

ommend talking with a priest or chaplain when you don't yet feel comfortable going to a therapist. Or, try them both! My point is this: there's always someone to talk to. There's always help. All you have to do is ask, even if it's only getting on your knees in the privacy of your home and going straight to your God one-on-one. Lord knows that very action saved my life several times!

Keep the faith. Believe in your dreams. Visualize what you want and don't allow yourself the habit of doubt or negativity. Read uplifting books; listen to uplifting tapes. Pray.

I think God works in miraculous ways, and I believe in looking for the positive and moving on. This can be challenging, for sure, but there's got to be a bigger picture here somewhere, which is especially important to remember when contemplating the subject of the next chapter...

The Will to Survive

CHAPTER VI
Suicide is Never a Dry Run

I have never seen my son's face. Nor have I ever laid eyes on my wife's beautiful smile. If I wanted to be really dramatic, that alone would be enough to make me stick my Glock 9-millimeter in my mouth and blow my brains out. I have found that never seeing my son laugh or even our dog's furry mug is reason to feel deeply sorry for myself, if I let it. Never experiencing the look of love in my wife's eyes as she looks at me makes me so sad.

For those of you who have ever loved a child, whether it was your own or someone else's, can you imagine having a baby and *never* being able to see its face? Think about how beautiful a sleeping infant is, or how cute a toddler is when he or she is learning to walk. How would you feel being so close to that little being, yet so far removed at the same time? I remember the joy of seeing my daughter, Kim, go off to kindergarten with her big smile and her front tooth missing. It was one of the most precious sights I had ever seen, and will forever be branded on my memory. Unfortunately I have never had that pleasure concerning my son, Brad. People have told me that he looks just like I spit him out of my mouth, but God, if only I could experience that for myself. What I wouldn't give to see our family portrait!

Now, obviously I'd never consider killing myself over not being able to see my family, despite the fact that it irks me and always will. But, I'll tell you, when emotional stresses stack up on top of each other, one after the other (with no end in sight), there's no telling what you'll do.

The Will to Survive

But It Will Never Happen to Me

Okay, I'm not going to lie to you. I'm sitting here in major discomfort trying to figure out what to put in this chapter. There's so much we could cover, but I don't want to write a word about suicide, and chances are you don't want to read about it either. Ethics vs. Corruption in Chapter One? Now that was fun stuff! Getting to talk about Clint Eastwood as *Dirty Harry* in chapter three—entertained even me, and I already knew what we were writing! But who the heck wants to deal with this topic? SUICIDE? Eek gads. Did someone turn out the lights because damn, it's dark in here?!

Well, I've got some good news. I'm just as surprised as you may be when I tell you that in my research, I've found a little bit of good news—cool news, even. Not about the numbers, because those are definitely too high. But about the WHYs behind this phenomenon of suicide. I think when you read about what's been driving this epidemic, you will breathe a sigh of relief and have more hope if the statistics have been bothering you. This chapter will take away some of the mystery and drama associated with suicide, which is a scary topic for us cops, based on the sheer number of us who fall victim to this form of self-destruction. How can we be so smart and yet do such a dumb thing? How can we be so tough, yet so weak as to destroy ourselves? This chapter will help you wrap your mind around the problem, ensuring that you'll be better armed so that regardless of what cards you're dealt, you will never be seriously tempted. You're reading about a guy (me) who has had every reason and then some to kill himself. Odds are that if I was seriously tempted (which I was) and didn't succumb (obviously), you won't either. Especially if you read on…

I know that some of you are still thinking, "Even so, Bobby, I think I'll skip this chapter because suicide will

The Will to Survive

never be an option for me." I used to think the same thing. I'd be at an officer's funeral and wonder why the deceased had taken the cowardly way out by leaving everyone in such despair. I absolutely couldn't relate. How could anyone be so short sighted? It made no sense. But I was soon to learn the hard way about the allure and temptation of the perceived "freedom" that comes with ending it all.

So, *please* **read this chapter in its entirety, even if you're hesitant.** Think of it like eating your vegetables. You don't always want to do that either, but you do it because it's good for you. Along with the good news, I'm going to be telling you the bad stuff, too, and straight up because, frankly, some of you don't have much time to waste. While I promise to keep it as short as possible, there are some things you *need* to know, especially if you're having a hard time or know someone who is. Even if you aren't anywhere near the danger point of becoming a statistic yourself, you could encounter suicide on the job at any time. In other words... suck it up. It can't hurt to read a measly little chapter. I promise that what you'll learn will be both fascinating and valuable.

We Are Our Own Worst Enemy

It is true that the majority of you reading this book will never attempt to take your own life, but that being said, nearly **one in a thousand cops will kill themselves this year** and every year after that, unless knowledge like this becomes commonplace. Knowing this information could be the difference between life or death for you at some point in the future. In case you think I'm being melodramatic about the psychological dangers we face, think on this (and the following points): Today, while you're reading this book, two or three cops will kill themselves! To put it in less dramatic language, my first little self-published autobiographical book, *Visions of Courage*, has sold somewhere around 22,000 copies. If you go by the stats that means that twenty-two cops who read my book will kill themselves. That's twenty-two sets of parents who will be devastated, and many more spouses, children, siblings, and friends who will forever miss their loved ones, some never getting over it.

A Few Alarming Points I Hear Frequently Throughout My Travels

1. Suicide has become one of the great "secrets" of law enforcement.

2. As many as 600-800 cops kill themselves each year, and that's a conservative estimate.

3. Out of 25,000 potentially lethal attacks on police officers in 2001, only approximately 150 were deadly.

4. Suicide is *the* leading cause of death for police officers.

5. *We* have the highest suicide rate of all professions. (Did you really believe that dentists could outdo us? Come on!)

6. We are the boogeyman waiting in the dark. Suicide kills more cops than all of the other dangers we face, combined.

In 2000, according to executive director, Robert Douglas, of the National Police Suicide Foundation in Pasadena, Md., 418 police suicides occurred that year. But the actual number may be closer to double that, as many suicide-related deaths are misrepresented as accidental shootings. (How many times have you questioned an "accidental death" when you heard the details: a skilled cop is cleaning his gun but somehow shoots himself in the temple; an officer's car hits a tree dead on, resulting in immediate death, but there aren't any skid marks to show that he tried to stop or swerve. You look a little deeper at the officer's personal life and hear about how he's losing his kids in a nasty divorce or being reprimanded publicly for a wrongful act on the job. Suddenly the "facts" of the case seem a little less factual and a lot fishier.)

Why the hush-hush? The stereotype that police are too tough to have emotional problems is a hard one to break, made more problematic by the fact that we don't typically acknowledge our stressors to anyone but each other. Talk about the blind leading the blind!

Very few of us want to talk about the fact that more cops die each year at our own hand than are killed in the line of duty. The stats are hidden, altered, eased, for the sake of the victims and those who love and employ us. The question becomes, why? Why do we do it? Suicide happens in great part because we don't know how to deal with the anger that comes from holding in all of the stress we deal with. According to recent FBI findings, **87 percent of American law-enforcement officers suffer from post-traumatic stress disorder.** In my counseling work with cops, I get to see the result of locked closets and the horrors of cops who never cry or get help and who eventually try to kill themselves, often succeeding.

In short, the most powerful perpetrator lives in the psyche of the officer, as the hazards of the job are often unbearable and our rage has few outlets. But it doesn't have to be this way.

Why Are We So Susceptible? A Bizarre, but Potentially Positive Twist

I'm about to tell you the "cool" news. It's rather tragic, actually, especially for the people affected by suicide in the part of the world I'm going to tell you about. But, for the rest of us, there is a powerful lesson here that can bring great relief and, I believe, hope.

On the South Pacific islands of Micronesia, suicide has truly become a phenomenon. Young men, specifically, seem enamored by the possibility of killing themselves, as if some great mythological power has them spellbound. Those who find themselves feeling suddenly powerless in a situation sometimes find the allure of taking control over their own death too tantalizing to ignore.

In a gripping account told by the author Malcolm Gladwell (*The Tipping Point: How Little Things Can Make a Big Difference*, Little Brown, 2002), the Micronesian epidemic of suicide and what it means to the topic in general is thoroughly investigated. It turns out that as recent as the early 1960s, suicide on the islands was nearly unheard of. Once it was introduced by one "heroic" seventeen-year-old boy named Sima, however, "it began to rise, steeply and dramatically, by leaps and bounds every year, until by the end of the 1980s there were more suicides per capita in Micronesia than anywhere else in the world." In comparing suicide rates between the islands and the United States, for example, a September 2003 report from *BMJ Publishing Group* (British Medical Journal) in Australia stated that for every 100,000 males between fifteen and twenty-five, there are 200 suicides in Micronesia, a number that exceeds U.S. rates by 20x. How could this be? We're talking about beautiful islands here, not some horrible place ruled by an evil dictator.

What makes these numbers even more staggering is that the suicides are often the result of "small" incidents: an argument with a parent, a breakup with a girlfriend, a failed grade. It has become a kind of ritual of adolescence. One eleven-year-old boy who lived through such an attempt

The Will to Survive

explained that he did not want to die, but was merely "trying out" hanging, as if it were an experiment. With each new suicide, the myth takes on greater allure and the rates continue to climb.

Although this almost casual way of viewing suicide in Micronesia is markedly different to the way suicide is seen in the United States, several similarities exist. As police suicide rates in America continue their yearly ascent, there appears to be a kind of cancer at work. **Suicide leads to more suicide.** It's as if the mere fact that it exists, like a cancerous tumor, feeds continued growth. According to anthropologist Donald Rubinstein, as quoted in *The Tipping Point*, "As the number of suicides [in Micronesia] have grown, the idea has fed upon itself, infecting younger and younger boys, and transforming the act itself so that the unthinkable has somehow been rendered thinkable." In a series of papers, he writes, "Thus as suicide grows more frequent in these communities the idea itself acquires a certain familiarity if not fascination to young men, and the lethality of the act seems to be trivialized."

What does all this have to do with us? Plenty! Have you ever stopped to think about how often the reality of suicide has come into your life? How many times have you answered a suicide call on duty? How many times have you heard your fellow officers talking about one of their suicide calls? How many funerals have you heard of or attended where the officer shot himself in the head? Chances are suicide has become all too familiar to you. Now, in comparison, how do you think your numbers rate against the general population? How often do you think your grandmother or your first grade teacher's life, for example, was touched by suicide? How many dead bodies do you think they have seen in their lives? Now you're getting the picture. The average person doesn't have this subject on their internal "computer screen" very often, if at all. For you, on the other hand, dead bodies and suicide are a real part of your everyday life, and one that has become far too real and WAY too much of an option. Especially when you're walking around with survivor guilt, repressed anger, and PTSD. **The unthinkable has somehow been rendered thinkable.**

The act of taking one's own life is obviously contagious under some circumstances, whether you believe that or not. Whether you like it or not. Because suicides invariably lead to more suicides, we need to be mindful of this epidemic and mentally and emotionally protect ourselves from being easily influenced by the mindless actions of others. All sorts of statistics exist that prove the contagiousness of suicides on our shores. Right after Marilyn Monroe's death, for example, Researcher David Phillips discovered that our nation's suicide rate temporarily increased by twelve percent—predominately from white women taking their lives in greater numbers that month (from "The Influence of Suggestion Suicide," in the *American Sociological Review*, 1974). And, think of how often you hear on the news that a man has shot his wife and his children before killing himself. These stories are becoming more and more common. This isn't just a problem concerning a small group of islands. This is a global issue.

But, this is good news for us. This is something that, once we are aware of, we can have power over! Now that we know that we're dealing with a virus, of sorts, we can choose the emotional vaccine. I can't tell you how exciting this is to me. Suicide has merely become an option for us because that's what we've seen. It's become an option for us because we've become numb to how truly outrageous this is! Are you listening to me? Do you see how crazy and unconscious this has become? Do you understand that we have had the act of taking our own lives as an option because we thought it was rational? What would you say to your young daughter if she said that she wanted to kill herself? You'd say, "What, are you kidding? Have you lost your mind? Nothing could be that bad. Don't take yourself so seriously!" But that's just what we do. We take it all too seriously, and that's crazy! Believe me, when you're suicidal, you're not thinking rationally. I know. I've been there.

Losing My Mind

When I was a kid, nighttime was always scarier to me than daytime. The closet that seemed totally safe and normal during the day was the place where monsters hid in the dark. From time to time, I would have myself totally convinced that evil, scary creatures were living and breathing somewhere in the space above my shoes and under my clothes.

In going back in time for a minute, one of the worst things about going blind was that it was always pitch black dark, no matter where I was or the time of day. Thus, I was often thrown right back into those childhood fears of hidden evil entities who were coming out to prey on my poor, helpless little self. After all, evil lurks in the darkness and is afraid of the light. I no longer had the ability to turn on the light switch and remove my darkness. Paranoia is a common after affect of trauma, and mine, encouraged by the onslaught of constant darkness and pain killers, started right away in the hospital (and still creeps in from time to time). I had to be watched twenty-four hours a day because I had been known to go into a rage and pull the IV's from my arms and tear the bandages from my face and hands. I had no consciousness of what I was doing, and when I'd awake, I'd be confused, disoriented, and sweating. One evening, I sat up and was told that my brother Terry was sitting at the foot of my bed, only I didn't know who he was.

"Who are you?" I asked.

"Bobby, it's me Terry," he replied. "What's wrong?"

"Why are you holding me here?" I asked.

"Holding you where?" he said.

"Holding me here, in this concentration camp," I said.

I was serious. I was certain that everything Terry was telling me about a shooting and about losing my eyesight was crazy, and that I was really being held against my will in a concentration camp. I wanted out something fierce! I stood up, pulled the IV's from arms, tore the bandages off my face and hands and yelled at Terry that he could no longer hold me against my will. I could feel pain, and suddenly everything got real confusing because I could "see" that the room was painted in yellow and black checkers. Talk about being paranoid! As the nurse rushed in, I growled at her to get away from me, and disregarded her assessment that I was hallucinating. It was only after they called in an officer that I knew I could trust, that my memories started returning and I began to believe their story and accept the fact that I had indeed been shot.

Returning Home Brought Its Own Kind of Paranoia

In the deep quiet and stillness of nighttime, without my wife's presence, I discovered that a mind can play horrible tricks on a person. Even though I couldn't see the difference between night and day, there was something sinister about nighttime now. Bad things always seemed to happen at night, and I couldn't figure out why. My paranoia was so intense that nearly every time I lay down, I would hear the most awful noises. (I could make a monster out of every sound.) I remember like it was yesterday, hearing footsteps of a heavy-set man walking down the hall. As the steps grew closer, I could hear the man enter my bedroom, walk over to me and stand right over my bed. I could actually hear him breathing right over me! Terrified, I lay motionless, wrestling with what to do, wondering if I should stay put or chance it by reaching for the phone. Sometimes I did nothing only because the fear was paralyzing.

I don't know what it was about the nighttime; if it was because the phone would stop ringing and the noise of the neighborhood would cease, but whatever the reason, this is when the dragon was unleashed, along with his buddies: fear, anxiety, paranoia and insomnia. I couldn't shake the fact that I was in this mess because I had been unable to see from the glare of the high beams that night on the highway, and now I *really* couldn't see. Did this mean I'd be harmed again? Could it be worse the next time? I was so worried, knowing that I wouldn't be able to arm myself against an attack if it was coming. Certainly my guns would be of no use to me now. I felt so vulnerable, and at the mercy of any psychotic madman who could decide to hurt me. It had happened once before, and now I was imagining 101 ways in which it could happen again. As you can imagine, my biggest fear was that I was going crazy and would end up getting beaten up somewhere in a nut house that I couldn't escape from.

Just Walking to My Mailbox Brought on Panic Attacks

Coming home was a brutal reality. I hated every minute of it! I was getting bruised shins by attempting to navigate my way past the coffee table to the television set. I was feeling like an idiot groping for the toilet seat and peeing on the floor (Have you ever tried to stand in front of a toilet with your eyes closed? Do I have to explain that one?) Hearing my wife sob hysterically in our bedroom down the hall before she gave up on me entirely, I knew that life would never again be lived on my terms. The smallest actions—getting the mail or going to the garage—became terrifying. Soon I developed agoraphobia and panic attacks, making it impossible to be self-sufficient. I was emotionally chained to the couch—my security blanket—and had to have my lifelines to the outside world, my remote control and phone, within reach at all times.

Couldn't Make It Through the Night Without Calling My Buddies

I don't think I'd be here today if it weren't for my buddies. These guys held my hands and held me up when I couldn't take care of myself another minute. When you've spent your entire career identifying with yourself as "the man," it's not easy to suddenly live life as a dependent person. My panic attacks were so relentless during the middle of the night that I often couldn't make it without calling my friends for help. Too many nights they had to race over and hold me, cry with me, and make sure that I felt safe. Trooper Mike Epps, for one, came over so many times between 2:00 or 3:00 o'clock in the morning that I just lost count. This guy worked deep under cover in narcotics for years; he is *not* a guy who's going to show you his emotions. He has these real dark, deep-set looking eyes and a linebacker mentality. Think Tommy Lee Jones. He's also a lean, mean, fighting machine, a real athlete. Believe it or not, his favorite snack was yogurt raisins, so that's the bait I used to keep him coming back. I would call him sobbing on the phone and although I couldn't even talk, he knew it was me. Who else would be on the line snotting and wailing in the middle of the night? Mike would be asleep and answer in his sleepy tone, saying:

The Will to Survive

"Bobby, Bob," I'll be there in about twenty minutes. I'm en route, but don't call Jackie. I don't want to have to deal with both of you wimps bubbling on the couch."

Of course, I had usually already called my partner, Jackie. What a mess we were! Mike would walk in the house and I'd be distraught with snot running down my face (sometimes Jackie would already be there, sniveling alongside), and he'd say, "Would you just stop all that damn crying." Without a beat, he'd walk straight to the pantry to the big container of yogurt raisins. He loved those things. As I'd hear him walk across the kitchen, I'd say to myself, "Oh God, I hope I'm not out of yogurt raisins because if I am, he's going to throw a fit."

"Bobby!" he'd yell, "This really pisses me off! You call me over here at 3:00 A.M. in the morning and you don't even have any damn yogurt raisins!"

What angels my friends were to me! I never personally heard Mike cry, but I know that he did. Jackie couldn't help but cry. He was always such a softie; I often wondered how such a nice, sensitive guy could be happy being a cop, but he loves it to this day.

Wrestling with the Five Stages of Grief

As we've already discussed, losses add up. I was starting to feel that mine had stacked so high that I was unable to deal with the enormity of my pain. Let's indulge in a brief recap, shall we? Let's see. I had never grieved the death of my mama, who had died on my tenth birthday. The only job I had ever loved had just been taken away from me because I could no longer perform the duties necessary to be a cop. I lived in a world of total physical darkness and dependency and would never again see *anything*. My second wife had just left me, and I was now living alone with terrifying panic attacks and agoraphobia. Oh, and monsters came to visit nearly every night. Dang, my life was nasty!

I'm sure you've heard about the five stages of grief. In a nutshell, none of us gets passed these suckers when dealing with trauma and devastating events. I had gone through several by this time, but I was far from being through with the grieving process! Let's look at the stages (four of which I had already encountered), and while you're reading, see if any of these are familiar to your life:

1. **Denial**. My best buddy! I loved hanging onto this one, but like all things, denial evolves, sticking around only until you're ready to deal with your loss. Eventually I had enough courage to stare reality in the face and look at my options, but that took a long time. Denial serves a purpose, however, and for a while it kept me from going totally mad by making me believe that I would get both my sight and my job back. In the end, it just wasn't worth trying to live in a fantasy world when the facts told a different story. That doesn't mean that I don't pray every day for the restoration of my sight, but I no longer depend on that outcome for my happiness. I no longer expect to be able to see again. If that happens, it will be icing on the cake of a good life.

2. **Anger**. Okay, this one is a given. As soon as the shooter's red car nearly hit us at the checkpoint, my blood was boiling. My memory is such that from the minute I woke up in the hospital, I was still furious. I was always a fighter, but my shooting put me over the edge. I began taking my anger out on the people I loved the most (especially my sister Betty), which made me feel terrible. She would cry and then I would cry, which fed into bargaining and depression, the next two stages.

3. **Bargaining**. This is one stage I embraced right

from the start! When I was face down on the highway, I bargained as if my life depended on it. Lying on the cold pavement, I told God I'd do *anything* if He'd just make it all okay and keep me alive. Later, my plea became more about, How can I get back what I've lost? I can't count high enough to tell you the number of times I begged and pleaded with God to heal my situation. Even though I was willing to do whatever it took to get my job and my sight back, we all know how that one turned out.

4. **Depression**. This is anger's twin, and where you end up when you realize that bargaining aint' getting you anywhere. You can't have depression without anger. Depression, as we discussed in chapter 5, is anger turned inward as a result of fear. It was pretty obvious that I had some attachment to this stage because any guy who curls up in the fetal position in the corner of his room to cry for hours at a time (which I did), has a little challenge with depression. Oh my Lord!

The stages don't necessarily follow chronological order, but all have to be fully worked through before the loss can become fully accepted. It would take some serious time before I explored the fifth and final stage: **Acceptance**. That, and the issue of finding hope once again, were a little more elusive.

I Had So Much Shame About Who I Had Become

It's safe to say that I hated myself. Not understanding that the nightmares, flashbacks, cold sweats and hallucinations I was experiencing were normal, I thought that I was the weakest cop ever to walk the earth. Another thing that was gnawing away at my self-respect was that I had lied about my shooting. It was a stupid lie, but an honest one (if that makes any sense) because it was a lie born out of denial. You see, when I was shot, the first bullet missed me, but I fell to the ground anyway. I had convinced myself that the first shot had ripped into my hand, spinning me around, and leaving me more vulnerable to the second shot.

The reality was that the second shot hit me in the hand *and* in the head. Even though getting hit by the first shot seemed like a stretch to me, that was my byline, my ten-second sound bite. Most everyone bought it, and that was fine with me because that's what I wanted to believe. I just couldn't accept that I fell from fear. "Bang, bang, you're dead" was too simplistic for my mind. It may have been the script we followed as kids playing cops and robbers (when falling to the ground upon hearing those fake bang, bang shots were part of the rules), but I hated to think that I didn't know better as an adult. It took me several years of therapy before I could admit that the first bullet (the one that brought me to the ground) missed me altogether.

Some of you may be thinking that we're trained to hit the ground when shots are fired, and you're right to think that. But I was still mad at myself for being so robotic in my response, and ashamed to admit, even to myself, that I had fallen out of fear. I couldn't get it out of my mind that the fact that my knees had buckled out from under me may have contributed to my getting shot.

So, Mr. Superman state trooper thought he was a coward. As I lay in my bed or on my couch and cried (something I didn't seem to have any control over), I knew that people were standing around me crying. I felt so badly for them. They hurt for me because I was hurting, and I hurt for them because they were hurting. It was a vicious cycle of spiraling emotions and helplessness. When I talked, they tried to console me. When they talked, I tried to console them. It was never-ending and totally depressing!

The Straw that Broke the Camel's Back

After Debbie left me, I didn't know what to do. It was obvious to everyone who knew me that I just couldn't stay home alone and do nothing. I needed a job; I was desperate to keep busy and to find value in my life again. Too much time on my hands had left me paralyzed with fear and self-loathing. I needed to find a way to be of service, to contribute to society and experience camaraderie with others.

Sgt. Aubrey Futrell, who trained me at the academy, and Sgt. Vic Summers came by one afternoon and asked me if I would be interested in going to Baton Rouge and doing a training video with the state police concerning my incident. Despite my fear of facing my memories in that kind of detail, I knew that I was getting stronger and that my story could help save lives in the future, so I agreed.

The ride was very enjoyable, and I thanked Aubrey for all of the training he had given me at the academy, telling him that if it hadn't been for the intensity of his leadership, I may not have survived that night on the highway.

The taping was a success and I was glad that I had made the trip. On the way back home, Aubrey asked me if I'd be interested in going to work for the state-police academy in Baton Rouge. I was so excited that I could hardly believe it! Maybe I could still be a Louisiana State Trooper after all! Even if I weren't in the field, at least I'd still be with the state police. I was elated, and we planned for me to move in with his family. It was fairly clear that I'd be a blind-school dropout anyhow because in the short time I had attended the building where they were supposed to teach me how to walk around with a stick and read little raised dots with my fingers (yeah, right), I had rebelled against all of the rules and kept arguing with the teachers. I was sure that I was about to become the first person on earth ever to be kicked out of blind school, so I had no qualms about leaving. Besides, I had a job to go back to now! This was a dream come true.

I Moved to Baton Rouge and Moved in with Aubrey and His Wife

The director of the academy, Captain Rutt Whittington, knew about my background interest in psychology and my experience with PTSD and thought that it would be beneficial for the training academy if I did some work with Aubrey, so he put a desk for me in Aubrey's office. It was so great to finally feel that I was a part of something again, especially being part of the Louisiana State Police! With time, I began to regain some of my old self-confidence. Captain Whittington came to me one day and asked me if I'd like to be a permanent part of the academy. Almost nothing could have made me happier, and I accepted right away. I was told that I would need to produce a proposal for the colonel, to show him how I could be of service to the department. I was determined to write the best proposal the department had ever seen.

Sgt. Vic Summers, who was an English major at LSU, helped me to complete my detailed proposal; we worked so hard on it and made sure that it covered every possible point that could help my case. On the day of my meeting, I was scheduled to speak to the new cadet class at the academy. My job was to inspire them to be the best cops they could be, and to learn from my example. It was a blast. In full uniform once again; my dream was already coming true. The cadets loved the talk. As I stood in front of the room, I was overcome by feelings of joy and tears began to well up in my eyes. These were happy tears. For once!

The Will to Survive

When I finished my presentation, Aubrey and I went straight to my meeting with the colonel. I walked into his office feeling confident, excited, and nervous because this guy had my future in his hands. It soon became clear that something was wrong, and that my future wasn't so important to this authority figure after all. I handed him my beautifully typed proposal, and he threw it across his desk without so much as looking at it.

"Bobby, I know why you're here. I received a call from the Governor. It's just not going to work out. Let me be very honest with you. We have the tape [referring to a training tape I made about my incident]; we just don't need you anymore."

Holding back the tears, I turned my back and walked to the door, thinking, "You don't deserve to see me cry." I was devastated, knowing that all of my dreams were now crashing around me. The daggers of his words had pierced my heart and I was furious that I had lost my eyesight in the line of duty and this was my thanks. He then informed me that he was in the process of finishing my retirement papers and that he wished me well. I wondered how someone could be so heartless, without empathy or compassion. *Sticks and stones may break your bones, but words will never hurt you. What a lie!*

I left headquarters and was suddenly thrust back onto the roller coaster of emotional turmoil. I had finally been accepting myself as a blind person and this one person had just taken a world of hope away from me. In a matter of seconds, what had taken six months to build was wiped away. To add insult to injury, I was told that I wasn't eligible for the retirement watch, even though I was now officially retiring, and I had to travel 230 miles to Monroe to sign my papers.

The Will to Survive

I couldn't believe what happened next. My colonel flew to the event in his helicopter with his personal photographer and had the audacity to take pictures of me shaking his hand as he handed me my retirement papers! In a big façade, the public was supposed to see how "gracious" the state police was being to a poor blind man.

I Sat On the Edge of My Bed With My Revolver In My Hand

I had never contemplated suicide before my shooting. As I said earlier, I never understood how anyone could be so irrational. But now, after being rejected, nothing seemed to be going my way. I felt like I was doomed to a life of failure and dependency. Thoughts that would have seemed totally irrational to me earlier now seemed completely rational. Death seemed like the only way out of my traumatized life. What was the point? My life only brought misery to me and all those I was dependent upon.

I knew it would be simple; countless cops before me had proven that. All I had to do was put my trusty loaded revolver in my mouth or hold it to my temple and fire. Quick and easy. I reached for my familiar Smith & Wesson .357 Magnum. I didn't want to die; I just wanted the emotional pain to go away. Since there was no light at the end of my tunnel, I figured I'd go looking for the supposed light on the other side. I saw death as my only real option.

Just as I was planning to put the gun toward my head, I heard a voice. There wasn't anyone in the room, so it appeared that the voice was in my head. But it didn't sound like my voice. It was strong and forceful and certain. It said, *"Go get the poem."* I remembered that my daughter had given me a poem after my shooting called *Footprints In the Sand*. I knew it by heart, and had been so moved at the end of the

The Will to Survive

poem where God reveals that the reason there is only one set of footprints in the sand during times of trouble is because God is carrying us. I hurriedly found the poem, held it to my chest and cried and cried. Kim was still alive at that time, and yet she had no idea how many times her small gift to me proved to save my life.

What Have You Done Lately to Reach Out to an Officer in Trouble?

I'd like you to think about your attitude toward officers who are experiencing trauma. Have you been willing to listen to a buddy in pain? Or, did you exit the east entrance of the station when you saw one of your troubled brothers or sisters coming in through the west entrance? If it weren't for my buddies, I never would have made it out alive.

I get letters all the time from cops who've heard me speak and want to share stories with me, often baring their souls concerning issues they've bottled up inside. One particular letter still stands out as one of the more heart wrenching.

A female officer wrote to tell me that she had gone to high school with a popular guy she didn't really know. A self-proclaimed "geek" back then, she wasn't included in his social circle. One afternoon she saw this man, now a fellow officer, at a police-sporting event. They had a great time talking about their children and about the many comical things they each experienced in their respective departments. He mentioned that he had been divorced, and before leaving that night, he gave her his home number, saying that he hoped they'd get together. She thought that was a great idea, and when she got home she put his number on her dresser so she'd remember to call him. She never got around to making that call, however, and it soon became too late because she heard that he had committed suicide. This woman was devastated and wrote to me about her regrets about not following up. She, like most people affected by suicide, wondered if maybe she could have made a difference.

We all get so busy; it can be hard to know when a situation is indeed dire. I'm quite certain, too, that in this man's misery, he never would have believed that in taking his own life, he'd be hurting people as remote as this female officer he barely knew.

If You Think You Are a Burden Now, Wait Until After You Pull the Trigger

Okay, you're doing dang well if you're still reading this thing! My hat goes off to you. Isn't so bad, is it? Now I have to talk with you a little bit about the stark reality of what suicide really looks like to the people left behind. Please indulge me. This is my feeble attempt to write my own version of *Scared Straight*.

Cops aren't afraid to die, but we don't handle death well either. We're mostly afraid of being weak, of feeling shame, of letting people down. Ironically, we're terrified of being a burden to others, but the reality of suicide is that you become the ultimate burden, as you'll see.

Think back to a time when you've felt badly about yourself. Maybe you felt fat or sick or depressed, and didn't think you were able to contribute enough joy or skill or money or emotional support to those around you. Maybe you felt that your life put undue stress on others: a spouse or co-workers, children or parents, and that life would be easier without you. I can see how that mentality forms. I've been there! When I had lost it all—my eyesight, my job, and my wife, I thought that killing myself would be a win-win situation of sorts: bringing peace and ease to those I was dependent upon, and the freedom from pain that I so desperately craved. Freedom is a big one for us cops because it ties in with being independent. I was used to being "da Man." Not "da burden."

I had never depended on so many people, from doctors, strangers, and co-workers, to my friends, my brothers and my sister. It seemed that no matter what someone offered, I always needed further assistance. Friends would bring me groceries but then I needed help putting everything away. Someone would help me find what I needed in a store, but then I couldn't count my money. If I asked for help getting to a bus stop, I then needed someone to make sure I was going to the right destination. I was constantly at the mercy of others and felt like a leach, which was ongoing and unbearable, Thankfully, however, I never totally lost sight of the bigger question...

How Do You Want to be Remembered?

It all boils down to this one question, doesn't it? What do you want your legacy to be? The sad truth is that most people who kill themselves are found by their children or spouses. I can't imagine a more selfish, horrible legacy to leave to your loved ones. Now, it's important to keep in mind that when you're depressed and suicidal, you are not thinking clearly. There's a chemical imbalance that takes place in the brain when a person is severely depressed. The only way to balance those chemicals is through medication, but medication is only a Band-Aid on a cancer if you do not deal with the underlying reason you're depressed. Cops are used to being in control, but when we're depressed and thinking irrationally, we deny that we have a problem. Suicide begins to look rational, and a cop will say to himself: "I'm the decision maker. I'm used to taking control. There is nothing wrong with thinking about taking my own life." It's like trying to convince a drunk that he's too drunk. He doesn't believe you because the alcohol has dulled his rational thinking.

So, in your irrational moment, maybe you don't think your family will be adversely affected if you die. Maybe you don't care what happens to them in that moment. Maybe you're mad at them; maybe they've hurt your feelings or let you down. You're so irrational that you can't even see that two days from now everything will look brighter. You're taking yourself WAY too seriously!

You Take Your Gun Out and Shoot Yourself in the Head

Once you actually pull the trigger, you are now a hideous mess—waiting to be discovered. Your youngest child finds you lying on the floor of your bedroom. She's terrified. But, you're not dead yet. You're bleeding to death and incoherent, but you're still alive, thrashing around and convulsing. The top of your head is blown off, splattered on the wall, and your daughter runs screaming from the room and calls in the rest of the family, who all scream and cry upon finding you. What happens next?

The paramedics come, as do the neighbors and the media who heard it over their police scanner. People are hysterical. Your family wants to ride with you to the hospital, knowing that this might be the last time they see you alive. But they aren't allowed to come. Why? Because your spouse and older children have to go into the station for questioning. The police on the scene can't be sure that you're responsible for your shooting. For all they know, someone in your family has tried to kill you. The investigators, who are your extended family, would sometimes rather believe that your wife killed you rather than imagine that you took your own life. Imagine the panic you've instilled in everyone involved. So, while you get wheeled away in the screeching ambulance, your family is hauled off in a somber squad car and taken in, where they will have to sit for hours in their bloody clothes, answering questions and trying to prove their innocence.

Do you really want to avoid being a burden? The only option is to get your act together and get some help! Suicide is an option, but not a very good one. There are better ways to leave an unhappy life, like divorce or a job change, for starters. The guy I just wrote about couldn't have left a more tragic and hideous legacy if he had paid Stephen King to write a horror movie of his life. His family will never forget that nightmare day and its aftermath. No matter how happy they may become down the line, these images will never, ever, fully disappear. This one very selfish act set this guy's wife and kids up for a lifetime of haunting flashbacks and regret. *Now that's irrational!* Is that really what you want to leave behind at the end of your life?

Unfortunately, this ripple effect is largely unimaginable to a suicidal person because desperate people don't see past their own misery. But, all you have to do is look around at your next suicide call and imagine those aftershocks taking place in your house.

If Kim's Death Didn't Push Me Over the Edge, Nothing Will

Thankfully, I had done a lot of work on myself and healed a lot of my old pain when I found out that my daughter was dying in the hospital. Probably because I had worked so hard on myself and learned how to handle the largest stressors that life could dish out (by grieving and facing all of my pain), Kim's death didn't take me out. Although I spent many dark moments grieving over the loss of her life, never once did I consider killing myself when she died. **Thank-**

fully, once again, the option of suicide had become unthinkable. (Later, I realized that she had previously been the one to stop me from killing myself with the poem, and that strength still held strong years later.) I have been able to stay rational and see the beauty of my life, even against the backdrop of the worst tragedy I had ever faced. Kim's death was emotionally devastating, but I had been to this place before; I had walked this familiar trail already. I could tell myself, "This is going to be hard, but it can't take me out."

In hindsight, Kim must have known on some level that she was going to die. On her last birthday she said to me very seriously, "You know Daddy, you're a much better dad blind than you were sighted." A month before her accident we had dinner together, and she told me that she was sorry for the bad choices she had made in her life, and that she had forgiven me for not always being there for her as a child. I had no idea it would be our last meal together.

I'm so grateful that my daughter and I were given emotional closure. Although I'd like nothing more than to have her alive, I found the strength to move forward, just as Kim would want me to. I think about my mama's words, oh so many years ago, and I now know what she meant when she said to me, "God never gives you more than you can handle." No matter how bad it looks, we have the fortitude to get through it.

Suicide is Never a Dry Run

No matter how bad it looks, suicide is never worth the aftermath. I pray that no matter how terrible your life might seem to you, no matter what you've done, who you've hurt, or what kind of mess you may find yourself in, you will keep your wits about you and remember my situation. Remember that the one pair of footprints in the sand are not

The Will to Survive

yours, but God's, as He cradles you.

If I didn't take my life after becoming a groveling, snot-nosed dependent wimp, you can get through whatever is going on with you. I never could have known at my lowest points the joy I currently live with. I have so much fun on a daily basis, so much laughter, such love and success around me that sometimes I feel like one of the most blessed men in the world. I challenge you to stay open to the good your situation can bring to the world and trust that there's a plan. There is always a plan, and being six feet under before your time ain't part of that plan.

I'm certain of it. Hang in there, no matter what, my brotha (I say that with affection for the ladies as well). This too shall pass. It's going to be okay.

The Will to Survive

CHAPTER VII
Protocol in Times of Crisis

Remember how I complained back in the last chapter about having to write about suicide? Somehow I got through that chapter, but now I'm stuck with possibly an even harder topic to write about! At least we had several positive points to discuss, like the discovery that by studying the stories of suicide in Micronesia, we can diminish suicide trends at home. By covering all sorts of ways to AVOID being tempted to commit suicide in the first place, chapter six had hope. But this chapter is about what to do when an officer or someone we are here to protect and serve is already dead. Whether dealing with funerals (from a death in the line of duty or the aftermath of a suicide) or notifying a family member about a death, there are no second chances here. It's just death, death, death. Give me strength!

So, why would you even consider reading on? Because, as always, you cannot heal until you feel, and there is a lot of healing that has to happen when dealing with the death of an officer or a death in the field. So, once again, I ask you to read about a topic you would normally avoid like the plague and step up to the plate. Being smart about the protocol surrounding a death can make a huge difference in the affect that event has on you and those involved. Just because most people ignore this topic, doesn't mean that it's not immensely important.

If you haven't already, there is a great probability that you will have to face the death of a fellow officer in the future (or notify a family about the loss of one of their own), and you might as well learn the protocol from those of us "experts" who have been there more than we care to remember. Along with some of the incredible work Concerns of Police Survivors, Inc. has done in the field of death notification, we will give you some tips for dealing with your grief and the many details surrounding a death. There are tried and true ways to make this easier on you and everyone involved.

Another reason to read this chapter now is because having to scramble to learn this stuff when you have to—when you're in crisis—is a pain in the butt. Many large departments have clear protocol steps set in place, but many officers don't know what those steps are. And, since most departments are quite small, consisting of only three to ten officers, there's a good chance some important steps will be missed. It's easy to assume that nothing bad ever happens in your small, rural area. Maybe you've never lost an officer to suicide or a gunfight. While that may be true so far, the stats are against you. And, everyone knows that those long rural highways are the scene of plenty of accidents, so this information is applicable to everyone.

In this chapter we will cover:

1. Dealing with abandonment: from the micro (your buddies) to the macro (the administration)

2. Protocol for death notification

3. Hospital protocol

4. Financial compensation for survivors

5. The role of the liaison officer, and why you need one

6. The important do's and don'ts of dealing with the media

7. Support groups

8. Protocol for funerals: in-the-line-of-duty deaths

The Will to Survive

9. Protocol for funerals: when an officer commits suicide
10. Department protocol procedure musts
11. Remembering our brothers and sisters

Abandonment Takes Many Forms

I went to a funeral once and heard the preacher say a profound thing:

"It's easy to be here for the survivors right now. It's easy to stop by with a lasagna and a bundt cake after the funeral, but the real act of love is showing up six months, a year, or two years from now, when most people will be gone."

How true is that? That has definitely been my experience. There were guys who were there for me from day one and who continue to be. But more often than not as time went on, people fell away. Not everyone, but some of those who did surprised me.

Abandonment is a big topic, and not one easily contained in a mere section of a chapter. Therefore, I'll start off with a personal story and as we discuss the different areas of protocol, the subject will make continued appearances. So, for starters, another painful chapter in the life of... me!

As you know by now, Jackie Coleman was my best friend. We lived and worked together, did everything together. After my shooting, however, Jackie would only come to my house when I called and asked him to. Why? Because he couldn't. He just couldn't deal with it. Not because he didn't love me or because he didn't care. It was just that seeing me sitting on the couch totally blind was too much for him. Truly, I think it was more emotionally difficult at times for him to deal with my shooting than it was for me. That still holds true today, over seventeen years later.

When I published my book, *Visions of Courage*, Jackie wouldn't read it. Wouldn't even open it, even though he's all over the dang thing, in word and in a black and white photo. I called him and said,

"Jackie, my book's in. I want you to be the first one to have a copy."

"Um, okay, I'll try and come by to get it," he said.

Try? We lived one and a half miles away from one another, off the same exit on the highway! What did he mean, try? Dang. My feelings were hurt. A day went by without a visit, so I called him at the troop and asked him where he was.

"You get your butt in the car and come pick up this book!" I said.

"Uh, okay," he replied.

Was Jackie stuttering? He sounded so strange. I felt so badly, like I was begging my best friend to be interested in my new life. Why won't he come get my book? I wondered. It took him two full days to make it over. Would you believe that he didn't come on his own? He brought another trooper with him rather than face me alone. The guy was a good friend of ours, so it wasn't too formal, but it was obvious to me that Jackie still wasn't comfortable with the way things had changed. Even after all the years and physical healing that had taken place, the emotional wounds were still raw. It wasn't like I was leading a horrible life and Jackie had to witness my continued devastating suffering. I was now happily married with a beautiful child and a thriving career speaking to cops all over the world. I was making good money and able to live in beauty and luxury. The book was a serious warning to cops about what to avoid, but also a celebration of all the good that had transpired since that tragic night on highway 15.

I Didn't Lose a Friend; I Lost a Relationship

I knew in my gut that Jackie would never read that book, and to this day, he still hasn't.

Jackie and I are still best friends. We always will be. But, there is sadness between us that time has not healed. On some level, we're both dealing with abandonment. He lost the ability to be with his best friend, Trooper Bobby Smith. It was like I had died. I couldn't be a cop anymore, and thus couldn't be the refreshing source of relief and play that he relied upon while on duty. We would never again protect each other as brothers in the field; heck, I would never even see him again.

From my vantage point, he died to me too—at least as the friend I had known. My shooting was so painful for him that he wasn't all that playful anymore either (which, of course, I understood). I'd call and instead of hearing the familiar, Hey, how ya doing enthusiasm in his voice, it was more like, Oh dang, what do you need now? It was the death of all we knew about being best friends.

"The strangest thing keeps happening." Jackie calls and says,

"Bobby, a buddy of mine saw my picture in your book the other day and wants a copy. Can you send me another one?"

One time Jackie was even telling me that "everybody" was talking about my book, and that he agreed it was very good.

"Jackie? How do you know it's a good book?" I asked.

"Cuz they say it is," he answered.

"You wimp," I said. "Why don't you just read the

damn book?"

"Cuz I don't want to," he replied. "I don't have to read the book because I know the book." Crud. I couldn't argue that.

As I'm sure you can imagine, however, Dr. Bobby Smith doesn't let too many things go unspoken!

"But Jackie," I continued, "Are you aware that you haven't really grieved what happened to me? Are you aware that your grief is locked up inside you and causing you pain?"

"I don't care," he said.

Just over a year ago I decided to update that book and spruce it up a bit with a new cover. Since other troopers had written segments about my shooting and how it had affected them, I begged Jackie to write something for the revised addition.

"Jackie, please, I'm begging you. I'm doing a revised addition about the night I got shot. You know how much I love you. I think it would be very powerful if you would talk about our relationship, our bond." He got real quiet.

"Would you do that for me, please? I know it's going to be difficult." I heard Jackie start to sniffle and choke up. He was crying.

"I can't. Please don't make me do this," he said. You know I will if you make me. But, Bobby, please don't…"

"Will you at least give it some thought?" I said. He never mentioned it again.

I've heard from our mutual friend that when he woke Jackie up at 12:30 A.M. on the night of my shooting, he answered the door saying, "Who's been shot?" When Jackie heard my name, I'm told he immediately collapsed to his knees and started crying.

Every cop knows that being shot in the head is not a

good thing.

The Dreaded Death Notification

I can imagine how hard it was for Jackie to get that news. There is almost nothing as painful as getting or giving the death or seriously injured notification. I hated this part of the job more than anything.

Every twelve minutes in the United States a cop arrives at a house unannounced, knocks on a front door and tells someone that his or her loved one is dead as a result of a car accident. (The death notification numbers are much higher if you count the deaths due to murders, rapes, suicides, and other accidents.) **According to my calculations, every thirty-nine hours in the United States a police officer is killed in the line of duty** and his or her family receives the dreaded knock on their door. (Again, the numbers are higher if you count the death notifications that result from officer suicides every 10-20 hours). Whether it's the mother and father of the deceased, or the surviving children, the family is almost always distraught. What a brutal situation. Life doesn't get much more serious than this.

How do you think it affects us to tell parents that their fifteen-year-old daughter who just got her driver's license last weekend, drove across the centerline and got herself killed? You think there might be some healing to do after that event? Do you think going to a bar with your buddies for a few cocktails afterward will make the sadness go away after this shift? What happens when you go home and see your own teenager sleeping soundly? Do you picture him or her lying there in the morgue?

One late night I had to notify a middle-aged couple that their sixteen-year-old boy, a new driver, had driven across the centerline and hit a car head on. Thankfully the other driver's injuries weren't life threatening, but the boy was killed instantly. When the parents opened the door and saw one of my sergeants and me standing there, they knew something was very wrong. Two uniformed cops (and a chaplain) don't knock on your door late at night unless someone is dead or fiercely injured. Most people know that. I said,

"Is your son named Jimmy?"

"Yes, officer," the father said. "What has he done? Is he in trouble?"

"Your son was involved in an accident," I said.

"Is he hurt? Is he okay?" the mother asked. There was great fear in her eyes. This couple looked like every parent I had seen or heard about in this situation; they didn't want to hear my answer.

When I told Jimmy's parents that their son was dead, the mother immediately covered her ears with her hands and collapsed to the floor, sobbing. The father just stood there dumbfounded, with a blank stare. They were so numb that they didn't ask too many questions, which was good. I didn't want them to know that when I got to the scene their boy was still in the truck, which was smashed in like an accordion. I didn't want to tell them that he was shattered in between the seat and steering wheel, and that the truck was still in a ditch. When I left, they were cutting him out, getting ready to put him in a bag and take him to the morgue. I just didn't want to have to tell them that.

I've had buddies in this situation who have been hit and screamed at when delivering a child's death notification. The father or mother becomes hysterical and starts swinging and screaming. A week later or after the funeral they will say, "I'm so sorry, I can't understand what happened to me." Believe it or not, this is fairly normal behavior under the circumstances.

The Will to Survive

What to Keep in Mind When Notifying Any Family—Cop or Civilian

There are so many things required in this situation, and it might be a good idea to dog-ear some of these pages for quick reference should you need to find this information in a hurry. And, check with your department to see if you have protocol procedures in place. If you don't, I strongly suggest that you take the time to set them up. Just because a department doesn't have a suicide or death notification protocol set up doesn't mean it'll never need one.

A few things to remember when delivering the death notification:

1. When at all possible, bring a chaplain with you to the home (if you're in a small enough place to know who people are, try to bring their own chaplain). Their presence can bring great relief to the family of the victim.

2. If there is knowledge of a medical problem with an immediate survivor, medical personnel should be dispatched to the residence to coincide with the death notification.

3. Notification must always be made in person and never alone. Bring another officer, a chaplain, a mental health professional, or a trained survivor of a slain officer with you.

4. If the above, suggested persons are not readily accessible, however, notification should not be held up until these people gather—especially if there is the opportunity to get the family to the hospital prior to the demise of the injured.

5. Never release the name of the deceased to the media before all immediate survivors living in the area are notified.

6. Always ask to be admitted to the house before giv-

ing the death notification. Never make the notification on the doorstep.

7. Ask that everyone in the home sit down, and then give the notification slowly and clearly. Use the victim's name, and avoid words like "gone away" or "passed away," which can give false hope. Use the words "dead" and "died" for clarity.

8. If specifics of the cause of the incident are known, the officer should relay as much information as possible to the family. (For heaven's sake, use good judgment and common sense. What would you want to hear if it was your loved one? The gory details are not necessary!)

9. The family should NOT drive themselves to the hospital. If they insist, please have an officer accompany them in the car when possible. (People have a tendency to jump in their cars, throw the car in drive, stomp on the accelerator, and drive a 1,000 miles an hour to race to the hospital.)

10. If the death of the officer is at all suspicious, the area should be considered a crime scene until proven otherwise. Doubt about the cause of death will interfere with department and family healing, so it's important to investigate immediately. Be careful to treat family members with great respect during this time, so that innocent victims aren't treated as criminals.

Assisting the Family of an Officer at the Hospital

The ranking public safety official at the hospital should meet with hospital personnel to arrange waiting facilities for the family that are separate, but not isolated, from co-workers. This official should also insure that medical personnel relay pertinent information to the family of an officer's condition on a timely basis.

The Will to Survive

If it is possible for the family to visit their loved one prior to death, they should be afforded that opportunity. It's the family's right to visit their loved one, and agency officials should "prepare" the family for what they might see. I caution you, however, to not be overly protective of the family. Sometimes the most comforting thing is to be present when death occurs, to touch and hold the body while there is still a presence, still life.

Helpful Hospital Protocol

1. The same ranking public safety official should see that the family is updated on the incident as soon as the family arrives at the hospital.

2. A ranking public safety official or designee should be present the entire time the family is at the hospital and should arrange whatever assistance the family may need at that time.

3. The people who made the initial notification should be among those at the hospital.

4. If the death of an officer is a result of a suicide, the department should quickly determine if a professional cleaning crew is necessary, which is likely due to the fact that most cops use guns to kill themselves. Make sure that the crew is dispatched to clean the area as soon as possible.

5. A survivor should not be sedated unless medication is requested by the survivor, and is recommended by the physician. (This decision should not be made by a hypochondriac auntie.)

6. Idle promises should not be made to the family at this time (i.e., "We'll promote him/her posthumously," or "We'll retire his/her badge").

7. Arrangements should be made for transportation of the family back to their residence.

8. Arrangements should be made for all medical bills relating to the services rendered to the deceased officer to be sent to the appropriate governmental agency for payment. The family should NOT receive any of these bills at their residence. Amen to that!

$$$ Financial Compensation for the Family

When a law enforcement officer is killed in the line of duty, it is the responsibility of the employing agency to file a claim for benefits with the <u>Public Safety Officers Benefits Program</u> at the Bureau of Justice Assistance (Office of Justice Programs, U.S. Department of Justice—see back of book for contact information). If approved as a line of duty death according to Federal government criteria, a Federal death payment is made to the survivors.

States also have benefits available to the survivors, however, state benefits are not uniform. Some states pay a one-time death benefit, while others pay in installments. Some states offer tuition-free education for surviving children and a few states include surviving spouses in this benefit. A continuation of health care coverage, a pension payment, the officer's badge and/or uniform, a waiver of property taxes, all represent different benefits that may be available to the primary survivors of a law enforcement officer killed in the line of duty.

Concerns of Police Survivors, Inc. (<u>www.national-cops.org</u>) has compiled information on benefits (including information on how to find out about continued health benefits and educational benefits for surviving children) available to law enforcement survivors in all 50 states, the District of Columbia, and Puerto Rico. Be sure to contact them if you have any questions regarding your coverage or the coverage of a fellow officer. (See back of book.)

The Will to Survive

I recently met a man at one of my lectures whose partner was shot in the line of duty and his family had only received a $5,000 check from the police association. No one had informed the family that they were entitled to over $150,000 from the state (it varies from state to state). They mistakenly believed that because the officer had no separate life insurance, the family wasn't entitled to anything else.

Take Care of Your Family Now... It Will Help Ease Your Stress

Even if your family is entitled to $150,000 on the event of your death, ask yourself if that's enough to keep them living in the manner in which they have become accustomed. Is that enough to keep your children in their schools and your spouse comfortable enough so that he or she won't have to get another job to cover costs? I know you may feel that you don't have enough extra money lying around to buy extra coverage now, but I'm telling you, look into it while you're healthy and strong. And, for God's sake, please get your will and/or your estate planning completed. Listen to what I'm telling you; don't depend on other people to make sure your family is taken care of!

Now What? What About Our Feelings?

Because delivering a death notification is so painful, you've got to give yourself room to grieve. Even if you didn't know the victim and his or her family personally, you can relate. You've got kids (or have felt love for a child) and you've got parents. It would be impossible not to put yourself in their shoes, or feel some of their pain. (If you don't feel anything, that's the first sign that you've shut down and need to investigate your feelings immediately.)

As we discussed in chapter three, where we talked

about the woman whose nine-year-old had died on the highway, it's totally appropriate in this situation to show emotion. It is okay to cry in front of the family. It is okay to share in their grief. If that's not comfortable for you, I hope you're able to tap into your sadness on the way home, or later in your own home. The sooner you face the pain of what you just experienced, the more you'll be able to enjoy the moments of your life unencumbered by this trauma.

The Liaison Officer

Choosing a liaison officer in the department is critical for the family (and, believe it or not, protection of the agency as well), and it should be someone who knew the deceased officer and is aware of his or her family relationships, but not someone so emotionally involved that he or she might be ineffective. This is not a decision-making position, but rather a facilitator role, to ensure smooth communications between the family, the public, and the safety agency. Also, it should be stated that this is a demanding role and the liaison officer should be relieved of all other duties in order to best serve in this capacity.

The Liaison Officer's Job Entails:

1. Insuring that the needs of the family come before the wishes of the department.

2. Meeting with the family to explain his/her responsibilities during this time.

3. Meeting with the family regarding funeral arrangements. (Most officers don't prearrange their wishes for handling their own funeral. If the family decides to have a "line-of-duty funeral" the department should make the family aware of what they can offer in the way of assistance.)

4. Being an immediate line of communication with

the agency headquarters and the family (pagers are recommended for this job). Being constantly available for family members during this traumatic time.

5. Knowing all information concerning the death and the continued investigation in order to answer all family questions.

6. Providing as much assistance as possible and overseeing arrangements for travel and lodging for out-of-town family members.

7. Ascertaining what the public safety, fraternal/labor organization involvement will be and what financial assistance they are willing to provide for out-of-town family travel, feeding the funeral attendees following the burial, and so on.

8. Making sure that the surviving parents are afforded recognition and have proper placement during the funeral and funeral procession.

9. Seeing that the family is briefed on the funeral procedure (i.e. the 21-gun salute, presenting of the flag, playing of "Taps," the ladder archway, etc.), and that all of those details are in place, including a suitable church with seating capacities large enough to accommodate attendance.

10. Ensuring that a departmental vehicle is made available to the family if they desire transportation to and from the funeral home, church, and or burial ground.

11. In the event that there is a trial in relation to the death, the family should NEVER hear of court or parole proceeding through the newspaper or television news. Perhaps a contact person from within the department should be assigned to notify the family of upcoming court proceedings.

Media

As previously mentioned, be certain to never report

an officer's name to the media until all surviving family members in the area have been notified. So many people have heard about a spouse or parent's death on the news, and that is something you want to avoid at all costs. It's just something they'll never get over.

Also, a commanding officer or public information officer should be designated to handle the media throughout this traumatic ordeal. In the unlikely event that the family should decide to accept an interview, this officer should attend and screen all questions presented to the family to ensure that any legal proceedings aren't jeopardized. In the event that the death is due to suicide, particular care should be taken with respect to the media. Be careful never to discuss the back-story of the case, the "whys" and "wherefores" of the emotional problems that led to the suicide. This is nobody's business outside of the family. Unfortunately, nearly all police suicides will involve media, as this is a "hot" story. Some of the smaller agencies may not have protocol and the news media may learn about it on the scanners. If they show up and hear some officer say, "Looks like he may have purposely checked out," and you've got a news camera rolling, it's not going to be pretty. There are some smaller agencies out there that have little experience in dealing with the media. Be careful what you say; there's no such thing as "off the air." Assume that the media wants you to say something worthy of the tabloids. Sensationalism sells, so think smart!

The response from the department should be brief, without speculation. And, if you're asking for no media involvement, it's wise not to have a long line of squad cars with lights flashing as part of the funeral procession.

The Will to Survive

Support Groups

It's a great idea to have a family support group organized in your department. This group can be assigned the responsibility of seeing that the home is prepared for the influx of visitors that will be arriving, and that ample food is available. (It would probably be in poor taste to bring in fast food burgers.) Babysitting needs for all family members should be met, as well as someone to screen all phone calls (which can be exhausting for the survivors). Make sure that someone is always at the home. Also, it is nice for the family to have access to other public safety survivors or other support groups (i.e. Concerns of Police Survivors, Survivors of Homicide Victims, Compassionate Friends, International Conference of Police Chaplains, National Police Suicide Foundation, National Organization of Parents of Murdered Children, and so on—see the back of the book for contact information).

Funerals: To Cry or Not to Cry… That is a Difficult Question!

Why is it that cops usually try so hard NOT to cry at the funerals of other cops? People will be crying all around us, but we remain stoic. What's that about? Put yourself at the scene: Your buddy has just been killed in the line of duty—a violent death, where two drug dealers put six slugs in the back of his head and shoulder blades with his own rifle. He was a ten-year veteran; someone everybody loved. He had three children, ranging from ages six to twelve, and along with his devoted wife, you and your fellow officers are vacillating between weeping and trying to be strong in the front of the room.

You are positioned near the family, alongside your troop. It seems like everyone, including the secretaries, have shown up to pay their respects. You're in your formal dress blues. The atmosphere is serious, totally solemn. You tell yourself that you've got to be strong because you know whatever you do will be contagious. Like a virus, each officer feeds off whoever they're standing next to. You want to stay strong for the guy to your right, and he in turn wants to be strong for the woman next to him, and so on. You don't dare risk being the first one to break down because the virus also works in reverse. Like dominoes, if you break down, the officer next to you probably will also. As long as you stay brave, everything is cool.

Is This Normal Behavior? Heck No. This is Crazy!

As a counselor, this is a horrible situation. It's not even remotely normal to be stoic at a loved-one's funeral. If you were standing there by yourself, you would probably weep like a child. Here's a guy you loved and worked with and you're trying to be brave and hold back your feelings of loss? Nonsense. But, I understand. Once again, we cops are faced with odd and difficult situations. It's the job.

How Many Times Can I Repeat Myself?

You cannot heal until you feel. There are no exceptions to this rule. And, I don't care about the location. It doesn't matter if you're not "supposed" to break down and cry. You had better let your guard down at sometime and the sooner the better. If it's not at the funeral, perhaps you can grieve at the gravesite. There's nothing like hearing "Taps" on the bugle or "Amazing Grace" on the bagpipes to help us feel the weight of our sorrow. This is usually when cops feel free enough (or can't hold it back any longer) to break down. Folding up the flag and handing it to the surviving spouse or parents or children as they lower the casket into the ground is a sure-fire tearjerker. If you're a real tough nut to crack and still haven't cried at this point, try acknowledging your feelings once you get quiet at home before bed. If you find that you need to scream and cry two days later sitting on the lake in your bass boat, then the Great Outdoors is going to be your audience. It doesn't matter where you do it. Just do it! Don't delude yourself into believing that you are an exception to this rule. You're not. You're only human.

The most emotionally difficult police funeral I ever attended was for Trooper Mike Keys of the Louisiana State Police. He stopped a guy for speeding on the interstate one night, and as he approached the car, the violator sped away. Mike jumped back in his trooper car and sped out after him. Now, Mike Keys was notorious for wearing his seat belt. As soon as he sat in his seat, that thing was the first thing he touched. He was so adamant about wearing his belt that as soon as anyone got in his car they heard, "Hey man, buckle up."

I'm sure you know where I'm going with this story.

Mike sprinted back to his car, slammed the door shut and took off after the perpetrator. This was no routine situation. As in my shooting incident, Mike was caught up in the thrill of the chase. I can bet one thing; the last thing on his mind at that moment was worrying about putting on his seat belt. He was in the game and fully engaged. How could he know that the creep he was chasing had just killed a woman and crammed her body into the trunk of his car? Chances are this guy was as nervous as could be when Mike stopped him. If Mike had actually had the time to question him, he would have sensed that something unusual was going on. I bet this guy's hands would have been shaking and his speech would have been choppy, nervous. The kind of nervous that nobody gets over a normal speeding ticket. Violators know that if they show any signs of stress, we are going to start asking a lot of questions. You kill somebody in the back of your trunk, trust me, you're not going to be too cool. This guy certainly wasn't going to take that risk, and thus took off like a bat out of hell.

Mike followed him to an exit off the interstate, into some backwoods, narrow state highway. At a high rate of speed, he chased the violator around some dangerous curves, and at one particularly sharp curve, Mike lost control of his cruiser and ran off the road, slamming into a tree. He was killed instantly.

I'm told that Mike's shadow box and mine are in the front of our troop, staring at each other across the foyer.

Mike's wife and his two small children (a boy and a girl) were a painful sight at his funeral. They reminded me of a photo I once saw of a little five-year-old boy at his father's funeral, standing on tip toes, trying to look into the casket to see his daddy. I could cry right now just thinking of it. Come to think of it, his death and others like his have brought up something other than tears from some of our fellow officers...

Holding Back the Anger

I have seen cops actually yell at a fallen officer in a coffin, angrily demanding to know why they didn't make different choices. On several occasions, I have witnessed an officer standing over a casket with tears flooding his eyes. While it's normal to cry over the loss of a friend, what amazed me was how the broken-hearted officer seemed to be screaming under his breath, cursing, saying things like:

"You bastard. How could you do this? Why didn't you call for back up?

The Will to Survive

Why'd you have to search the car by yourself? Why couldn't you have waited
    for back up to arrive?"

The anger is followed by depression, as survivor's guilt sets in and the officer is haunted by flashbacks, where his or her mind won't seem to stop replaying the scene.

Can You Say Uncomfortable? The Funeral of an Officer Who Commits Suicide

There is a lot of honor involved when someone is killed saving someone's life or chasing a murderer down a dark road or alley. There is honor and dignity in the fact that they gave their life in the pursuit of making the world a safer place. At the funeral, the family is given a beautiful folded flag and a medal of valor for the fallen officer.

Suicide is a whole other ballgame. What do you do at this funeral? It's far more difficult to say, "Officer Jones committed suicide" than, "Officer Jones was a hero to us all, and his death was not in vain." These funerals are often loaded with guilt and shame as everyone, from the parents, friends, co-workers and family members wrestle with the issue of whether or not they could have done more to save this person's life. Even the surviving children will feel that it's their fault—and every eye in the place is watching their pain. If you had the ability to hear their thoughts, it would sound something like this:

"If only I had been more lovable, quieter or better in school, maybe Mommy
    or Daddy wouldn't have been so stressed out."

What a miserable situation! (Remember how in the suicide chapter I gave you a bunch of reasons not to kill yourself? Well, I just gave you another one!) One of the most painful things about these funerals is the absence of an uplifting final sentence to leave the survivors with. How do you close the ceremony? Everyone knows that the victim didn't die in the hail of some heroic gunfight. The opposite is true, in fact. He or she probably died with their gun aimed at their temple. What are your beliefs about that? Do you secretly believe that's a coward's way out?

I personally feel that when an officer loses his or her life to suicide, it's truly another example of an in-the-line-of-duty death. I'm not saying that I condone suicide by any means, but as far as I'm concerned, it's a byproduct of the job, just as my shooting was. Let me tell you why. If you look at any case of police suicide, behind the scenes you will see that it's all about the accumulation of grief that results from any combination of the countless instances of loss, death, unspoken and unwritten rules to stay quiet, a lack of connection with significant others, a lack of support from the administration, and chemical brain imbalances that cause the irrational to seem rational.

Imagine an empty glass with a small floating plastic blue ball inside. If you begin pouring water into the glass, as the cup begins to fill up (emotionally), the ball will start to rise. As it does, symbolically, it makes sense that the magnum also rises to the head.

What Should I Be Doing and Thinking at This Ceremony?

That's a good question, and one that I'm frequently asked as a therapist. You honor the officer by going, by showing up, and by comforting the family. By reminding everyone of the strength and valor this officer showed in their stronger hours. You walk with an open heart and a non-judgmental attitude that says:

"There but for the grace of God go I. Officer Jones's

cup was too full, which is not uncommon in our line of work. That could be any one of us lying there in that casket."

Now, sometimes the nonjudgmental part is not too easy. Sometimes you will feel the need to blame someone. I once worked with a great guy, a young husband and father, who was loved by everyone on the troop. This guy was positive, loving and good looking. He seemed to have everything going for him, especially with a beautiful wife and three young children. For reasons at first unknown to us, his marriage started falling apart, and he would show up at work sad and confused. It turned out that his wife was having an affair. He was devastated. I didn't know the details in full, but I knew that she complained that because of his job, he wasn't at home enough. He was desperate to fix the rift between him and his wife and started spending more time with his family, devoting himself to making the marriage work. His wife promised him that she had stopped seeing the other man, and that she, too, wanted to heal their relationship. He believed her and brightened up a bit at work.

To make a long story short, he found out that she was lying, sneaking around behind his back and continuing the affair with her lover. When faced with that truth, she admitted that she was in love with the other man, and wanted a divorce. The trooper couldn't handle it and called his best friend, who was also an officer, to tell him that he was going to kill himself. While the officer was en route to his home, talking to him on the phone and pleading with him not to do it, the trooper took his gun and shot himself in the head.

The funeral, as you can imagine, was horrible. Of course we all knew "why" he had shot himself. The wife knew that we knew, and the children looked like the ultimate victims. No one said anything, except the minister, who was especially somber. It was a mess. Through my studies and work as a therapist, I no longer choose to hold blame for the wife. While I don't agree with what she did, I have stepped back some and can see that they were both victims. One of the reasons I decided to write this book is so that officers in similar situations will see another way out. There are so many other options, as I'm hoping are clear by now, since we're almost at the end of this book. While the difference between this funeral and one for an officer shot in the line of duty is night and day, it's not healthy in the forgiveness process to hold blame for anyone. Sure, it's easy to say that she was the "bad guy" in this situation (and we all did), but there were a multitude of human frailties at work on both sides. It's good to see that now because the blame was eating us all up. Speaking of blame, that's a subject I know intimately…

The Governor Called, but My Superior Didn't

It is quite common for the families of injured or deceased officers to say that they feel abandoned by the administration, or that they experience insensitivity on the part of the administration in dealing with their loss. Again, this proved true in my case. (It's not enough that we are abandoned by friends and often family members, but our own administration!) Positively everyone showed up for me, literally or figuratively, in one way or another. My wife ultimately couldn't handle the stress of my situation, but she tried. Troopers, police officers and deputies lined the corridors of the hospital, often on both sides. Everyone with a title was there for me: everyone, that is, except my own superior. The troop commander came immediately, the regional commander got to the hospital almost as fast. Even the governor made sure that I knew he was praying for me, by calling as soon as he was allowed to talk with me.

Can someone tell me why my colonel never called or

came to see me? How is it that he totally ignored the fact that he had a trooper who had been shot in the face and blinded? How is it that I never once heard from the man who is appointed by and who answers to the governor, and yet the guy he answers to made the effort?

I believe the truth lies in the reality that sometimes the people at the top can be insensitive to those of us on the streets. Too many administrators, once they get to the top, have other fish to fry and cannot be bothered with our independent needs. Many of them got the top because they are politicians. For those of you who worked your way up in an honest and ethical manner, I honor you, so don't get offended. You know who you are, so don't sweat the small stuff. For those of you for whom the shoe fits, however, own up to it and put that sucker on.

Think about politics for a minute. Can you name one politician who is not somewhat bigheaded, self-centered, and narcissistic? I don't think you can. You can't make me believe that a person would turn down a multi-million dollar CEO job to take $100,000 paycheck as a senator unless there were some ego issues going on. I'm not saying that they don't want to do good or cause healthy change in the world. I'm just saying that these people have an "I am the man" mentality. Hey, if I end up running for senator one day (which I may very well do), you can say the same thing about me. Am I arrogant and full of myself sometimes? You bet! If you think for a second that I won't be full of myself and or in your face if I become a senator, you're mistaken.

Certainly people can accomplish a lot of good things with the "I am the man" or "I am the woman" mentality. But some of it is all about me. The ultimate "I am the man" job is a senator or the President. And I have observed that when people get to these positions of power, they get very separated. The same thing happens in the upper echelons of law enforcement, as I imagine also happens at the top of many fields. (We've all heard stories of celebrities who scream and yell at their assistants and make unreasonable demands on everyone around them. Do you think they get to the top with that behavior? Something tells me that the more powerful they become, the more the "us vs. them" attitudes take over.)

We Have Our Own Version of "Us vs. Them" Within Our Ranks

I have learned that there is a reason that our administration, for the most part, likes to keep separate from the line personnel. If they have relationships with us and we screw up, they won't be comfortable taking appropriate disciplinary action. That's one of the reasons why our supervisors are not part of our union. It is mind blowing to me that with all of the stressors we face in law enforcement we have our own *us vs. them* within our ranks. I guess you could say that it's the people on the street vs. the administration, or as I like to say, the "Uniforms vs. the Suits." I think it's so odd that these men and women trade their uniforms in for suits. It's almost like some of them are saying, "I'm a business executive now. I'm too good to wear that."

It took me years to get over most of the anger I carried about being sent into early retirement. I felt like a soldier on a battlefield, fighting for and defending the people of the state of Louisiana. While the commander was sitting atop a white horse overlooking the battlefield from a nearby hilltop, I was going down in the hail of gunfire. Instead of riding to my rescue, he turned his horse around and trotted off back to his mansion.

The Will to Survive

Do the Ends Justify the Means?

While I will never sing the praises of a man like that, I do acknowledge that the bigger picture probably intended for me was to have the destiny of a blind man. If you think of everything I went through in my life, from my mother's illness and death on my tenth birthday, to losing my eyesight and my marriage, to the death of my daughter (who, by the way, pulled away a great deal from me for years after my shooting because she was scared to look at me and scared that I couldn't see her), none of those losses made me want to kill myself. But when told that I was no longer wanted, that the troop no longer needed me, that about did me in. If you're an administrator reading this, I hope you can see with new eyes the importance of your words and actions. The tongue has incredible power.

Unfortunately, in the broad separation between the officers and the administration, we don't know each other anymore. Some of us feel that once an officer gets stripes on his or her sleeve and some bars on their collar, they forget where they came from. I know this is true because every time I lecture to officers (at least ten times a month) I ask: "What is the number one stressor in your career?"

The number one response, above the danger element and every other stressor we encounter is: "The administrative staff."

Recently I was in Minneapolis talking to 650 administrators, sheriffs and chiefs (the administrative bosses), and I asked them the same question. "What is the number one stressor in your career?"

Their answer? "Personnel."

I've noticed that the guys on the street give the administrators some status by calling them "staff." To me, the

The Will to Survive

word personnel sounds like we're just a number, which in some sense is the attitude we feel. Neither of us can survive without the other. We need leadership and they need officers on the street. I hope with time, the rifts between the two will disappear.

What the Governor Did Right

The Governor must have understood what his call would mean to me. I have always felt that if a man or woman has done their duty, and pulled the right strings to get the top paying job in the department, he or she can surely get their butt out of bed to check on their troops in times of crisis. There are plenty of top brass in this country who say, "If I have an officer who's injured, I had better be the first person called." When something happens to that officer, he or she is en route immediately. That's the way it should be. That's what we need to see from our leaders. You show me an administrator who does that and I'll show you a well-oiled machine between the administrative staff and the officers on the streets. We've all seen or heard of the sheriffs who don't show in times of crisis until the media arrives. They are nothing but supportive when the cameras are rolling. Don't be one of those people. A lot of officers are depending on you to lead by example.

Remembering Our Brothers

A Part of America Died
Somebody killed a policeman today,
and a part of America died.
A piece of our country he swore to protect,
will be buried with him at his side.
The suspect who shot him will stand up in court,

The Will to Survive

with counsel demanding his rights,
While a young widowed mother must work for her kids,
and spend alone many long nights.
The beat that he walked was a battlefield too,
just as if he'd gone off to war.
Though the flag of our nation won't fly at half-mast,
to his name they will add a gold star.
Yes, somebody killed a policeman today,
It happened in your town or mine.
While we slept in comfort behind our locked doors,
a cop put his life on the line.
Now his ghost walks a beat on a dark city street,
and he stands at each new rookie's side.
He answered the call, and gave us his all,
and a part of America died.

Copyright 2004

National Association of Chiefs of Police, Inc.

Originally written by the late deputy Harry Koch,

Maricopa county Sheriff's Office, State of Arizona

Printed by permission of Jim Gordon, the American Police Hall of Fame

Every year on May 15th, Washington D.C. is the site of Peace Officer's Memorial Day during National Police Week. This is the time to honor all of America's fallen officers, usually between 150-165 men and women per year. I attend as often as I can, when my speaking schedule allows. I have been fortunate to share the stage and podium with some incredible speakers at this event, but I'm told that I missed one of the most remarkable.

Each year, the main speaker is the President of the United States (remember, the president is the Commander In Chief, after all). In 2003, President George W. Bush was the main speaker, but unlike the usual ten- or fifteen-minute appearances made by supposedly most former presidents, George W., who reportedly loves the police, stayed for two and a half hours. The crowd of survivors was shocked when the President got down from the podium and shook hands with every survivor, hugging people's necks and meeting every last person. Event coordinators said that no previous president had ever displayed this magnitude of support for our uniformed officers before. I don't know if it's because George W. is from Texas, and because southerners are known for loving their police, but his display of compassion and the time he spent was greatly appreciated. I'm told that there wasn't a dry eye in the place when the President started shaking hands.

This is an example of the system working as it should, if only for a few hours. The tip-top brass honored and cared for the officers on the street. The machine was at least momentarily well oiled. If only it could be like this day in and day out.

I was invited to the White House to meet with President Ronald Regan after my shooting, and I felt that kind of love and appreciation from him as well. The president told me that he loves cops and believed that if it weren't for us, he would have died during his assassination attempt in 1984. When we met, there were a dozen men standing at the ready, poised to protect him in a split second. With great respect in his voice, he said to me:

"Bobby, a secret service agent pushed me to the ground and jumped on top of me as soon as I heard the shots firing. Every one of those guys was willing to die for me. Bobby, I honor you guys so because I wouldn't be here if it weren't for you."

We all know what those agents were thinking: "Oh

The Will to Survive

God, he's not going to die on my watch. I've got to save the president." Only then, maybe, did they think about themselves: "I hope I don't die trying to protect him. I hope I don't get hit." Notice how the first response is to protect others?

Occasionally, agents will decide to resign or retire shortly after such an incident, a very unfortunate thing indeed. Which leads me to...

The Will to Survive

CHAPTER VIII
Everything Else: Promotions to Retirement

Congratulations! You're almost through with this thing!

You may have moaned and groaned about this book being too long when you started, but I told you it was a pretty fast read, didn't I? I am a practical joker—no one will deny that—but my word is as good as gold. I knew you could get to this point if you just sat still for a few hours.

Well, now that we're almost done, what's left to cover? Plenty. In this chapter we'll talk about valuable information concerning your future—things like promotions and retirement. And, God forbid, should you get yourself injured in the line of duty, that's covered here as well. Mostly, we'll cover hints and revelations to help you continue on with a greater sense of purpose and enjoyment in your day-to-day life as a cop. Then, before we close, we'll talk about how to prepare to leave this job (we all have to retire sometime) so that when your tasks of "protecting and serving" are officially complete, you'll know that you did everything you could to empower your future and end your career on the strongest possible note.

Once a Cop, Always a Cop

You've heard the saying "Once a cop, always a cop," and that's so true. How do you show up day in and day out, always wearing the uniform and the badge, learn the zillions of details we have to know in this incredibly demanding career, do the job of several officers (you know you do) by being there for nearly everything and everyone, and then suddenly turn it all off one day just because you're fifty-eight or sixty years old? It's nearly impossible. You can't just turn this all off. I've got news for you; you will never *not* think like a cop. Even if you can't wait to retire and live a leisurely life on a golf course or at the beach somewhere with your nights filled with homemade gourmet dinners and grandchildren, in many ways you will continue to see the world from a cop's eyes. Unless you truly disliked your job and never quite felt that it suited you (which is rare, in my experience talking with thousands of cops), you will forever remain a cop in your heart and mind.

Knowing this can help sustain you through times of stress when you may question your career choices. I am in the fortunate position of having gone through many of the stages of being a cop, and now experiencing so much through the lives of those of you I work with and meet on the road—putting me, I believe—in the fairly strong position of being able to shed a little light on what's to come.

Let's start with one of the most rewarding and/or troublesome stages of life in law enforcement: Moving up in the ranks. First we'll do a broad sweep of the benefits and challenges, and then we'll go into a little more depth in the following pages.

Promotions: The Good, the Bad, and the Ugly

It can be a very positive thing to be promoted up the ranks in police work. For one thing, other than having a thriving business on the side (yeah, right) or a wealthy benefactor (uh, uh), this is the route to making more money. If your peers feel like you've earned this new position, they will support your forward movement and show you the loyalty and respect you deserve. And that's good because your job *can* get easier and somewhat less dangerous once you get promoted, which your family will love. But heaven help you if your rise appears to have been the result of sucking up or favoritism, in which case it's not a very pleasurable job leaving the "safety" of the group. Some officers in this situation have told me that they've never experienced a let-up from the resulting peer pressure. Ouch. That, my friend, can make retirement seem like a very long way off.

First impressions in police work will stay with a person longer than skunk on a dog, and it works from either spectrum, whether you're the chief's favorite or a screw-up. I bet you can imagine where it all starts. You guessed it... at the academy. This is where your career-long reputation begins, where others get a sense of who you are. You had better make a good impression there because if you whine like a baby and expect preferential treatment at the academy, you may just be stuck with a bad rap for the rest of your career. As far too many unassuming officers have found out, how others view you—your reputation—is paramount. It can be the difference between loving your job and feeling like you're living a nightmare.

So, what's the key? What's the object of the game? It's real simple. Here goes:

You want to be respected and loved by the other officers, and you want to be respected and loved by the administration. *At the same time!*

Holy you-know-what! How is that possible, you might be asking? Well, it can be a tightrope walk, but you can do it. For most of my career, I was in that very good position, even though I didn't shy from fighting with my supervisors when I felt strongly about a topic. (There's a fine line between courage and stupidity!) The camaraderie I experienced made my life on the force a great ride, both with my fellow officers and with the brass. You're never going to have 100% acceptance when you get a bunch of macho people in one department, but you can shoot for the odds being in your favor.

I'm about to share with you what I did to bridge the gap between the "personnel" (us) and the "staff" (them). Maybe you'll be able to grab hold of a few tips for your own career.

It's All About Being Real

As you know by now, I excelled in the academy and was well liked. And, I worked my butt off, too! But, this in itself can pose a challenge. Jackie Coleman, for instance, had been in the military and was taught a lesson there: Don't stand out. Don't be bad and don't be good. That way you wouldn't make any enemies. That was all well and good for Jackie, but that's just not my way. I wanted to excel in everything I did. How can you do that and still be seen as a team player?

The answer is that you do it with class.

There's a big difference between trying to outdo everybody (thereby wanting everyone to *see* that you're "da man") and just doing your best (so that your team *knows* they can depend on you no matter what). Officers who are promoted by the administration, and loved and accepted by their peers, are above all else real and true-to-the-core with everyone they come into contact with. No game playing and no B.S. (hey, those are my initials!). Again, the way to remain "one of the boys" (ladies, that includes you) *and* a friend to the administration is by being the best of who you are.

Now, before you go thinking I was born Mr. Self-Confident, Leader-Man-All-the- Time, let me tell you that my sergeant at the academy, Aubrey Futrell, had to push me forward. Two or three weeks into our training, he looked at me and said, "Bobby, you're obviously a leader and it's time for you to show it. I want you to step up to the front of the line." That's encouragement, and I knew he was right. But I also knew that I had to show my leadership without bragging. Without being a jerk and acting as if I was better than everyone else. Fortunately for me, Aubrey didn't make a big stink out of it. He didn't blatantly show favoritism or overt kindness toward me, which would have hurt my career. He used discretion.

I have seen sergeants and captains put an officer in the awful position of unashamedly giving an officer the favorite details and new car that everyone else wished they had, thereby putting him or her in the terrible position of being ostracized by their peers at no fault of their own. You can see how this messes with the officer's head. He or she wants the easier shifts and can't help but like the complimentary treatment, but you can almost hear them thinking, "Oh God, I wish the Captain wouldn't do that."

Who Says You Are More Qualified?

For a little more analysis, why is it that some officers seem to have all the good fortune and easily rise up within the ranks?

Many departments base their promotional system on seniority, but obviously that's not all that counts or you wouldn't see so many young officers making their way up the ranks. As you know, everyone has to pass whatever tests correspond to the rank they're hoping to attain, and all work records and disciplinary actions (if there are any) are reviewed.

But beyond the basics are issues of likeability and fairness (or, unfairness). Sometimes the officer who is the most popular with the colonel is the one who gets the promotion. It can be that simple. What a drag if you're not that person, but that's life.

Let's get one thing straight right here. In case you didn't know this already.

Life is not fair. Did you get that? Did I make myself clear? If not, let me say it again.

Life is not fair!

Now that we've got that pesky little fact out of the way, we can simply acknowledge that if you're waiting for fairness to come up, knock on your door and hand you all of your dreams, you might stand waiting forever. But, then again, if you have a great attitude and do your job with professionalism and enthusiasm, you might not have long to wait at all.

Either way, there are no guarantees. Sometimes, people who are less qualified than you will rise in the ranks like a rocket. And when that happens, just know that it hurts. It hurts when life kicks us to the curb, and allowing yourself to feel your emotions and deal with your anger and disappointment (hopefully not in front of your new superior) will help you to ultimately rally and continue working toward the next rounds of promotions.

While you wait, you can look on the bright side (because every situation has one). There are, as I've stated, challenges that come with higher rankings. For one thing, it's only natural that the officer with the new title will experience some distancing between himself/herself and the group they've been working with—the group they most likely came in with. When you're promoted, you're now in the strange position of telling officers you were hired with what to do. Now, it might suit you just fine to have them calling you "Sarge" instead of Mike, Bob, or Kay, but understand that

The Will to Survive

they may not love it. Your buddies may resent the fact that now it's you who are "da man." It shouldn't be surprising to find out that someone, somewhere is not exactly overjoyed about your new position.

When it's your turn to be promoted, if you find yourself being treated unfairly by your former peers, just be aware of the fact that whomever is giving you a hard time is dealing with his or her own feelings of loss. I'm not telling you to coddle an officer who acts jealous, wishing they had your job. But I am telling you not to take it personally. Be honest with yourself. If you're walking with an attitude—like you own the troop or precinct—tone it down immediately or you'll never have the respect you want. If, however, you are doing your best, you can even address an officer's concerns privately to them, letting them know that you understand how they feel, but that their time would be better spent proactively concentrating on how they can be the next one promoted.

All Promotions Are Not Created Equal

Even though I stress the importance of realizing that life isn't fair, within that wisdom I want you to consider another idea—to trust that there's a bigger plan. You know by now how I feel about being blind—it sucks—but I really do believe that it is God's will for my life. I have to believe that there is a benefit that I can offer that could only be expressed in this particularly dramatic way. Had I been conscious when I was signing on for this role, you can bet that I would have chosen to be an actor like Tom Cruise or Colin Farrell playing a blind man instead, but oh well.

Most likely, you'll never face anything as remotely unfortunate as my circumstances, so let me say this: If the worst thing that ever happens to you is that you get passed over for a few promotions, don't be calling me for sympathy. We all have our crosses to bear and I'd prefer to bear yours any day of the week. It may sound harsh, but if you've ever heard one of my talks, you know that I often tell officers to quit whining and complaining. "If you think your job is so bad, I'll meet you at the front of the class and change shoes with you this afternoon." I've said that over 1,500 times now and I have yet to have one cop come up and offer to take me up on that challenge.

Getting Ostracized by Your Buddies

What if you were the favored child of your class and the chief, from the moment you were hired, would say things like, "This is my boy/girl right here." I always felt badly for these officers because if they ever did accomplish anything, the attitude was, "Yeah, but he/she is in the chief's back pocket," or "He/she has got their nose up the chief's butt." No matter what these officers accomplish on their own, no matter how many innovative ideas they come up with for running the division, their fellow officers will never give them full credit.

If you're a woman, I think you know what you're up against. Talk about an up-hill battle! In law enforcement, we have quotas just like most professions. We've also got affirmative action. A certain amount of minorities and females must be promoted by law. Sometimes those women and minorities are more than qualified for the job, and sometimes quotas prohibit more qualified people from moving up. When a woman is promoted over a man with better abilities, how difficult do you think her job becomes? Have compassion for these women. You know how gossipmongers sometimes accuse women of sleeping their way to the top. Those jerks don't care how smart or rich or talented that woman is on her own—she was promoted because she bedded down with somebody important. Hogwash. It can be a double-edged sword for a woman who gets promoted in law enforcement, and it's highly likely that her job will no longer be as much fun as it used to be.

Regardless of gender or race, if there are two of you competing for the position of lieutenant and you don't have equal time on the force (maybe you've been pounding the streets as a cop for five years, but your buddy—who's a little less rough around the edges than you—has only been at it for three), what can you learn from the experience if he's chosen instead? Even if you have more credits than he does, more training, and you scored higher on the tests and have better attendance, there's a reason he got the job and you didn't.

A Few "Left Coast" Ways to View the Apparent Injustice

If you're like most cops, you probably lean toward being politically conservative, as I do. But take a leap with me here…

Maybe God has something better waiting for you in the near future?

Maybe this officer's talents will be necessary for the dept. at this particular time?

Maybe there is some destiny you are meant to have with someone on the beat?

Maybe you're being protected in some way that you cannot yet know?

Or, maybe you're just getting the short end of the stick. But, I have to believe there is a bigger reason you didn't move up and that something good will result if you learn and grow through the experience.

The Will to Survive

Since this is a mental-health book, and I want you to be healthy, it's wise to take a breath before you get reactive in these situations of apparent injustice. Sometimes that's easier said than done. What are you going to do, for example, when a guy you've gone fishing with a million times is now your superior? Are you going to be pissed off when you call for a break and he says no? Are you going to blurt out to anyone who will listen,

"Hey wait a minute, I've been working with so-and-so for three years and now I don't even get dinner! Ever since they put those stripes on his sleeve, he's forgotten where he came from."

Or, are you going to take a breath and remember that another officer called in sick, the department is understaffed, and your new superior (who is probably nervous about doing a good job) is just trying to cover his bases? Realize that it's possible you don't know all of the details. Taking a moment to consider all sides and breathe will help you think about how to best be a team player.

I was fortunate enough to have the kind of personality that could handle the pressure of getting along with most everyone. In case you're wondering, I liked being a street cop and didn't have feelings on the positive or negative side about being promoted. You may have noticed by now that I was always Trooper Smith (not Sgt. or Lieutenant Smith) and that suited me perfectly and probably helped me to always have good relationships with people in the department. But I mostly think I got along well with my peers and the administration because I was either courageous enough or stupid enough to show my true colors to just about everyone, all of the time.

I've got a crazy story about this that you might enjoy.

The Will to Survive

Fighting with My Field-Training Officer

I had been a cop for six years before becoming a trooper. Even so, when it was time to be given my own unit, I had to drive around like everyone else with a field-training officer to make sure that I knew what the heck I was doing. One of my assigned guys was a serious ticket writer. He wrote a ton of those things. Even though he was supervising me at this time, I didn't see him as "above" me in any way. Technically, I had to please him because he would be writing progress reports each day that would either allow me to keep my job or lose it, but because he had no prior police experience before becoming a trooper, in my mind he wasn't any "better" than I was. In fact, I had more overall law-enforcement experience than he did.

As you probably know, after a certain period of training, I was basically left on my own in the unit while my training officer watched me like a hawk. (These officers don't want us looking to them for answers; we're supposed to be on our own to see how we handle each new experience. Their job is primarily to observe.) I was a few weeks into my six-week training period, and it was understood that this guy wasn't going to interject unless I got into big trouble.

As we were driving the interstate, we clocked a ratty old car doing 84 mph in a 55. (This was during a slower driving era.) I immediately stopped this guy and from the second I laid eyes on him, my heart went out to him. He stuttered, had a speech impediment, and a cleft lip. He was tall and lanky—in his mid-twenties—and seated next to him was his young wife and little girl in an infant seat.

After talking to him for a minute, I found out that he had recently lost his job and had been collecting unemployment. He was headed to a little general store in the isolated country community of Calhaun, Louisiana, hoping to get a job. Everyone in this little, bitty town knew he was looking for employment and the owner of the general store had just called him saying: "We lost our cashier. If you can get here by 1:00, the job is yours."

Because he was hauling butt to see if he could earn money in order to take care of his family, I wasn't going to be the one to keep him from being able to do that. I said,

"Look buddy, here's your license. Good luck on your job. You can't very well take care of your family if you all get killed on the way there. Please slow down and be careful."

Feeling good about myself, I walked back to the car and sat down next to my field-training officer. Remember how I told you that this guy was a serious ticket writer? I forgot to mention that I was just the opposite. I knew that I had just done the "right" thing by letting this young man go, but I also knew that I might hear a few complaints about what had just transpired from my "boss" man.

"You better have a damn good excuse why you let him go," he said.

"I don't have an excuse, but I do have a good reason," I said before telling him the story.

"That ain't good enough," he said when I had finished. I was starting to get mad. The word I use all the time is discretion. If you take away a cop's discretion, he or she becomes a robot.

As you know, I can be a little overly self confident, so I gave him the Bobby Smith glare, threw my car into drive from the shoulder of the interstate, and stomped on the accelerator.

"You think he deserves a ticket?" I yelled, "Then I'll give you the opportunity to write him one." (Just how stupid could I be? My fate was in this guy's hands. All he had to say was, "Bobby Smith is a disrespectful smart-ass who doesn't listen to authority" and I was toast. Gone. End of story. End of career.) In that moment, however, all I cared about was the difference between right and wrong.

"You ever heard of double jeopardy?" he yelled, as we were racing ahead. We were like two snapping turtles, snapping at each other. "You've already stopped him once, you can't stop him a second time. Just forget it. But it better not happen again."

It was 3:30 P.M. and we weren't scheduled to report back to the troop until 5:30 P.M. From 3:30-5:30 P.M, not a word was spoken between the two of us. Not one word. I was furious and I'm sure he was too. We headed back at 5:30 P.M.; I pulled up to the gas pumps and he started to get out.

My attitude was, "If you don't agree with me to do things the right way, you must be a total idiot." That was just my personality.

"Excuse me," I said. "Before you leave, can I have a word with you?" (We're talking about a serious role reversal here, where he suddenly looks like the cadet and I'm the officer.)

"I've been a cop for over six years," I began. "I've been out here on the road a lot longer than you, and there's something you need to consider when you go home this evening and stand in front of the mirror while you're brushing your teeth. I want you to look at yourself real good and ask the guy staring back at you one thing: Do I like who I see? If you do, let's go back to work tomorrow, but if you don't like who you see in the mirror, I suggest you make some serious changes."

He glared at me and without saying anything, slammed the car door and walked into the troop. "My brother," I said to myself, "Have you lost your damn mind? I think

241

you have just screwed up." I parked my car, went into the troop and told Jackie what had just happened. He freaked out.

"Please don't tell me you did that," Jackie begged.

"You know that I did," I answered.

"I believe you, Bobby, that's what bothers me!"

The next morning, five of us new troopers were sitting in the lobby as the field- training officers were about to have their regular morning meeting with the captain. Jackie was sitting across from me, and we were both saying silent prayers that I wouldn't get fired. I had been doing so well. I had already developed a reputation for doing my job and doing it well. What a waste it would be if all of that were about to be thrown away.

The door opened that led from the lobby into the hallway and I could see directly into the commander's office. The captain, a small but tough guy, was standing in front of the open door glaring straight at me with an "I will eat you, son, and spit you out" look on his face. For five seconds he just stood and glared at me. Then he turned toward his office and closed the door. Jackie and I looked at each other as if to say, "Oh crap."

I Was Sure I Was Fired

When the meeting was through, everybody filed out of that same door. I was as nervous as a cat on a hot-tinned roof. I heard them say, "Let's go guys." My field-training officer walked over to me and said, "Bobby, you ready?" We got our coffee and started walking out of the building. Here I had been thinking I was going to be called into the captain's office and fired. Instead, every step that I was moving toward my unit was helping me to feel better about myself. I was thinking, "Hmm, this ain't gonna be too bad after all."

The Will to Survive

He and I got into my unit and I cranked it up, put my seat belt on, and put the car in drive. Suddenly he reached over to me and said, "Bobby let me talk to you." I could feel the blood rush out of my face. "Oh my God, here it comes."

"Bobby," he said. "I did what you said. I went home last night and I stared in the mirror. I'm going to be honest with you, Bobby. I didn't like who I saw." He took a long pause. I didn't breathe. Then he said, "Let's go out and have some fun today."

Can you believe that one? I nearly fainted! This guy and I were never best friends, but the mere fact that he did that gave me great respect for him.

It's hard not to be reactive when a fellow officer or superior acts like a jerk. Sometimes it's best to stand up for what you believe in. Trust yourself. I was lucky not to have lost my job in that instance, but then again, I don't really believe in luck. I believe in destiny.

Sometimes destiny can be brutal, as is the case when an officer is injured in the line of duty.

When S%#@ Happens: The Disabled Officer

Some of you know an officer who has become disabled on the job. In the Louisiana State Police alone there were five of us in a twelve-year period (from 1986-1998) who were "tragically" or "catastrophically injured." This is a high number, but is not unusual. The first injury during that time was me. Then another officer was getting a camera out of his trunk on the side of the road, when he was hit by an approaching automobile, cutting off his leg. Another was intentionally run over by bad guys, leaving several of his internal organs seriously damaged. The next guy was shot in the chest and paralyzed from the neck down. The fifth was shot in the head and has resulting mental defects. His case was especially sad to us because he was young—in his twenties—and would never again be able to live by himself. An only child and unmarried, the question on everyone's mind was, "Who will care for him when his parents die?" His medical retirement wouldn't be enough to do the job.

Serious injury is undoubtedly our greatest fear, even more than getting killed. Cops are an independent group, and none of us wants to lose our independence. The thought that we may be unable to take care of ourselves and earn our way in life is terrifying. As in all other areas of law-enforcement, the administration has a lot to do with the future of many disability cases. Some cops go on to thrive in their departments, despite being injured. Some, like me, are forced to retire.

The Other Blind Trooper

"Is this Trooper Bobby Smith?" the voice on the other end of the phone asked. It was 1990 or 1991, four or five years after my shooting. My first thought was, "Well, yes, but I'm not technically a trooper anymore. Truthfully, I'm just Bobby Smith again." (It's interesting to me that I'm now a "doctor" and have replaced one title for another. Guess I've got to have something in front of my name.)

"Yes it is," I said.

"Bobby, this is Lieutenant Karl Wade of the Alabama State Troopers. I just found out that you had a similar incident to mine."

Karl went on to tell me that he had been on a SWAT team that had been brought in to get an eighty-eight year-old mentally ill man out of his home, where he had barricaded himself. The old man had already shot several officers earlier that day, and Karl was another victim—hit at close range from only five feet away. Like me, he was now blind as a bat.

The Will to Survive

"You've got to be joking," I said.

"I wish I were," he answered. "I was curious as to what the state police did with you, Bobby. Did they let you come back to work or make you retire?

"They told me I had to retire," I said.

"Why?" he asked.

"Because I'm blind," I said.

"What difference does that make?" he said.

"I asked to be transferred to our training division," I said, "but my request was denied. I wasn't given any other option."

"Bobby, I got shot just like you," he continued, "and now I'm totally blind. When I got back from the hospital and got back on my feet physically and emotionally, the colonel called me and he said, 'Lieutenant, what do you want to do?'"

Lieutenant Karl Wade was fortunate enough to have someone who backed him all the way and gave him several options. Options that many disabled officers aren't given. First, he was told that he was free to retire, if he wished. But, seeing as how he had a wife and two small children to support, the medical retirement salary (which was even less than regular retirement) wasn't attractive to Karl. Besides, he was only thirty-eight or thirty-nine years old, and in his mind, "too young to retire." He didn't want to go home and just sit down.

"Bobby," he told me, "There was a slot open in the department for a Communications Coordinator, and they asked me if I wanted the job, telling me that they would get me the adaptive aids (computer, scanner, speech software, etc.) to make the work possible. That tickled the devil out of me because law enforcement is all I ever wanted. My father was in law enforcement and I hadn't done any other work since I was eighteen—other than the three years I took off to be in the military, but even then I was with the military police in the army."

As of this writing, over thirteen years later, Lieutenant Karl Wade still works for the Alabama State Police. He's now in recruiting, which he "absolutely loves." At the time of his shooting, he was a sergeant who was slated for a promotion. Regardless of his disability he was promoted to lieutenant and treated as someone of value. Not only did he remain an Alabama State Trooper, but he also never lost a day's pay. He was sent on Administrative leave for three months, where he attended the VA hospital blind rehabilitation school, and was taught mobility, orientation and typing. Then, he was sent to a school for deaf and blind people in Alabama for computer training. Talk about a healthy dose of support! This officer received bucket loads.

You may be wondering if Lieutenant Karl Wade encountered any opposition from within his department when he was brought back to work. You bet he did! Some argued that if he were allowed to remain a trooper (thereby requiring that certain "rules" be waived—i.e. handgun qualification and an up-to-date driver's license), it would establish a precedent.

You're damn right it would establish a precedent! And what a great precedent to set!

Why Some Keep Their Jobs When Other Can't

Speaking for those few minutes with Lieutenant Karl Wade took me right back in my mind to all of those hours I sat feeling sorry for myself, wrestling with the demons and wondering what the heck I was going to do with my life. Even though my life had great fulfillment at the time he called (Brad had just been born, we had just moved into our dream home, and my career was going strong), I couldn't help but hurt for all of those lost days and months I had endured without any certainty about how I would take care of myself. It felt like lost time—time that wouldn't have been sacrificed to desperation and hopelessness had I been able to keep my job. I ached remembering all those failure-filled hours, sitting in the "pity position" on my couch with the remote in one hand and the phone in the other—just waiting for someone, anyone, to call or come by.

Other than destiny (if you believe in that, and I still do), the future of a disabled officer often boils down to leadership (or lack thereof). Simply stated, Karl had a different administrator than I did. Being disabled doesn't automatically mean an end to an officer's career. In most cases, there are creative ways to find them new roles.

At least one or two cops cry to me after every lecture I give, and one twenty-three-year-old guy recently about broke my heart. He was all bandaged up, having been shot in his right arm. A bullet had shattered his bones, and although his doctors had operated and put pins in his bones and fixed his arm the best they could, he would never again be able to use it to full capacity.

"All I've ever wanted to do is be a cop," he told me (sound familiar?), "but six months ago I was involved in a shooting and now I can't squeeze or use my right hand. I can't hold my weapon anymore. They're going to make me retire."

I don't understand this! Why couldn't his department make him an investigator or allow him to push papers? He could be a DARE officer or a radio operator. There are many other jobs in law enforcement besides carrying a weapon, especially at the larger agencies. But his chief said that they had to follow "policy"—that everyone must be able to qualify with weapons in "both hands."

Policy is Merely a Stroke of a Pen!

There are exceptions to every rule! I know cops who have switched gun hands. All it takes is training. (We have to qualify with both hands anyway before we can have the job.) Can't administrators be lax on one policy when it's important to do so? Sure they can! They are lax on policy all the time, all over the country when they want to be, which is not always. If an agency like Karl Wade's cares enough (and understands the serious financial investment they have in an officer like Karl), they can make exceptions to the rules for heaven's sake! But some administrators would rather use the rules against us, seeing us as damaged goods.

I challenge that mindset. If I were so damaged, would you be reading this book right now? There is no telling what talents lay within any given officer. In my opinion, we deserve the right to find out how to serve in a new capacity. I guarantee that somewhere in many agencies, you can pull someone off an "easier" detail and put him or her back on the street, making room for a disabled officer. But what if the person you're moving doesn't want to go back on the street? Tough. All I have to say to that person is, "Can't you give up your place for an injured brother or sister?" Look at how blessed you are, and be grateful to do your part.

What about the small departments around the country, where only two or three officers are on duty at any one time? There may not be room enough in the budget to buy a pack of chewing gum, much less keep a disabled officer on the payroll. What then? That is a good argument and poses a great challenge, but I bet there's something you can do to help. You could check to see if there's a position at the recreation department that can be filled. Maybe the mayor knows of a job that will be opening up soon. This is the government we're talking about—a large system. See what you can do, and let the officer know that you've tried your best to find a place for him or her. At least they won't feel abandoned and forgotten by the administration, like I did.

I no longer believe in walking with a victim's mentality. Personally, I don't think anyone "owes" me anything—that's why I went back to school. But I'd appreciate knowing that you've tried to keep me within the system that I gave my eyesight for. I may be unable to protect the masses, but I am an expert lip-reader, and therefore would make a great spy (okay, just checking to see if you're paying attention). My point here is that there's a lot we can do if someone will give us a chance!

Certainly, not everyone who is injured in the line of duty can be kept within the system. Some, unfortunately, are mentally ill or too physically dependent. And some just plain old have a bad attitude. I have run into disabled officers who are so disgruntled, sour and angry that I wouldn't give them a job on my payroll! Administrators have said to me, "Bobby, we tried to employ so-and-so, but he/she bitched, bellyached, and whined every day." I wouldn't expect an officer with a bad attitude to be allowed to remain on any force—blind or sighted, disabled or not. I even heard of one disabled officer throwing tantrums (and papers) in the department, basically spitting in other officer's faces. For officers like that I say, "You best not bite the hand that feeds you." Well, duh!

I Had to Sell Nearly Everything I Owned

People outside of law enforcement often assume that I was given a huge sum of money for being shot. Some think I must be a millionaire because of it. How I wish that were true! The reality is that many of us find that our retirement isn't even enough to live on. This is one of the reasons cops fear getting injured. We have seen cases where grown men and women are forced to move back home with Mom and Dad or even become institutionalized because loved ones cannot handle the burden of care giving. Can you imagine a worse fate for an officer used to being "Superman" or "Wonder Woman?"

I was lucky. Only by the grace of God did I recover without brain damage or paralyzation. But my retirement was nothing short of measly (less than $1,100 a month). Talk about falling through the cracks within the law-enforcement family. I couldn't even pay my bills with what I was given, and thus had to sell most everything I owned.

Civilians ask me why I didn't have a separate long-term disability plan in place that could have given me extra coverage. That would have been great, but could you imagine paying those types of premiums on our salary? Heck, even people with office jobs have huge premiums if they smoke or fly gliders. Imagine covering a man or woman who is dealing with bad guys all day long. The long-term fees can be astronomical.

They Changed the Laws for Me

When I say that policy can be changed, I know from personal experience because I was, eventually, one of the fortunate ones for whom policy was rewritten—twice!

Soon after Brad was born, I was invited to work in the training division of the West Monroe Police Department, and as fantastic as it was working in law enforcement again (training new officers), to do so meant that I was getting a paycheck, and thus was forced to give up the money that exceeded my monthly medical retirement check.

A Louisiana state representative from Lincoln Perish

heard about my dilemma in the media (which, thankfully, followed my story relentlessly for a long time) and called me out of the blue. He told me that he wanted to make sure that I had the opportunity to make additional money without losing my retirement. His feeling was that I had more than earned my retirement. To think that by my working, I would have to forgo what little money I had been guaranteed from my disability was unfathomable to this man and to his fellow representatives.

In the late 80s, a bill was passed through the Louisiana State legislature that exempted me from the law that says that if you take a medical retirement, any monies you make above your retirement check are deducted from that check. Then, in July of 2003, the Louisiana State Police Retirement Board presented legislation to pass a bill to add a catastrophic injury addendum to the disability retirement bill, stating that if an officer is catastrophically injured in the line of duty, they now receive a radically significant increase.

How did these advancements happen? The state police are funded by the legislature, and the legislature decided to make it happen. They passed the legislation because they didn't think it was fair that we had to accept less. Some representatives basically said, "Come on, how can a guy be expected to live on this?" You see, rules can be altered if the right people say so. Once the legislature stated that Bobby Smith was exempt from the policy, my bosses had no choice but to oblige.

I worked in training at the West Monroe Police Department for six years, and as much as I loved being there, it couldn't last. The world of speaking was opening up for me daily, and frankly, I could touch more people's lives and make more money as a speaker. Destiny had new plans for me.

The Will to Survive

Some of you, however, will remain with a force or troop until the day you retire. Lucky you! If you think you're going to be in law enforcement for the long haul, you will definitely want to read on...

Retirement: Start Preparing Now!

Most of us have a countdown in our heads about when we're going to retire. We talk about it all the time. How many times have you said (or heard another cop say), "I've got fifteen years to go" or "I've got five years to go." There are more than a few reasons for this. One is because everyone we know—from our spouses, children, parents and friends—worries that we might end up shot on the job and *not* make it to retirement. They all look toward the day when they can stop worrying and know that we're either home re-doing the garden or on that golf course (hey, isn't that where a lot of people get hit by lightening?). When you have that many people worried about your physical safety, it's easy to keep an eye on the prize—a time when most physical dangers will cease.

Another reason for the countdown is because with the majority of cops, once we've been on the force for five or six years, it's normal for us to lose a bit of our enthusiasm. We start to come off the high. Reality hits us: "Man, I'm working the nightshift fighting drunks and drug addicts in dark, sleazy bars. I'm missing my kids' ballgames and dance recitals. I'm not getting paid but peanuts, and then I come home and, man, I can't even afford to pay my bills!"

If we determine that we can't or won't leave our job, this is about the time when we will notice our thoughts increasingly focused on retirement. Most of us won't want to give up our jobs at this point, but we're less idealistic than years prior, leading to minutes or hours of daydreaming about easier days, where things like fishing, traveling, and plain old downtime dominate.

Once you get past ten years, your daydreams of changing jobs, if you had them, are mostly behind you. It's *really* hard to leave at this point because you've made a huge emotional, mental, and physical commitment toward this career, and you've paid a lot into your retirement. You might hear yourself saying, "I've already got ten years in; I can retire in ten more."

The closer we get to our actual retirement, the more we realize that we've been talking about it for twenty years.

"I've got five years to go."

"I've got three years to go."

"This is my last year."

Since it's hard to be on the force for a long time without rising in the ranks (unless you're a screw up or don't want to be promoted) it gets even harder to walk away or retire because your job, due to promotions, is probably easier. I've heard shift commanders say,

"Well, my job's not that difficult anymore, but I've been telling everyone that I'm outta here as soon as I hit twenty years. Now that it's almost up and my pension plan is nearly complete, I'm not so sure I *want* to retire."

One guy in this position said to me, "But Bobby, I've *got* to retire. I've been saying for years that I will leave this year, and I'm a man of my word." Can you believe that? He had changed his mind about leaving but was too embarrassed and too prideful to follow through. In order to save face, he was therefore willing to spite the rest of him.

The Will to Survive

As I see it, this guy (and others like him) had three choices:

1. He could have swallowed his pride and told everyone that he had changed his mind, and then just stayed on the job, probably happily.

2. He could have remained on the force, as an unpaid volunteer (in the reserve/auxiliary police).

3. He could have retired like he said he was going to do, keep his pride intact, and be miserable because he missed his job and didn't have anywhere to go or anything to do.

For those officers who can go ahead and retire, their biggest challenge is often in their minds. Oh, how easy it is to forget how much we love being needed—until, that is, we no longer are.

The Sweet Little Old Lady on Apple Street

Most of us come into this job with our hearts in the right place. We sincerely *enjoy* public service. Not just putting bad guys in jail, but also helping to feed war veterans, return lost children into the arms of their grateful parents, and comfort little old ladies who call because they are afraid of the bumps in the night that come with living alone.

Speaking of little old ladies, we had the funniest woman on my route when I worked with the Monroe Police Department! For as long as I live, I will never forget Miss Graves—a lonely eighty-year-old widow who lived on Apple Street in the poor section of town. I imagine that most departments have someone like her. Miss Graves would call almost every night around 9:00 P.M. and say that someone was on her front porch, outside of her bathroom window, or in the backyard. There probably wasn't a cop in the department who hadn't been there a million times, and we never

The Will to Survive

did find anyone present, other than Miss Graves.

Remember my comment from chapter two that no one ever calls the police to serve us baked goods? Well, this woman was the one exception to that rule. She'd call and we knew darn well that there were no dangerous perpetrators lurking in the shadows. She just wanted someone to visit with, and we'd always go. This is the softer side of cops that most people don't see.

We'd knock on the door. "Miss Graves, this is Officer _____, coming to check out the place." She was always standing right at the door, having probably waited by the window until we arrived. "Oh, Officer _____, come right on in." We'd ask her what the problem was, and then go outside and act like we were looking for bad guys. We'd take our flashlights and search the ground for footprints; check the side yard and back porch, shake the windows and doors, and then tell her that it was probably "just those kids."

Miss Graves was the typical grandmother. When we walked in, we would always smell cake or cookies baking. Her husband Joe had died forever ago, and she'd make some comment about how "Ever since Joe died," there were more hoodlums in the neighborhood. "I just baked these cookies," she'd say, and we'd grab a few before telling her that she'd be put down on the extra patrol list. Then later, if we were on that side of town, we'd drive by and shine our light on her front porch. I bet there were nights when she waited up for that light—her nightlight, her security blanket.

Doing this kind of work gets to you, in a good way. Not to say that it's never irritating checking up on people who are paranoid or even mentally ill. But mostly these types of calls give us a serious reason for waking up in the morning. Checking up on people like this is about as meaningful as life can be, outside of taking care of our own families. Cops get used to being needed, and take great pleasure in making a difference in people's lives. Upon retirement, when we wake up in the morning and no longer have that sense of purpose, it's not uncommon to start feeling as if our life doesn't carry the same level of value.

Losing Our Identity

Sometimes in retirement, we don't know who we are anymore. We're so used to being Officer- or Captain so-and-so. Men, especially, get their identity from their career. There's a lot of status in being a cop. We're important people, for heaven's sake. We save lives. We've got status ("Hey Captain!" "Hey Major!") and we love our rank. When I ask an officer his or her name and they say, "Sgt. Jones," I reply, "Your mama name you that? You got a first name that goes with that?"

We cops are used to being the center of attention everywhere we go. Think about your career. No matter where you're at, everyone watches the cop in the room. Positive or negative, you're the focus of attention, much like a celebrity. Do you want to give that up? I surely didn't!

Truth be told, aren't you used to walking into your local diner and being catered to? What happens when you retire and go into your favorite coffee house where you've been eating for twenty-five years and there's a new waitress on staff who treats you just like any regular person. You say, "Give me the usual," and she says, "Excuse me, Sir?" Suddenly it dawns on you that you don't have a uniform on and she doesn't know who you are. You've lost your identity. The waitress is new, and wouldn't have known you as "Officer Smith" without your uniform anyway. But she would have known you as "Officer Somebody."

Now who are you? A regular everybody?

The Will to Survive

Leaving the Family, the Hard Way

It can be depressing to lose this status. I don't think anyone bothers to keep statistics on retired officers, but we hear about many who commit suicide—who can't handle being out of the "family." It's not unusual for these officers to give up entirely.

I was in the Midwest recently giving a lecture on retirement, talking about how this job gets in our blood. Everyone agreed that we get used to a certain level of excitement and camaraderie that can be very painful to give up. Now, I should digress a minute and tell you that I'm a very emotional speaker, and after hearing me talk, a lot of feelings get stirred up. Cops know they can be real with me and let out some of their bottled-up emotions, and there's always two or three officers standing off to the side, waiting to connect with me. Whoever is assigned to help with my book sales is usually also a cop, and therefore trained to read body language. At some point he or she will leave me alone so each officer feels safe enough to approach me.

So, that day in the Midwest, when I got through with the lecture on how *not* to be depressed, I could literally feel depression welling up around me. Turns out that a guy was standing near my book-signing table hanging around waiting for people to leave so that he could bare his soul.

Man, I get emotional even thinking about this guy. I could feel him walk up to me, and I said, "How ya doing, Buddy?" "Not very well," he answered. I stuck out my hand and he immediately started crying when he grabbed it. I didn't pat him on the back because I wanted him to deal with his feelings without me patting them away. I just stood there and waited, saying, "It's okay; go ahead." Some people need permission to break down.

After he gained his composure, he told me that he

had retired the previous year and that everything I had said about feeling left out of the family and feeling ostracized through his vacancy was true for him. He was at this police conference, not because he had to be there for continuing education, but because he wanted to feel like part of the family again.

"Bobby," he began, "when I retired a year ago, they threw a big party for me. The guys who worked on my shift said, 'Hey Captain, I'm sure going to miss you.' 'Well, I'm not going to miss you boys,' I told them, feeling in reality like their daddy. Deep down I knew that I was going to miss these kids, but I blew it off. One of the guys said, 'Don't forget where we're at, you better come by and visit us.' I wanted to believe that, but knew that I'd just get replaced with another captain and that they'd forget about me within a few weeks.

"I got up that first morning after retirement at 5 A.M. like I always did and then it hit me, 'Where do you think you're going? You got nowhere to go.' I tinkered in my shop, ran to town, and by midmorning I didn't have a damn thing to do. I did that for about a month. I missed the boys, the laughter, being in the know. I missed knowing who was stealing from whom, what VIP they took to jail, that kind of stuff. All of a sudden I'm just another citizen who's out of the loop.

"One morning I just walked into the station like I was going to a briefing. I entered the break room and sat down, got my coffee, and everybody was all smiles. 'Hey Captain, we sure miss your grumpy-old ass.' Isn't it funny how we put down the people we care about? Everybody came out and shook hands and patted me on the back. A couple of officers sat down and asked me if I was fishing, and what I was up to. After half an hour they got in their cruisers and went to work. I felt good; not necessarily needed, but still well liked.

"A couple of months passed and I did the same thing. This time when they all saw me, only about half of the officers came in (the others yelled as they walked by... 'Hey Captain'). They were cordial, but kept moving. I noticed the change, but justified it. Rationalized it as in, 'Uh, they must be backed up with a bunch of calls to make. They don't have time to shoot the bull today.'

"Six months later, I walked in and sat down. When they came out this time, even their faces were different. They were talking more with each other and not with me anymore. Only one person sat down, just for a moment, though. By this time, I was realizing that it was no longer the same. The guy who just sat down suddenly looked like he was in a hurry and said, 'Gotta go,' as he slapped me on the back and took off.

"Directly in front of me was a cigarette machine with a mirror in it. I had seen that machine for thirty years, but when I saw my reflection in the mirror it startled me. It was then that it dawned on me that I had become one of THEM (as in, us vs. them). I was no longer one of us.

"I saw tears streaming down my cheeks in the mirror and I got out of there as fast as I could. I haven't been back since."

Retirement: Preparation Equals a Happy Ending

How can you avoid the pitfalls you've just read about? First of all, realize that life goes on! It's nothing personal, even though it feels like it is. We bond with whoever is physically closest to us, and you've been out of the group lately and someone else had to take your place. Did you ever stop to think that these officers you miss might assume that you've also got other people besides them filling up their spots in your life? Friendships are reinforced by repeatedly sharing time and space. If you're in a night class, for example, doesn't it make sense that you'll form relationships based on who you sit next to and the number of times you see people in class? Think back to your past. How many people do you hang out with from high school? Probably one or two at the most. But when you went to school together every day, I bet you were practically glued together at the hip! It's natural to become separated by absence.

It will never do you any good to see life from the vantage point of the victim.

If leaving the force sounds like a horrible option for you, as I mentioned before, you can ask to stay on the job as a volunteer. You may not get paid, but you'll still be part of the family and be able to wear a uniform and continue to put people in handcuffs. You'll have to work a certain amount of hours to remain on the schedule, but you might find this work very rewarding.

If that doesn't suit you, you could simply just enjoy your retirement! Some officers are overjoyed when their retirement begins because they have planned for it. The house is paid off. They don't owe anybody a thing, and, it's travel time. I have a buddy in this situation. He and his wife are happily married and have decided to live the "easy" life. They sold everything, bought a motor home, and all they do is travel. I call him on his cell phone and say, "Hey man, where you at?" He might answer, "Me and mama are on the Harley in Seattle, Washington." They have nowhere to go in particular, and with money in their pocket, they just crank that baby up and look at each other and say, "Where we goin' sweetheart?"

For those of you who don't want to or can't afford

to retire in style, but who are really done with a career in law enforcement (either because you're tired of the beat or because you're even more tired of your loved-ones lecturing you and worrying about you every day), there is an easier way to transition than to quit cold turkey—without a plan. In my lecturers I say, "If you weren't a cop, realistically, what would you be?" I ask you now the same thing. What would you be? If you're fortunate enough to be able to answer that and still have a few years of work as an officer ahead of you, start planning now.

In a perfect world, about five or ten years before you're scheduled to retire, I suggest going back to college or to a trade school part time and learning about something you've always been interested in but have never had time for. Maybe you're good with numbers and want to pursue accounting or investing someday? Maybe you're good with your hands and have remodeled your kitchen, but have regretted not having the correct credentials to do similar work for your friends when asked. Getting your contractor's license won't be the easiest thing you've ever done, but it could open up a world of creativity and financial freedom for you down the line.

Maybe you love doing finish work on Craftsman homes, or tinkering with cars, or programming computers? Maybe you've always sensed that you'd be a good counselor or a college professor? Well, pursuing avenues like these long before you're set to retire will give you plenty of time to find out the possibilities, and the necessary hours it will take to become adequately skilled. Best of all: It will take some of the worry and uncertainty out of your future. You will be able to relax in the knowledge that you've got something else to do when this "cops and robbers'" gig is up.

Personally, I don't care what you do when you

retire. You can buy one of those embarrassingly large, gas-guzzling motor homes and tour all fifty states if that's what floats your boat. You can even trail a boat behind you and paint it bright red with a fire-breathing dragon on the side. Or, you can go the altruistic route and feed hungry children, hungry vets, or hungry orangutans. It doesn't matter a lick to me if you shave your head, pierce your nose and open an orphanage in Uganda. Just do something! There is no reason to hang up your badge and feel old, left out and sorry for yourself. There is a big, wide world out there waiting for you to be of service. All it takes is a little forethought, planning, and the ability to figure out what else you want to be when you grow up. Yes, you're going to miss police work sometimes, maybe even often, but do you really want to be snatchin' and grabbin' bad guys at ninety? Come on!

For me, I'm not going to want to continue lecturing all over the world over 150 times a year when I'm an old fart. Eventually I'm going to want to slow down. To prepare for that (and continue with my goals of helping the largest number of law-enforcement professionals possible), I'm putting a lot of my energy into the FORTE Foundation. I work on our trauma center project night and day when I'm not speaking, and nothing but this book has had me this excited in a long time. That's a good thing because I know that my level of passion for this new phase of my life will carry me through any sadness I will experience when I stop touring and hanging out with my huge extended cop family every day across this country.

But Bobby, what do I do if I have no idea what I want to do?

Pretend that you do know, or that you're capable of finding out, and just start somewhere! After all, no one is

The Will to Survive

going to do this for you. I'm not promising that you won't "waste" some time, but is it going to kill you to take an unnecessary pottery class? No. Whatever you try will lead to something else, even if it's only the knowledge that you definitely don't want to go down a certain road.

The only chance you have of being truly miserable all the time when you retire is if you set it up that way.

Hobbies are good, but only if they make you feel productive. Even going fishing gets a little old, and can end up feeling like a job. Creating something with your hands (and getting paid for it) is always better than hearing your wife say, "I'm tired of watching you sit in that recliner; do something with your life," or your husband say, "Stop spending so much money." They aren't used to having you home every day, and you aren't used to being told what to do, so get on with your life and maybe even become your own boss. Doesn't that sound intriguing?

Retirement isn't always the fun we think it's going to be unless we love to travel or have a very fulfilling hobby or a second career we find exciting. Whether it's rebuilding kitchen cabinets and traveling regularly to your local Home Depot, or collecting model trains and traveling all over the country to different shows, you can always find a group of people who are interested in you and what you do, and you're bound to form new and satisfying relationships. They may never be as intense as the ones you formed as an officer, filled with drama, high stakes and the kind of humor that goes with that territory, but I'm willing to believe that your need for speed will have lessened significantly by then, and there will be fulfillment on levels you haven't yet experienced.

That has certainly been the case for me. But, I'll tell you something. I will always be a cop in my heart! You can

263

take the cop out of the job, but you can't take the job out of the cop. It doesn't matter how long it's been since I held a gun or sat in my unit, F-18, or answered a call for help. I will be a cop until the day I die and hopefully beyond that.

There's one other role that means even more to me than being a police officer. I'm hoping that some form of my following story applies to you.

Please indulge me one last time and put yourself at the scene: It's a warm spring day and the sun is shining and the birds are singing. I sit down on the grass next to the sidelines at my thirteen-year-old son's soccer practice after school and notice the smell of blooming honeysuckles drifting through the air. I can hear boys laughing and running and the coach calling out drills. Brad yells out, "Hey Dad!" as he sails by and whacks me lovingly on the arm, and I return the salutation. After sitting down and "watching" practice for about forty-five minutes, a mother of one of Brad's teammates comes up and sits beside me.

"Excuse me, Sir. Aren't you that trooper who was shot and blinded?" she asks. I look up at her with a smile and say, "Yes I am."

"Do you mind if I ask you a personal question?" she says.

"What other kind is there?" I reply.

"Are you totally blind?"

"YES I AM. Blind as can be. Can't see a darn thing."

"Well that's what I thought," she said. "Do you mind if I ask why you're here all the time if you can't see your son?"

"That's an easy one, Maam. I'm not here to see my son. I'm here for my son to see me!"

No matter what kind of cop you are—just out of the

The Will to Survive

academy or about to retire—I suggest that you have someone to love. While being a cop may be the most rewarding thing you ever do with your life, true fulfillment in your professional career is about balance, about having time at the end of the day to connect with those dearest to you. That, to me, truly fulfills the highest ideals of our oath to protect and serve.

It is my hope and my prayer every day for you that God will assign His angels to you to give you courage, strength, and wisdom, and deliver you home safely to your family at the end of every shift.

God bless you and stay safe!

The Will to Survive Resource List

FORTE Foundation
Dr. Bobby Smith, Founder
P.O. Box 14753
Springfield, MO 65814
(417) 887-1142
www.VisionsofCourage.com

International Conference of Police Chaplains
P.O. Box 5590
Destin, FL 32540
(850) 654-9736
www.icpc4cops.org
icpc@icpc.gccoxmail.com

National Organization of Parents of Murdered Children, INC.
Error! Unknown switch argument.
100 East Eighth Street, Suite B-41
Cincinnati, Ohio 45202
Email: natlpomc@aol.com
(513) 721-5683 (phone)
Toll Free: (888) 818-POMC

National P.O.L.I.C.E. Suicide Foundation, Inc.
Robert E. Douglas, Executive Director
8424 Park Road
Pasadena, Maryland 21122
Toll Free:1-866-276-4615
www.psf.org
redoug2001@aol.com
Office for Victims of Crime,

The Will to Survive

National Criminal Justice Reference Service
P.O. Box 6000
Rockville, MD 20849-6000
1-800-851-3420
AskOVC@ojp.usdoj.gov.

COPS: Concerns of Police Survivors, Inc.
National Office
P.O. Box 3199 - S. Highway 5
Camdenton, MO 65020
(573) 346-4911
www.nationalcops.org
cops@nationalcops.org

The Compassionate Friends, Inc.
P. O. Box 3696
Oak Brook IL 60522
(630) 990-0010
Toll Free: (877) 969-0010
www.compassionatefriends.org
nationaloffice@compassionatefriends.org

U.S. Department of Justice
Office of Justice Programs
Office of the General Counsel
810 7th St., N.W.
Washington, D.C. 20531
www.ojp.usdoj.gov
askojp@ojp.usdoj.gov
www.policepoems.com

The Will to Survive

About the Authors

Dr. Bobby Smith is a hero to countless cops, and one of the most sought after law-enforcement speakers in the world, with over 150 dates a year in the U.S. and abroad. As the founder of the **FORTE Foundation** (Foundation for Officers Recovering from Traumatic Events), Bobby is fulfilling a fifteen-year goal of building the first residential treatment center for officers dealing with Post Traumatic Stress Disorder and other hazards of the job. FORTE is a 501(c)3 non-profit corporation dedicated to providing counseling services to police officers, firefighters, and their families at little or no cost to the individual. A police officer from 1975 to 1986, Bobby's career was cut short when he was shot and blinded in both eyes in the line of duty. After losing his career, his wife, and suffering numerous additional traumatic events, Bobby felt that he had two choices: to end his life or start over. Bobby chose the latter, and since getting his masters in education, and receiving his Ph.D. in counseling psychology from Pacific Western University (and authoring his first book, *Visions of Courage*), his focus for helping cops has never wavered. Bobby and his wife of eighteen years, Janie, and their son, Brad, just recently moved to Marksville, LA after spending four years in Springfield, MO. He can be reached through his Website at www.VisionsofCourage.com.

Linda Sivertsen is an award-winning author, ghostwriter, speaker, and the West Coast Editor of *Balance magazine*. She has been featured on CNN, *Leeza, Extra*, E!, and in the *Star* & *the New York Post* as an expert author on living a charmed life. Her goal, which she accomplished with her first book, ***Lives Charmed: Intimate Conversations With***

The Will to Survive

Extraordinary People (and continues to strive for in her celebrity cover stories with *Balance* magazine), is to inspire readers through uplifting interviews with beloved role models, of which Bobby Smith is her "all-time favorite." Linda lives in Los Angeles with her husband, Mark, and their son, Tosh, and many animals. Aside from founding an educational environmental foundation, they are currently putting the finishing touches on the screenplay about Bobby's life, and can be reached at www.LivesCharmed.com.